Welcome to

THE

EVERYTHING

DOG BREED GUIDES ®

AS THE OWNER of a particular type of dog—or someone who is thinking about adopting one—you probably have some questions about that dog breed that can't be answered anywhere else. In particular, you want to know what breed-specific health issues and behavioral traits might arise as you plan for the future with your beloved canine family member.

THE EVERYTHING® DOG BREED GUIDES give you clear-cut answers to all your pressing questions. These authoritative books give you all you need to know about identifying common characteristics; choosing the right puppy or adult dog; coping with personality quirks; instilling obedience; and raising your pet in a healthy, positive environment.

THE EVERYTHING® DOG BREED GUIDES are an extension of the bestselling EVERYTHING® series in the pets category, which include *The Everything® Dog Book* and *The Everything® Dog Training and Tricks Book*. These authoritative, family-friendly books are specially designed to be one-stop guides for anyone looking to explore a specific breed in depth.

Visit the entire Everything® series at www.everything.com

THE
EVERYTHING®

Boxer Book

Dear Reader,

Growing up on a cattle and wheat farm in North Dakota, I was exposed to dogs at an early age—not only my father's herding dogs but also the many retrievers that hunters brought into the area. A chance encounter with a boxer changed my dog life. Previously enamored of herding and sporting dogs, I fell totally in love with a plain dun boxer bitch. From the moment I laid eyes on that dog, I knew that, someday, I'd own a boxer. As it turns out, they are now "my" breed.

From Cleo, whose white coat was a disqualifying factor in the show ring, to Huxley, my beautiful black brindle boy, each of my boxers has taught me more about this whimsical working breed. They bolt. They fight. They work either like a clown or a dream, like my Harpo, the breed's first UDX male. Harpo was so charismatic that he knew more people at the dog shows than I did! And they love, like my Gracie, the first puppy I bred, with a heart so big and true that it's breathtaking.

More than any other breed I've known, boxers need clear, consistent training to keep them out of trouble. Otherwise you'll find them chasing cars, eating the tires off your truck, or chasing the neighbor's cat, all with a look of total innocence. Enormously sensitive and intelligent, boxers also have a sense of humor. A wonderfully endearing and smart breed, they frequently exhibit the independence of cats. This book will tell you all you need to know about this fantastic, dynamic breed of dog—the boxer.

Karla Spitzer

THE
EVERYTHING®
BOXER
BOOK

A complete guide to raising, training,
and caring for your boxer

Karla Spitzer

Adams Media
Avon, Massachusetts

Thanks, Dad, for giving me your great love of dogs.

. . . .

Publishing Director: Gary M. Krebs
Associate Managing Editor: Laura Daly
Associate Copy Chief: Brett Palana-Shanahan
Acquisitions Editor: Kate Burgo
Development Editor: Katie McDonough
Associate Production Editor: Casey Ebert

Director of Manufacturing: Susan Beale
Associate Director of Production: Michelle Roy Kelly
Cover Design: Paul Beatrice, Erick DaCosta, Matt LeBlanc
Layout and Graphics: Colleen Cunningham, Holly Curtis, Sorae Lee

An Everything® Series Book.
Everything® and everything.com® are registered trademarks of F+W Publications, Inc.

Published by Adams Media, an F+W Publications Company
57 Littlefield Street, Avon, MA 02322 U.S.A.
www.adamsmedia.com

ISBN 10: 1-59337-526-3
ISBN 13: 978-1-59337-526-3
Printed in Canada.

J I H G F E D C B

Library of Congress Cataloging-in-Publication Data
Spitzer, Karla.
The everything boxer book : a complete guide to raising, training, and caring for your boxer / Karla Spitzer.
p.   cm.
Includes bibliographical references.
ISBN 1-59337-526-3
1. Boxer (Dog breed) I. Title.
SF429.B75S66 2006
636.73--dc22

2005033329

This publication is designed to provide accurate and authoritative information with regard to the subject matter covered. It is sold with the understanding that the publisher is not engaged in rendering legal, accounting, or other professional advice. If legal advice or other expert assistance is required, the services of a competent professional person should be sought.
—From a Declaration of Principles jointly adopted by a Committee of the American Bar Association and a Committee of Publishers and Associations

Many of the designations used by manufacturers and sellers to distinguish their products are claimed as trademarks. Where those designations appear in this book and Adams Media was aware of a trademark claim, the designations have been printed with initial capital letters.

Interior Photographs courtesy of Jean Fogle, *www.jeanfogle.com*

This book is available at quantity discounts for bulk purchases.
For information, call 1-800-289-0963.

- **Height:** Males 23–25 inches; females 21½–23½ inches

- **Weight:** Males 65–80 pounds; females 50–65 pounds

- **Head:** The muzzle is a third the length of the head; the bite is undershot; and the boxer has a black mask.

- **Ears:** The ears are customarily cropped, cut long, and raised when alert. If uncropped, the ears should lie flat and close to the cheeks, falling forward when alert.

- **Expression:** Intelligent and alert and curious.

- **Tail:** Docked—3 to 6 inches, and held erect.

- **Coat:** Short, shiny, and healthy. Colors are fawn or brindle. White markings should not cover more than a third of the coat.

- **Topline:** The back is short, straight, and muscular, slightly sloping when the boxer is at attention and leveling out when in motion.

- **Movement:** The gait is firm yet elastic and smooth. It covers a lot of ground quickly and easily—athletic.

- **Temperament:** The boxer is a hearing guard dog. He will initially exhibit curiosity and then fearless courage if threatened. He is playful and generally very patient and social with children. Intelligent, loyal, affectionate, and trainable, his curiosity remains a part of his personality throughout his life.

Acknowledgments

I would like to thank the board of the American Boxer Club and member friends who have taught me so much about this wonderful breed; Richard Tomita of Jacquet Boxers and Betty Aikenhead of Sandhill Boxers for being the best friends and mentors anyone could ask for; and Janice DeMello, one of the best obedience instructors in the nation. Jan has taught me the joy and elegance of obedience training my boxers and has been a true friend to me in my many ups and downs on that path. Thanks also go to Gary Steele and the Steele family for helping me through conformation hurdles and hassles; Kate Burgo, my editor, for her patience through my struggle in organizing the material for this book; Kathy Cognata, of *The Boxer Review*, who has been a great friend and fan; my students, members of the ObedcompBoxer newslist, and the many rescue boxers who have helped me learn how to communicate more effectively to humans and boxers; my many friends and club members in Southern California; Louise Brady for being the best friend and training buddy in both obedience and conformation that I could ask for; my own boxers—Waldo, Cleo, Bonzo, Harpo, Groucho, Gretel, Kosmo, Helio, John, Cello, Grace, Charm, and Huxley—who have taught me, well, everything else I know about boxers on an up-close and personal basis. And last but not least, I thank my husband, Scott, who does most of the dog-show driving and is the major dog-walker and pooper-scooper.

Contents

Introduction

There I was, at the border of the Principality of Liechtenstein, staring at a dun-colored boxer bitch. I had never seen a dog like her. I stared at her, and she stared at me. The guard commented that she usually didn't take as much interest in strangers as she had in me. I don't know exactly how she felt about it, but for me, it was love at first sight. I knew from that day in 1976 that I'd fallen in love with a new breed of dog. Sure enough, I'm now on my twelfth boxer.

If there's one thing I've learned through my experience with boxers, it's that they need a job. If you don't give them one, they will make one up for themselves, and chances are you won't like it. A beautifully athletic member of the dogs classified by the American Kennel Club (AKC) as the Working Group, boxers give life their all. This is why they need clear, consistent training early on and throughout their lives in order to be the good dogs they really, truly are. Once you get through the silly stages in your boxer's life, you will have a companion dog second to none. You'll also have a working dog that can compete in conformation, obedience, or agility; a search-and-rescue or therapy dog; an assistance dog; and just an all-round great pet.

Boxers were the original Seeing Eye dogs. The breed was developed to work, which originally meant anything from herding to hunting to guard work. As a "gentle" guard dog, boxers alert on sound, and they attack via a body slam rather than with jaws and teeth.

You will learn all you ever needed and wanted to know about boxers right here in this book. First, you'll discover the history of the breed—where they came from and why. Next you'll learn about their breed characteristics, including the features that distinguish the boxer from other dogs. This book also covers health problems. Like all purebred dogs, boxers have several genetic issues that breeders can avoid with careful screening. You'll read about training issues; although they are highly intelligent, boxers do belong to the Working Group, which means they tend to have a somewhat flat learning curve. You'll find out what makes this breed so lovable and loyal and where you can find your own healthy boxer.

Meet the Boxer

The link between humans and dogs dates back to prehistoric times. The earliest accounts of selective dog breeding come from ancient China, Egypt, and Mesopotamia. Broad-muzzled dogs are shown in carvings and paintings dating from about 4000 B.C. Dogs resembling boxers have been found in archeological grave sites around the world.

Boxer Popularity

A lesser mastiff-type breed called the bullenbeiser ("bull baiter") can be traced back to the Assyrians (2300–600 B.C.), who went to war with heavy-headed, short-muzzled dogs with a powerful build and great courage. These dogs were also used to run down and hold game such as bear, boar, and bison until the hunter could slaughter the animal. Later, the bullenbeiser herded cattle, becoming one of the first dogs to do all the basic dog tasks—herding, hunting, and guarding.

Although the exact origins of the boxer are unknown, it is generally accepted that the breed descended from the bullenbeiser. According to the American Kennel Club, the boxer is a working dog that developed in Germany. Boxers were recognized as a breed in Germany in the late 1800s. The AKC registered its first boxer in 1904, and the first championship in the breed was finished in 1915.

Cropping and Docking

The decision to crop dogs' ears and dock their tails goes back to ancient times. These modifications helped the dog avoid injury while baiting bull, boar, bison, or stag. Long, thin tails are easily broken, and floppy ears are easily torn. They also helped ensure stability within the pack, as injured dogs often fight with or are attacked by other dogs. A dogfight might result in the loss of the quarry being hunted and could also result in an injury to a valuable working animal. Worse would be the damage to the cohesion of the pack.

Who Owned Dogs?

Before the early 1800s, dog ownership was a privilege that, in many parts of Europe, was restricted to land owners and noblemen. After the Napoleonic wars, during which many of Europe's large estates were broken up, the ordinary citizen could own dogs. A movement developed across the continent whose goal was to standardize many of the indigenous dogs into different breeds. This standardization resulted in the weimaraner (from the Weimar Republic), the viszla (from Czechoslovakia), and the dalmatian (from Dalmatia).

The Early German Boxer

The bullenbeiser was another of the many indigenous dogs that became standardized. Known for its ability to bring down stags, bulls, and even bear, the compact, muscular body of this medium-sized dog was aided by a strong undershot jaw. The bullenbeiser packed a lot of strength and power into a relatively compact package, and the breed's power and intelligence were highly prized.

A Bulldog Named Tom

In the 1830s, the Germans imported a British dog that strongly resembled the bullenbeiser. This white bulldog, named Tom, appears twice in the early German pedigrees and is probably responsible for the white markings in what would become the boxer. Tom more nearly resembled the modern American bulldog than the English bulldog, a look similar to the bullenbeisers of the time, so the decision to incorporate Tom in breeding programs was not as unusual as it might sound. The first boxer entered into the German studbook was a dog named Flocki, son of Tom, the white bulldog. Many early studbook entries were Tom's progeny.

 **Fact**

Boxers come in two colors: fawn and brindle. Fawn is a reddish- to a golden-brown color, like the coat of a young deer. The richer the color, the better. Brindle is a reddish to golden background striped with black. The stripes should be distinct and tend to form a unique pattern. A reverse brindle is a black base coat striped with red or gold.

Developing the Breed Standard

A breed standard is the list of elements a dog must have to be a desirable member of any particular breed, compiled by breeders, judges, and fanciers of the particular breed. The standard serves as a basis of comparison, a model of the ideal example of that breed. It describes the breed's physical characteristics, such as coat color, way of moving, conformation, size, and the number and size of teeth. Also described are the breed's ideal temperament, working ability, and intelligence, all expressed in terms of suitability for the breed's original purpose. The standard also lists minor and disqualifying faults of the particular breed—that is, the characteristics that would cost a particular dog points in the conformation show ring or that would result in his being disqualified from competition entirely. The current official boxer breed standard can be found in Chapter 2.

 Question?

If the boxer is German in origin, why is its name English?
There are two theories to explain this. One is that the word boxer came from the German word Boxl, which described various types of German dogs in existence around the time the boxer breed was being developed. The second theory is that the name "boxer" came from the characteristic way in which the boxer uses its front paws in playing or fighting.

Not every purebred dog meets the breed standard. Though an individual dog may have numerous faults, he should not be considered any less a member of the breed or any less loveable. A standard is an ideal of what breeders should strive to achieve, and the show ring is a determination of which dogs, in the judges' opinions, most closely meet that standard.

The Early Standard

In 1904, when the AKC registered the first boxer, most representatives of the breed where white or checked (a pinto pattern) rather than today's fawn or brindle.

 Fact

A studbook lists all of a breed's producing sires and dams (males and females) and thus provides a genealogical record for the breed. For most breeds, including boxers, the studbooks go right back to the very first dog considered to be a representative of the breed.

In the early days, solid black was a disqualification. The reason for this had something to do with "unacceptable" behavior on the part of a Herr Shactner, the owner of the black boxer, Graf Blitz von Grauding. White, on the other hand, could be registered and did not become a disqualifying fault until about 1936. It is speculated that white fell out of favor because of the boxer's wartime duties. The boxer was the original World War I German war dog; a white coat was a disability because the enemy could see it more easily at night. However, a dissenting opinion suggests that disqualifying the color white in boxers was one way to distinguish the breed from the English bulldog, which it then resembled.

 **Alert!**

White was originally the only disqualifying fault of boxers in the conformation ring. Although solid black coats are no longer seen, white boxers are still quite common. When two boxers with white markings are bred, approximately one in four of the pups will be white. More than one-third white ground cover remains a disqualifying fault in the boxer conformation ring today.

The AKC Breed Standard

The Deutscher Boxer Club, formed in Munich in 1896, was the first German boxer club. In March of that year, the first boxers were registered and the first official boxer show was held. By January of 1902, a boxer breed standard was developed.

Until the 1940s, when the boxer became popular in the United States, Germany was instrumental in the development of the breed. The period from 1902 until 1911 saw great growth, development, and homogeneity in the breed. Less desirable traits became breed disqualifications through revisions of the written standard.

Frau Stockmann's Influence

The artist and sculptor Frau Friederun Stockmann was probably the single greatest influence on the world of American boxers. Her heartwarming autobiography, *My Life with Boxers*, exemplifies the European movement at the turn of the last century to champion a breed or indigenous type and promote it through showing and breeding. This work is described through her account of her life, including her struggles to help the breed survive the two world wars. Her autobiography includes stories of how she trained her dogs specifically to be of benefit to the war effort and details her heroism in caring for them under difficult situations, including barrages of enemy fire.

 **Fact**

Frau Stockmann's kennel name was Von Dom (sometimes called "Vom Dom"), meaning "of the cathedral." It is believed that the kennel was named for her first boxer, Pluto, famed for his many dogfights in the vicinity of Munich's cathedral.

Frau Stockmann's life was a study in determination and dedication to the breed, and she managed to survive both wars with at least some of her boxer kennel intact. However, she found that to survive and to enable her kennel to thrive, she was forced to sell her best dogs to America and Canada to support the others—perhaps to their benefit and the world of dog breeding today.

Sell the Best to Support the Rest

Frau Stockmann's philosophy was, "Sell the best to support the rest." She recounts many times when a proven champion or a promising youngster was sold to pay for the lesser lights in the kennel. This policy continues today among many successful, ethical breeders. They sell their best boxers to support the rest of the kennel family.

 **fact**

The foundation studs of American boxers are sometimes referred to as the Four Horsemen of American Boxers. They were all German-bred dogs: Sigurd Von Dom of Barmere, a fawn dog imported in 1939; Dorian von Marienhof of Mazelaine, a brindle dog imported in 1935; Lustig Von Dom of Tulgey Wood, a fawn dog imported in 1937; and Utz Von Dom of Mazelaine, a fawn dog imported in 1939. All four of these dogs can be found in most American pedigrees if traced back far enough.

The Original German War Dog

Frau Stockmann's husband Phillip, also an artist, was drafted early in World War I. Photographs of him in uniform on guard duty surrounded by numbers of boxers still exist today. The Stockmann's trained champion boxers and pets were both drafted by the German Army in World War I. Champions were the first to be taken since in those days, the German championship requirements included demonstrations of working ability, or what was then called "man work" (the equivalent of modern-day Schutzhund).

 **fact**

In World War I, Phillip Stockmann led the Munich Boxer Club to mobilize all useable and fit boxers in the German Home Guard. The dogs helped guard against enemy snipers and enemy infiltrators who were firing on German soldiers during guard duty.

Accounts of boxers of the early 1900s stress the boxer's agility, power, speed, and intelligence, all of which proved invaluable against snipers and spies. Sniper attacks dropped substantially once soldiers began using boxers on patrol. In her book *My Life with Boxers*, Frau Stockmann expresses pride in the fact that she and her daughter spent a great deal of time training the dogs to do such things as carry messages between points, track, jump, fetch, discriminate scent, and attack an enemy.

One of the best of the original war boxers was CH Roll von Vogelsberg. His ability to discriminate scent and his good instincts helped him round up and hold whole groups of smugglers and snipers by himself until soldiers arrived to assist him. Roll was also known for catching live hand grenades out of the air. He survived World War I, so he must have been very intelligent and capable! That amazing ability to assess and handle dangerous situations still characterizes the breed today.

Boxer History in the United States

The very earliest unofficial accounts of boxers in the United States mention two boxers being shown at the Westminster Kennel Club Show in 1898. AKC Judge Charles G. Hopton remembers the two boxers being shown in New York City. Judge Frank Begler recalls rumors of boxers being shown in Chicago in 1904. The first recorded boxer to finish a championship in the United States was German Champion Damph von Dom in 1915, a dog that belonged to New York Governor Herbert G. Lehman and his wife.

 **Alert!**

The boxer is known as a gentle or sometimes a hearing guard dog rather than a biting guard dog. While some boxers certainly will bite, boxers as a breed tend to guard by standing their ground. If pushed, they have been known to body slam assailants. Bitches as small as twenty-two inches have been known to slam a misbehaving horse to the ground.

The 1930s were a period of great development for the American Kennel Club and dog shows in general. Obedience regulations were adopted in 1936, and professional handlers were required to be licensed. By 1938, the AKC was issuing championship certificates. Because many of the top winning dogs were from Europe and not registered by the AKC, the AKC began offering cash prizes for American-bred dogs. As a result, many parent clubs of all breeds were formed in the 1930s, including the American Boxer Club (founded in 1935).

Although the early American boxer was greatly influenced by the German boxers, the people founding the American Boxer Club were more influenced by the Austrian boxer breeders, who followed a much plainer standard. When Austria revised its standard to be in line with Germany, the United States continued under the greater influence of the German Boxer Club. The American Boxer Club is still in existence today and is the parent club to the many local AKC boxer clubs around the nation.

 **Essential**

Some people are surprised to learn that boxers did not begin to catch on as a breed in the United States until the 1930s. Boxer popularity has since grown and attracted owners, breeders, and trainers with many different interests.

Boxers were the AKC's seventeenth most popular breed in the early 1990s. At the same time, the popularity of other guard dogs began to wane, including rottweilers, chow chows, pit bulls, Dobermans, and German shepherds. This may be because boxers, as a gentle guard breed, were perceived to incur less liability. What surprised many owners interested in the boxer's guard capabilities was the breed's high energy level. That drove some people who simply wanted a guard dog away from boxers and back to their more familiar (and lethargic) breeds.

Understanding the Boxer

The boxer is complex, intelligent, and frequently misunderstood. While we no longer have need of its bear-, bull-, and boar-baiting abilities, the breed retains its powerful mental and physical characteristics. This sometimes causes problems for boxers in a world that no longer has a need or outlet for their tremendous skills.

▲ The boxer is a dignified and intelligent breed.

All boxers need a job, and if they aren't given one, they will make one up. Thousands of boxers across the country end up in rescue programs every year because their owners failed to take these latent abilities into consideration when their boxers were still adorable puppies. As a result, they failed to provide these pups with the stimulation and education that every boxer needs to keep from getting into trouble. Without sufficient attention and training, boxers tend to exhibit problem behaviors, especially the following:

- Aggression, usually the result of unrestricted territoriality
- Unrestrained physical energy (such as jumping up and knocking people down)
- Excessive barking
- Uncontrollable and inappropriate chewing (as of furniture, car tires, linoleum flooring)

Your boxer's job doesn't have to be as dramatic or interesting as what his ancestors were used to doing every day. What he does need is basic obedience training (at least) so he knows how to be a canine good citizen. In essence, every boxer should be busy being a good, well-trained dog and a wonderful family companion.

 **Fact**

Every boxer needs to know the obedience basics: come, sit, stay, down, leave it, get off, and walk nicely on leash. In addition, your boxer should know how to get along with other dogs and should willingly accept handling and petting from anyone approved and introduced by the owner. These are basics skills every new dog or puppy should learn.

With all their sensitivity, complexity, energy, and drive, boxers generally need more of their owners' attention than other breeds that might settle down more readily after adolescence. Unlike those dogs, most boxers remain puppies until the end. This comes as a surprise to people familiar with other breeds who expect a mature dog to become a couch potato. First-time boxer owners are usually in for quite a shock.

Special Needs of the Boxer

The boxer is a short-coated bracycephalic breed. Unlike breeds with coats that act like a heated blanket in winter and a cool coat in summer, the boxer does not have much natural insulation because of its short coat. Coupled with its undershot jaw and smushed nose, this puts the boxer at great risk of overheating in hot, humid weather.

 **fact**

Behavior that vets, trainers, and behaviorists might otherwise characterize as hyperactive in other breeds is, in boxers, just a normally high energy level. For this reason, boxers need extra play time, attention, and training.

All bracycephalic breeds have some difficulty breathing efficiently in extreme heat because of their shortened noses and the extra tissue that fills their nasal cavities and throats. (The extra folds on the outside of the muzzle are mirrored by extra folds on the inside.) As a result, you must always be sure that your boxer has ample fresh water and a cool place to lie down in summer.

CHAPTER 2

Looking for a Boxer

Before you fall for the first puppy you see, keep in mind that you have some important homework to do. Boxers, like many other breeds, have their fair share of genetic health problems. Their hearts, hips, thyroids, and spines are all subject to various issues, some of which are life threatening. Temperament is also something you have to evaluate thoroughly. This chapter describes how to find the boxer that's perfect for you.

Is the Boxer Right for You?

If you are interested in the boxer's history and you want a smart, loyal, energetic, opinionated, sensitive, strong dog, the boxer is just the breed you're looking for! You can expect to train your dog throughout his life to keep him mentally and physically stimulated. Without that kind of devoted attention, your boxer may become destructive or may begin to age before his time.

The first way to ensure success with a dog is to be sure you're getting a good example of the breed. Working with a reputable breeder is the best way to find a healthy boxer. Chapter 4 describes all the hallmarks of the reputable breeder. You can find one through the American Kennel Club (online at *www.akc.org*), your local AKC-affiliated boxer club, or by visiting an accredited show.

 **fact**

In 2004, the boxer was the seventh most popular breed registered with the American Kennel Club. Over the last decade or so, boxers have risen in popularity from seventeenth to seventh. As the breed has become more popular, however, the number of boxer rescue organizations has increased dramatically as well.

The Official Boxer Breed Standard

The breed standard for the boxer describes the physical and temperamental characteristics of an ideal example of the breed.

 Breed Standard

The current breed standard, as published by the AKC (and quoted from the organization's Web site), reads as follows:

General Appearance:

The *ideal* Boxer is a medium-sized, square-built dog of good substance with short back, strong limbs, and short, tight-fitting coat. His well-developed muscles are clean, hard, and appear smooth under taut skin. His movements denote energy. The gait is firm yet elastic, the stride free and ground-covering, the carriage proud. Developed to serve as guard, working, and companion dog, he combines strength and agility with elegance and style. His expression is alert and his temperament steadfast and tractable.

The chiseled head imparts to the Boxer a unique individual stamp. It must be in correct proportion to the body. The broad, blunt muzzle is the distinctive feature, and great value is placed upon its being of proper form and balance with the skull.

In judging the Boxer first consideration is given to general appearance and overall balance. Special attention is then devoted to the head, after which the individual body components are examined for their correct construction, and the gait evaluated for efficiency.

Size:
Adult males 23 to 25 inches; females 21½ to 23½ inches at the withers. Proper balance and quality in the individual should be of primary importance since there is no size disqualification.

Proportion:
The body in profile is square in that a horizontal line from the front of the forechest to the rear projection of the upper thigh should equal the length of a vertical line dropped from the top of the withers to the ground.

Substance:
Sturdy, with balanced musculature. Males larger boned than females.

Head:
The beauty of the head depends upon the harmonious proportion of muzzle to skull. The blunt muzzle is 1/3 the length of the head from the occiput to the tip of the nose, and 2/3 the width of the skull. The head should be clean, not showing deep wrinkles (wet). Wrinkles typically appear upon the forehead when ears are erect, and are always present from the lower edge of the stop running downward on both sides of the muzzle.

Expression:
Intelligent and alert.

Eyes:

Dark brown in color, frontally placed, generous, not too small, too protruding, or too deep-set. Their mood-mirroring character, combined with the wrinkling of the forehead, gives the boxer head its unique quality of expressiveness. Third eyelids preferably have pigmented rims.

Ears:

Set at the highest points of the sides of the skull, the ears are customarily cropped, cut rather long and tapering, and raised when alert. If uncropped, the ears should be of moderate size, thin, lying flat and close to the cheeks in repose, but falling forward with a definite crease when alert.

Skull:

The top of the skull is slightly arched, not rounded, flat, nor noticeably broad, with the occiput not overly pronounced. The forehead shows a slight indentation between the eyes and forms a distinct stop with the topline of the muzzle. The cheeks should be relatively flat and not bulge (cheekiness), maintaining the clean lines of the skull as they taper into the muzzle in a slight, graceful curve.

Muzzle and Nose:

The muzzle, proportionately developed in length, width, and depth, has a shape influenced first through the formation of both jawbones, second through the placement of the teeth, and third through the texture of the lips. The top of the muzzle should not slant down (downfaced), nor should it be concave (dishfaced); however, the tip of the nose should lie slightly higher than the root of the muzzle. The nose should be broad and black.

Bite and Jaw Structure:

The boxer bite is undershot, the lower jaw protruding beyond the upper and curving slightly upward. The incisor teeth of the lower jaw are in a straight line, with the canines preferably up front in the same line to give the jaw the greatest possible width. The upper line of the incisors is slightly convex with the corner upper incisors fitting snugly in back of the lower canine teeth on each side. Neither the teeth nor the tongue should ever show when the mouth is closed.

The upper jaw is broad where attached to the skull and maintains this breadth, except for a very slight tapering to the front. The lips, which complete the formation of the muzzle, should meet evenly in front. The upper lip is thick and padded, filling out the frontal space created by the projection of the lower jaw, and laterally is supported by the canines of the lower jaw. Therefore, these canines must stand far apart and be of good length so that the front surface of the muzzle is broad and squarish and, when viewed from the side, shows moderate layback. The chin should be perceptible from the side as well as from the front. Any suggestion of an overlip obscuring the chin should be penalized.

Neck:

Round, of ample length, muscular and clean without excessive hanging skin (dewlap). The neck should have a distinctly arched and elegant nape blending smoothly into the withers.

Back and Topline:

The back is short, straight, muscular, firm, and smooth. The topline is slightly sloping when the Boxer is at attention, leveling out when in motion.

Body:

The chest is of fair width, and the forechest well-defined and visible from the side. The brisket is deep, reaching down to the elbows; the depth of the body at the lowest point of the brisket equals half the height of the dog at the withers. The ribs, extending far to the rear, are well-arched but not barrel-shaped.

The loins are short and muscular. The lower stomach line is slightly tucked up, blending into a graceful curve to the rear. The croup is slightly sloped, flat and broad. The pelvis is long, and in females especially broad. The tail is set high, docked, and carried upward. An undocked tail should be severely penalized.

Forequarters:

The shoulders are long and sloping, close-lying, and not excessively covered with muscle (loaded). The upper arm is long, approaching a right angle to the shoulder blade. The elbows should not press too closely to the chest wall nor stand off visibly from it.

The forelegs are long, straight, and firmly muscled, and, when viewed from the front, stand parallel to each other. The pastern is strong and distinct, slightly slanting, but standing almost perpendicular to the ground. The dewclaws may be removed. Feet should be compact, turning neither in nor out, with well-arched toes.

Hindquarters:

The hindquarters are strongly muscled, with angulation in balance with that of the forequarters.

The thighs are broad and curved, the breech musculature hard and strongly developed. Upper and lower thigh are long. The legs are well-angulated at the stifle, neither too steep nor over-angulated, with clearly defined, well let down hock joints. Viewed from behind, the hind legs should be straight, with hock joints leaning neither in nor out. From the side, the leg below the hock (metatarsus) should be almost perpendicular to the ground, with a slight slope to the rear permissible. The metatarsus should be short, clean, and strong. The boxer has no rear dewclaws.

Coat:
Short, shiny, lying smooth and tight to the body.

Color:
The colors are fawn and brindle. Fawn shades vary from light tan to mahogany. The brindle ranges from sparse but clearly defined black stripes on a fawn background to such a heavy concentration of black striping that the essential fawn background color barely, although clearly, shows through (which may create the appearance of reverse brindling).

White markings, if present, should be of such distribution as to enhance the dog's appearance, but may not exceed one-third of the entire coat. They are not desirable on the flanks or on the back of the torso proper. On the face, white may replace part of the otherwise essential black mask, and may extend in an upward path between the eyes, but it must not be excessive, so as to detract from true boxer expression. The absence of white markings, the so-called plain fawn or brindle, is perfectly acceptable, and should not be penalized in any consideration of color. Disqualifications: Boxers that are any color other than fawn or brindle. Boxers with a total of white markings exceeding one-third of the entire coat.

Gait:
Viewed from the side, proper front and rear angulation is manifested in a smoothly efficient, level-backed, ground covering stride with a powerful drive emanating from a freely operating rear. Although the front legs do not contribute impelling power, adequate reach should be evident to prevent interference,

overlap, or sidewinding (crabbing). Viewed from the front, the shoulders should remain trim and the elbows not flare out. The legs are parallel until gaiting narrows the track in proportion to increasing speed, then the legs come in under the body but should never cross. The line from the shoulder down through the leg should remain straight although not necessarily perpendicular to the ground. Viewed from the rear, a boxer's rump should not roll. The hind feet should dig in and track relatively true with the front. Again, as speed increases, the normally broad rear track will become narrower. The boxer's gait should always appear smooth and powerful, never stilted or inefficient.

Character and Temperament:

These are of paramount importance in the boxer. Instinctively a hearing guard dog, his bearing is alert, dignified, and self-assured. In the show ring his behavior should exhibit constrained animation. With family and friends, his temperament is fundamentally playful, yet patient and stoical with children. Deliberate and wary with strangers, he will exhibit curiosity, but, most importantly, fearless courage if threatened. However, he responds promptly to friendly overtures honestly rendered. His intelligence, loyal affection, and tractability to discipline make him a highly desirable companion. Any evidence of shyness, or lack of dignity or alertness, should be severely penalized.

The foregoing description is that of the ideal boxer. Any deviation from the above-described dog must be penalized to the extent of the deviation.

Disqualifications:

Boxers that are any color other than fawn or brindle. Boxers with a total of white markings exceeding one-third of the entire coat.

AKC Approval: February 11, 2005
Effective: March 30, 2005

Where to Look

The best source for a healthy boxer puppy is a reputable breeder, who is likely to be a member of an AKC-affiliated boxer club. Try paying a visit to a licensed show (all-breed or a boxer specialty) or trial, and make your way to the boxer ring. Certain dogs will catch your eye, and you can then seek out their owners or handlers for a reference to the breeder. This is a good way to find a breeder with a new litter "on the ground" or on the way. Refer to Chapter 4 for a list of questions you should be prepared to ask all breeders before you consider buying one of their dogs.

 Alert!

The terms "dog" and "bitch" describe males and females, respectively. These are generic terms and should not be used or interpreted as an insult of any kind! These designations tell you where a dog fits in the show schedule, which is known as a "premium list."

You should also ask to see the pedigrees of the dogs in line with the puppy you would like to own. Preferably the pedigree of your puppy should have at least one parent who was shown ten times or more in conformation or had a CD (Companion Dog) title from the AKC. Either will be a sufficient test of temperament so that you know the parents are of sound temperament. It is preferable that at least a quarter of the dogs in the last four to five generations have titles.

Longevity and Vitality

If a breeder cannot or will not answer questions about health or longevity, she might be hiding something, or she might not be experienced enough to know that there are at least four major health-related conditions that every boxer should be screened for and found clear of before it is bred. The only exception to this

is if the breeder can prove definitively that she has *many* generations of boxers who live past ten years of age who are very vital
and healthy. This is most important if you want to do performance
events. The golden age of all obedience dogs tends to be from
ages six to ten. If the puppy you are looking at comes from a line
that is old at age six, you may want to pass on that puppy because
there are lines which are filled with vitality until past ten which
would be a better choice for competition purposes.

 **Essential**

> Be prepared for a reputable breeder to ask you many questions, such
> as these: Do you own or rent your home? Do you have a fenced yard?
> Will someone be home to house train the puppy in the early days?
> Do you have a veterinarian to treat the puppy? Do you want to show
> a boxer, or do you just want a pet? Will you take the pup to puppy
> classes? Can you afford to show a dog? Can you afford veterinary
> care for your boxer, including expensive specialized care?

Longevity (in a boxer, ten years old or older) and longevity with
vitality (a dog that is infirm, arthritic, or chronically ill, is not particularly vital, but a dog that still plays, works and is in good physical
shape meets this criteria) is the best health test in boxers, and there
are long-lived lines out there. If you look, you can find them.

You can ask friends or people you see in obedience or agility
rings where they have gotten their boxers if you like their dogs and
their dogs have the performance attitude and longevity that you
are interested in having for yourself. However, if you live outside
of an area where there are many reputable boxer breeders, you
might wish to call the American Boxer Club for information on
clubs and breeders near you.

You can search the Internet as well, but when you do that you
might want to ask for references from happy puppy buyers. You can

contact any of the Internet resources and ask questions of breeders on any of the boxer lists or who belong to the American Boxer Club.

A Quality Puppy

A quality puppy is one that has the potential to be a healthy, good tempered, positive representative of the breed. If one or both of the parents are breed champions, then you know that the puppy in question has correct type in its near genetic makeup and probably a good temperament.

If one or both has done an obedience title, then you know that the puppy has intelligence, biddability, and working ability in its near genetic makeup. Similarly, an agility title in the parents indicates that the puppy has good athletic ability.

 **Fact**

Type suggests those qualities that consistently distinguish one animal from another. Repetitive type is usually the result of inbreeding or line breeding. Biddability refers to how readily and willingly a dog can be trained.

A Good Breeder

A good, reputable breeder is one who has, to the best of her ability, had both parents health-screened before the breeding. A reputable breeder will stand behind her line and guarantee the health of the puppy for at least the first forty-eight hours, until you can take the pup to your vet.

A good breeder will tell you if there were any heart- or thyroid-affected individuals in either of the parent's littermates, parents, or grandparents. The same is true of hip problems, cancer, or any other disease or illness.

A good breeder should be able to tell you if there is spondylosis or degenerative myelopathy in the line (both causes of going down in the rear, a phenomenon that affects a lot of boxers). In other words, a reputable breeder will give you a full disclosure on the health and well being of her dogs. If the breeder can give you direct answers in all of these areas, she is probably a good, competent breeder. The puppy she sells you will probably be healthy.

In the end, a good, reputable breeder should be a constant resource for the puppy buyer for the boxer's entire life. Additionally, a good breeder will take your boxer back if you cannot keep him at any time during his life, for any reason. This shows that the breeder has the dog's best interests at heart.

Where Not to Look

First and foremost, you want to avoid any backyard breeder who is breeding just to make money without regard to the health, welfare, and well being of the boxers she is breeding and the breed as a whole. You also want to avoid anyone who does not screen for health-related issues, who does not know the boxer standard, is unfamiliar with the common boxer health problems, or who produces boxers with the genetics for common health problems.

Also, regardless of how cute they are, always avoid getting puppies from a pet store. These generally come with no health history on the parents, and therefore, no idea of what the pup's genetics are. If you have no clue about the puppy's genetics, you have no guarantee on the inherited health issues and you may not even get an AKC pedigree. In many cases, by buying a puppy that is not from health-tested parents, you are buying a lifetime of major veterinary bills with the pup. And while there are no absolute guarantees of health even if the parents and grandparents have passed all the boxer health screening tests, the chances are much better that you will have a boxer with better health longer if one or both of the parents were screened for the inherited health conditions that shorten the lives of many boxers and/or cost their owners a great deal of money to treat. Your boxer's health is too important to leave to a less-than adequate breeder.

▲ Always learn about a puppy's parents before selecting your boxer.

Finding a Healthy Boxer

Find out which lines live the longest with the greatest vitality. Some people will tell you that if you find any boxer line that lives past six, you are lucky, but that is not true. Many live to ten years of age and beyond with good health and vitality. This is the line that will be most likely to be able to provide you with the boxer puppy of your dreams.

 Fact

You can ask your veterinarian if she knows of healthy long-lived lines of boxers that she may treat in his or her practice. This is one good way to find out from an objective outsider who is not involved with the dogs directly and who has nothing to lose by being honest about health issues and longevity. Your vet will only give you names of healthy dog's owners or breeders, and you won't have to wade through those that are not healthy and long-lived.

Again, by contacting the American Boxer Club for breeders in your area, or contacting a local boxer club, you will have a better chance of finding those lines that have greater health and longevity and those breeders who value health, type, and temperament. These are also the breeders who can help you raise a sound puppy and who can give advice on a number of breed-related health and behavioral issues.

Dog Ownership: A Family Affair

Before you even think about getting a boxer, the decision should be discussed with all members of the family, as everyone will need to be involved in the dog's care. All members of a household should attend the first puppy socialization classes and later basic obedience classes so everyone in the family learns how to deal with the boxer. That said, the adults in the family are really the ones who are ultimately responsible for the boxer.

 Essential

Puppies grow exponentially. When they are little, it is hard to imagine that a tiny male puppy will grow from eight to ten inches tall at eight weeks old to twenty-five to twenty-six inches tall by eleven months old and will ultimately weigh sixty pounds or more. A female boxer puppy will grow from eight to ten inches at eight weeks old to twenty-one to twenty-three and a half inches tall at eleven months and will weigh in at fifty pounds or more.

At eleven months of age, your boxer is still very much a puppy, but in a large, rambunctious body. The puppy should be trained so that anyone in the family can handle or direct him should the need arise. Each member of the family should be able to walk the family boxer down the street (on leash) safely, and each should be able to give commands the boxer should obey.

"Come," "Sit," "Stay," "Down," "Off," and "Leave it" are the essential commands that every good boxer needs to know and begin to learn in puppyhood. Under no circumstances should the family get a boxer because only one member of the family wants a puppy. And you shouldn't get a boxer puppy if mom and dad had one when they were young, but the rest of the family wants something else like a cat or an iguana or even a different breed of dog. No boxer should just belong to just one member of the family. Instead, it should be a family dog that everyone loves and cares for.

 **Fact**

Boxers "kidney bean" when they are happy. This means your boxer is wagging his tail so hard that his shoulder is about to touch his hip, and his back looks like the shape of a kidney bean. This is a strong characteristic of a happy boxer and one of the fun, joyful characteristics of the breed.

Pros and Cons of Boxer Care

First of all, boxers, like most purebred dogs, have some very specific genetic problems as a breed. However, there are health tests that can help the breeder screen for these problems.

Second, the boxer is a high-energy breed that some people consider hyperactive. Many boxers slow down only at a very advanced age, so if you are looking for a calm, quiet dog, the boxer may not be for you. This is an important consideration when getting a pet of any kind. There will be a lot of years (if you are lucky, and have chosen your pup well) during which the boxer is not a cute little puppy. So be very sure that the adult boxer is right for you. You must be able to protect your boxer from overheating in the summer and getting too cold in the winter. The boxer is not a candidate for an outdoor dog that can live in a doghouse in the back yard.

 **Essential**

Like all dogs, boxers need baths, nail grooming, walks, training, and cleaning up after. Luckily, boxers are very trainable, and training any dog is part and parcel of having the dog of your dreams. But you must be willing to dedicate the time that it takes. Owning a boxer, or any dog, is a lifestyle choice, so make your decision carefully.

Generally speaking, the great parts of owning a boxer are that it is an intelligent, short-coated breed that tends to be good with children and relatively easy to train if you are consistent with training. The downsides of owning a boxer are that this is a high-energy dog that is curious to the point of being nosy. Boxers can become destructive when bored and aggressive without direction and training and they have, as a breed, a number of inherited health issues.

Choosing Your Dog

The decision to get a boxer, or any pet, deserves careful consideration. No dog should be an impulse buy. It is up to the owner to provide a dog with the best care possible, which is easier if you're very sure that you truly want a boxer. You will be making a ten- to fifteen-year commitment to walks, training, veterinary bills, and food costs, so you want to be sure of your choice. This chapter includes all the information you need to know before taking the plunge.

Important Considerations

The biggest considerations in choosing a boxer are health, longevity, energy levels, and training needs. The boxer is a higher-level energy dog than many other dogs of its size, so be sure that you are prepared to deal with this fact. Read on for detailed information on health concerns, aging issues, and expenses associated with boxers.

Health

Health in a boxer is extremely important. The inherited diseases that the boxer fancier can screen for are heart health, hip dysplasia, and hypothyroidism. These conditions should be checked for using the following health tests:

- Twenty-four-hour Holter monitor with a resulting PVC (pre-ventricular contractions—also known as VPC) rate of fifty or less
- Clear echocardiogram or auscultation administered by a canine cardiologist
- OFA (Orthopedic Foundation for Animals) with hips evaluated "Fair" or better, or PENNHIP (the University of Pennsylvania Hip Improvement Program) reading
- Normal thyroid test results from the Michigan thyroid panel, evaluated by Michigan State University

Other health problems that are relatively common in boxers include spondylosis, degenerative myelopathy, epilepsy, cancers, Cushing's syndrome, and colitis. Boxers may also be prone to other health problems, most of which have no definitive screening tests at this time. The best option is to ask a breeder if any of these conditions are evident in the line that she breeds.

 **Fact**

A line is the family or generations of dogs that have the same kennel name or that come from the same breeder or cobreeders. In your search for the perfect boxer puppy, you will find that some lines show up in other lines' pedigrees again and again. Some lines are just longer lived and healthier, and some win more often than others.

Some health problems can be treated effectively and inexpensively, as in the case of hypothyroidism. On the other hand, health problems such as boxer cardiomyopathy, subaortic stenosis, degenerative myelopathy, or the many cancers that boxers can get are generally quite expensive to treat. It pays to ask what the breeder's line tends to die from, or what inherited illnesses they get before you purchase your puppy.

Aging

In addition to energy levels, ask how the line ages. It they're still running around with the younger dogs at ten and beyond, that's great. Then all you need to do is decide if you have the energy to deal with a dog with that much life and vitality.

As for training needs, ask how the line tends to train. Are they easy to housetrain? Obedient? If they seem too independent-minded, they may not be the right line for you.

How much time will you be able to spend with your boxer? Boxers are a people-needy breed. In other words, they want to be with you as much as possible, and they tend to get themselves in trouble when they can't.

 Essential

> If you want a dog that will just be happy spending time in the back yard, boxers will not work for you. If you want a dog that is curious to the point of nosiness, companionable, that you can take with you wherever you go, and that will appear to feel entitled to be a part of every aspect of your life, then a boxer is the dog for you.

But do you have the time and energy to deal with a high-level energy dog? Do you have time for training and walks? Do you have the personality that goes with not minding a dog that is always in your face wanting to know what you are doing? For those of us who love boxers, this is part of their charm, but for people who want a dog that is happier in the back yard on its own, the boxer is not a good choice. In fact, this is a reason many boxers end up in rescue each year.

Expenses

Boxers can be a bit like expensive sports cars in that they're somewhat high maintenance. Still, if you love them, you've got to have one. Some rescue organizations will not adopt a rescue boxer to a family that does not have at least $3,000 in the bank available for potential emergency veterinarian problems. While it is always a good idea to have money in the bank, emergencies don't always happen. However, in most parts of the country, good basic veterinary care that includes a once- to twice-yearly visit with inoculations against common diseases, some form of heartworm preventive, flea repellents and incidentals tend to cost about $300 to $500 per year. While that may be a little high for some parts of the country, it is not an unusual amount, so you need to consider what you can spend and what you are willing to spend on veterinary care should your boxer need it. One accident injury, or gastric torsion surgery alone can cost from $1,500 to $2,000. Good veterinary care will be an expense.

The same goes for premium-quality dog food. Most boxers, like expensive sports cars, run best on the higher-grade fuels. In fact, most reputable breeders have a particular brand of dog food that they feel their line does best on, and they will recommend that you get that food for your puppy. Or some will have fed their dogs on a raw-food diet, which is an expensive and time-intensive choice in itself.

Puppy or Adult?

It can be difficult to decide between a boxer puppy and an adult boxer. People are often sucked in by a boxer puppy's big eyes, wiggly little body, and sweet puppy breath, but they easily forget that the cute little pup will quickly grow into a hyper, rowdy canine in six to ten months, ultimately weighing somewhere between fifty and eighty pounds. With that in mind, others prefer to start out with an adult dog so they know what they're getting from the start. Clearly, this decision takes careful consideration.

Getting a Puppy

If you choose to get a puppy, you will need to start training the moment the pup walks in the door. This does not only mean housetraining, which the puppy will most certainly need, but also basic manners and skills, such as how to walk on a leash, how to come when called, how to get off or leave it, and how to stay.

 Question?

How old should a puppy be when you take it home?
No reputable breeder sells a puppy before it is eight to ten weeks old. Many backyard breeders will sell their puppies at six weeks because that is usually when the mother will stop feeding the pups, and the backyard breeder does not want the added expense and bother of feeding a litter of puppies for a few weeks. However, this is very irresponsible.

It is best for the pup to remain with its littermates and mother until at least eight weeks of age because there are many crucial lessons that a mom imparts to her pups about how to be a good dog between the age of six to nine weeks. A puppy also learns a lot about getting along with other canines in his own family pack during that time. To deprive the pup of those lessons is to risk ending up with an antisocial dog that is not able to get along well with other dogs, or with people, in the real world.

If you have the time, energy, and willpower to raise your puppy well, then a puppy is a great idea and will be tons of fun. Also, if you want an obedience-competition dog, you may want to get it at an early age to begin its competition training. But if you want a show-prospect puppy, you might want to wait until a bit later when more mature physical promise for the show ring is evident.

Getting an Adult

Some people decide to get an adult boxer as opposed to a puppy because they want a more mature, calm dog. However, boxers mature mentally and emotionally more slowly than some breeds. Essentially, what this means is that they are puppies longer, and they often keep their puppy-like traits until the day they die. This is just the reality of the breed, and you have to be able to handle this responsibility whether you get a puppy or an adult.

 Fact

You can teach an old dog new tricks! It is a myth, and not a very intelligent one, that old dogs can't learn new things. Actually, many trainers find it much more rewarding to work with an older, sensible dog that isn't going through growth stages of puppyhood or canine adolescence. Older dogs tend to have more focus and memory retention.

If you are leaning toward getting an adult boxer, go for it! This is a great thing to do. Puppies are quickly given homes because they're so cute, while perfectly sweet adult dogs are often ignored or forgotten. There are many boxer rescue organizations around the country where you could go to find a wonderful adult boxer. All that most of the rescued boxers need is a little love and some basic manners, or information on how to be a good, pleasing boxer, to make them into perfectly wonderful dogs. You might even find a show breeder who has an older puppy or an adult that may not be doing well in the show ring, or that might have actually finished its championship, but will not be used in a breeding program. These are also great candidates for pets.

Young Puppies Versus Older Puppies or Adults

Of course, very young boxer puppies are downright adorable. They are playful and will bond readily. However, older boxers are usually already housetrained or generally more easily house-trained than a puppy. Older boxers are also playful, and are relatively easy to train in general. The majority of older boxers will bond and respond to kind, firm treatment.

▲ **Playful and enthusiastic, boxers are often called "puppies for life."**

The downside of little puppies is that they need housetraining and socialization. They will need to work through teething, chewing, fear periods, and adolescence. The cons of older boxers are that they are not cute little pups, and they may have learned bad habits with previous owners. Even so, both puppies and adult boxers need training.

Male or Female?

Male boxers are larger, bigger boned, heavier, and more powerful than female boxers. Many people think that male boxers are less manageable than females. It is true that if left intact, untrained, and unsupervised, males will sometimes mark in the house. Males tend to be more wildly enthusiastic and sillier than females, which some people equate with being unmanageable. If unchecked or untrained, males may have a greater tendency to lunge at other dogs and to be aggressive. All of these behaviors, however, are very manageable with training. On the other hand, some people feel that that enthusiasm makes for a great performance or conformation dog.

 **Essential**

Despite the common (uneducated) belief, male boxers can be very sweet pets. If you start your little boxer puppy in puppy socialization classes at an early age and work with him consistently, you will have a wonderful, loyal, and affectionate companion once he is an adult. Male boxers are very loving.

Female boxers, like the females of most breeds, are considered to be more docile and affectionate, although some boxer bitches can be just as wild, energetic, and territorial as their boxer brothers. The female boxer's ingrained concern for the young of all species makes them good with children. Their smaller size, lighter weight, and lesser strength may make them more manageable. But just like their boxer brothers, they need lifelong training.

Other Pets and Children

Boxers, when raised with other species of animals, tend to be very good around those species. This tends to apply to cats, other dogs, horses, rabbits, and many other kinds of family pets. If you need your boxer to get along with other animals, you should ask the breeder how the puppy's parents interact with other animals, such as cats, for instance, as that will be a clue to how your puppy may respond.

If you have children, there are other guidelines to keep in mind. Although boxers have a longstanding reputation for being a good breed for children, it is very important to supervise children and dogs at all times as neither the boxer nor the children have adult judgment. There is no point in taking the risk that either one of them could make a mistake that could result in an injury to either.

 **Alert!**

Children and dogs must be supervised! Some boxers become very protective of their family's children, to the point that they do not even want the children's friends to come around. Remember that your boxer still has guarding instincts and may not always understand that rough behavior that children consider play is just that. An inexperienced boxer might see a childish disagreement as a genuine threat without other supervision from a sensible adult.

It's important to teach your children to treat the new puppy or dog gently and with respect. No pulling ears, tail, flews (lips), or private parts. Children must be taught not to tease the dog, hurt it, and not to take its food away while it is eating, as all of these things could provoke a bite. Children must be taught to respect the boxer as a dog with a dog's instincts and needs just like they must be taught to respect all other things they will encounter in life.

It is important that children learn to give the boxer basic commands such as sit, down, stay, off, and leave it. The reason for this is that dogs tend to see children as pack members rather than superior members of the pack, so it is important to be aware of this. One way to elevate the children's status in the pack is to have them feed the boxer (under your supervision, of course!), and of course, to be able to get the boxer to obey basic commands from every member of the family.

Make boxer ownership a family responsibility. Children can help to prepare the boxer's food and help the boxer learn to sit and to wait while the food is being prepared. Learning to sit and wait calmly for food helps to take the edge off of food challenges. If the boxer knows that waiting patiently will result in him getting his dinner, he will not mind it so much, and he will learn that waiting can produce good things. These simple commands and exercises will go a long way in telling your boxer that the children outrank him, and this will go far in preventing problems from arising.

Choosing a Boxer Puppy

There are a number of factors to consider in choosing a puppy. The first and most important one when choosing a puppy for the family is temperament. The other is looks. You want a good, easily trained biddable dog, and you want one that will represent the proud, confident image of a boxer as an adult. If you are getting a boxer for the first time from a reputable breeder, the breeder should be able to assess both you and the available puppies and come up with a wonderful match for both.

 Essential

Don't get the bravest puppy in the litter. He is the most independent and will probably be harder to train for a first-time puppy buyer. However, don't get the shyest puppy in the litter, either. He may never gain the confidence you need to work with as a first-time puppy buyer.

If you are not an experienced dog person, and have never even thought about the real issues of temperament before, much less wanted to test a dog for one, don't despair. The Volhard puppy aptitude test, one of the longest-standing temperament tests for puppies, is available to anyone. This test is still used by service dog organizations to help determine the reliability of the temperament of the puppies being evaluated before entry into the program. You can find more information about the Volhard test online at *www.volhard.com*.

If the litter you are looking at has a forward-looking breeder, the litter will have been evaluated by in independent evaluator at forty-nine days of age for temperament. The ideal puppy for you is partly based upon your experience with dogs. In general, the ideal puppy is one that is neither shy nor overly confident, and one who is high in pack drive and moderate in prey drive. This type of temperament profile will give you the puppy that will bond and be easily trained, generally with no aggressive tendencies.

 **Fact**

If the litter has not been evaluated, and you don't feel confident to do it yourself, or the breeder does not feel comfortable with the evaluation, then you are best off explaining in as great a detail as you can to the breeder what you want out of a puppy. A reputable breeder wants the puppy to have a great home just as much, if not more, than she wants you to find your dream dog.

Looks

The boxer is a head breed, which means that the correctness of the head is very important to the dog's look. The boxer profile is unique in the canine world, and it is the broad head, expressive eyes, and the undershot jaw that gives the boxer its distinctive appearance.

From the looks perspective, you want your purebred boxer puppy to grow up to become a proud, beautiful example of the breed. Fawn or brindle or white, flashy or plain, you want the world to know the dog on the end of your leash is a boxer.

Balance

You want your puppy to have good overall balance. Your first impression of the puppy should be a pleasant one. The muzzle should be broad and deep. A bump above his nose suggests that the puppy will probably have a good stop. The stop in a boxer is where the skull meets the muzzle. If it's too shallow, the boxer is spoonfaced or dishfaced. A high occiput (similar to a high forehead in people) is a prediction of a good ear set. The expression should be pleasing, and the puppy should have some wrinkling on his face and jowls. A boxer puppy's neck should be arched, and his topline should be straight with the tail set high and at right angles. He should have good rear angulation and sloping shoulders.

Markings

If you are getting the puppy to show, you should get the deepest red fawn or the most pleasant, richest brindle. Whichever color you are leaning toward getting should be richly pigmented on the puppy's head and back.

White markings can range from little to one-third of the dog. Remember, more than one-third white is a disqualifying fault, but only in the breed ring, never in your heart. Most conformation champions have a substantial amount of white on them. At this point in time, it is harder to finish a plain dog, or one with little or no flash, than it is to finish a flashy one, all other points of comparison being equal, but by no means impossible.

 Question?

What does "flash" mean?
White markings on boxers are called flash. More than one-third white markings on a boxer are called a disqualifying fault in the conformation ring. Dogs with more than one-third white can still be shown in obedience, rally, agility and tracking, and they still make wonderful pets and companions. A disqualifying fault in any breed is one that renders the dog ineligible to show in the conformation or breed ring of AKC shows. It is a fault that is believed to be detrimental to the breed.

The puppy's eyes will be blue, but should be as dark a blue as possible. Those puppies with dark blue eyes grow up to have dark brown eyes. Those eyes that are gray will often turn out to be a light brown or yellow, which is considered a fault.

Choosing an Adult Boxer

Let's say you have the time for a dog, and want a dog in your life, but you don't have time for all the training, socialization, and house manners that a young puppy requires, or you'd simply like to give an older boxer a home. How do you go about finding the dog of your dreams? The answer is boxer rescue.

Boxer Rescue

The America Boxer Rescue Association can refer you to an ABRA member rescue organization in your area. You can visit the ABRA Web site, at *www.americanboxerrescue.org*. You could also contact the Boxer Rescue Foundation for a list of rescue organizations that have earned grants through BRF in your area. The BRF Web site is *www.boxerrescuefoundation.com*. Finally, the largest and oldest consistent boxer rescue organization is Boxer Rescue of Los Angeles, Inc. (*www.boxer-rescue-la.com*). These organizations have a proven track record of rescue at a local and regional level. These organizations are able to evaluate the temperaments of the dogs in their care.

 **Alert!**

It is very important to be very clear with boxer rescue organizations about your needs concerning what kind of boxer you want. Let them know the extent of your experience with dogs, your questions, and so on. Like reputable breeders, they will have as many or more questions to ask you about your ability to care for a boxer.

In addition, it is possible that a breeder or a person who shows boxers may have an older puppy that did not make it as a show prospect or a finished champion that they will not be using in their breeding programs. If you are interested in this option, it is probably best to go to a show and to talk to breeders around the ring if they know of anyone who has an older boxer that they would like to place in what they will call a pet home.

Whatever way you acquire your adult boxer or older puppy, the best test of whether the particular dog is for you is whether you (or you and your family) and the boxer click. It is not so different from making human friends. Some times you just click, and sometimes you do not. Trust your instincts on this. Do you trust him, and does he trust you? The answer to that question will probably be the best test of compatibility with an older boxer.

 Question?

In what situations is it a bad idea to get a dog?
There are several. For example, never surprise a family member with a dog. Any individual who is not involved in the plan for a new pet will not be prepared to handle the responsibility. Likewise, never get a child a dog with the goal of teaching the child how to be responsible. Such a goal is rarely achieved this way. Finally, don't get a dog when a new baby is on the way thinking how cute they'd be together. Adjusting to life as a parent while trying to train and care for a new dog will cause nothing but stress—for everyone in the household.

Boxer Buying Etiquette

There is probably nothing more discouraging to a breeder or a rescuer than to get a call from a prospective buyer who goes on at length about exactly how the dog should look: "I want a flashy fawn male, with high white stockings and a full white collar, but I don't want to show." Most reputable breeders will be more likely to keep the flashy dogs for the conformation ring. Many breeders have spent their lives improving the breed, and they want the pups to go into the show ring to help them prove it. If you don't want to show, then you will probably not be the right home for them. Looks don't indicate temperament. The advice here is that the paint job is not important when you look for your first boxer.

Rescue organizations often face a similar of challenge. They may have a boxer that is perfect for you and your family in every way—good with children, loves cats, knows all basic commands—but it's not the right color. Don't take the chance of losing the dog of your dreams because it's a color you weren't expecting or lacks the kind of markings that you think you would like. Give that wrong color boxer who is right in every other way a chance.

Reputable Breeders

A reputable breeder is one who shows a genuine love of her chosen breed and her individual dogs. This love should be evident in the quality of veterinary care and the quality of life that she provides for her dogs. A reputable breeder is really the only source for a healthy boxer puppy with a good temperament. Before you go out in search of a reputable breeder, you need to know what you're looking for. This chapter explains all you need to know about breeders, breed registries, pedigrees, and contracts.

What Is a Reputable Breeder?

First and foremost, a reputable breeder is one who puts the welfare of the breed and the individual boxers above monetary gain or quest for titles. Any person breeding solely for money or titles is likely to be overlooking some aspects of the boxer's health or well-being.

A reputable breeder *adores* boxers, supports the welfare of the breed, is a member of a local boxer club and probably the parent club (the American Boxer Club), and supports boxer rescue attempts and organizations. Also, a reputable breeder will take back any dog she has bred regardless of the circumstances. That is part of her commitment to the breed and to her own personal breeding program.

Alert!

Minimum health screening tests used to plan a healthy, well-bred boxer litter include the Michigan State thyroid panel (to determine a healthy thyroid and absence of autoimmune antibodies), OFA hip evaluation or PennHip (to determine that there is no hip dysplasia), twenty-four-hour Holter monitor (to help establish that the boxer does not have boxer cardiomyopathy), and auscultation for subaortic stenosis (to rule out that possibility). A reputable breeder will take these precautions with her dogs.

Questions to Ask a Breeder

As you talk to people about where to find a boxer puppy, you should be asking questions. Not only will this give you the specific information that you should get about every breeder, but it will provide you with a way to start a sensible sounding conversation that should appeal to the responsible boxer breeder. Here are some questions to ask:

- How long have you been breeding boxers?
- Do you show in conformation, obedience, or agility? If so, how many titles have you produced?
- What is your dogs' average longevity?
- What are your dogs' general health problems and causes of death?
- Are any of the siblings of the parents or grandparents affected by either boxer cardiomyopathy or subaortic stenosis?
- May I see Holter monitor and electrocardiogram results on your breeding dogs?
- May I see the results of the Michigan thyroid panel?
- May I have the OFA or PENNHIP numbers?
- May I talk with owners of other boxers you've bred?
- Do you require a contract? If so, what are the conditions?
- When will I get the AKC registration papers?

Also be sure to thoroughly discuss cost before signing a contract or making any other binding agreement. If a breeder tells you one thing and then does another, find another breeder who deals with you honestly.

Questions a Breeder May Ask You

A high-quality boxer puppy will likely come from only one source: a reputable breeder, who will have just as many questions for you (or more). You should welcome this kind of interrogation, which is a strong sign that the breeder cares about her puppies and is looking for the best possible homes for them. All reputable breeders do their best to avoid having their puppies end up in rescue or abandoned. Here are some questions a breeder might ask you:

- Do you own or rent your home?
- Do you live in an apartment?
- Do you have a fenced back yard?
- Do you have a reputable veterinarian?
- Do you have references?
- Have you ever owned a dog before? A boxer?
- Have you ever trained or shown a dog before?
- Have you ever obedience trained a dog before?
- Can you afford veterinary costs?
- Do you have a reputable obedience club or trainer to help you train your puppy?

Boxers are big strong dogs that need plenty of space, attention, and training. If you can't provide any of these necessary elements, the breeder may decide that it's not in everyone's best interest to give you one of her dogs. Again, this signals that the breeder cares about her dogs' welfare above all. If the breeder meets all the criteria described in this chapter, her estimation may be valid, and you may want to consider another breed more suited to your situation.

◀ A good breeder will ensure that her dogs are happy and healthy.

The American Kennel Club (AKC)

The AKC is the oldest kennel club registry in the United States. The founders were reputable breeders with a great love of purebred dogs. They saw the AKC as one way of bettering breeding practices everywhere in the United States.

History of the Club

J. M. Taylor and Elliot Smith called the first meeting of the twelve original founders on September 17, 1884, in the rooms of the Philadelphia Kennel Club. Each member of the group was a delegate from a dog club that had recently held a benched dog show or run field trials. This new "club of clubs" would eventually become the AKC.

 **fact**

In October of 1884, the newly organized AKC met at Madison Square Garden to adopt its constitution and by-laws. Major James M. Taylor became the club's first president.

By 1887, the AKC had an office in New York City. Around this time, it became apparent that the club had to maintain complete studbooks to record the history of each recognized breed. In January 1889, the *AKC Gazette: The Official Journal for the Sport of Purebred Dogs* was first published, with listings of AKC events. It has been published continuously ever since and is one of the oldest dog magazines in existence.

Registrations

One of the AKC's most important and basic functions is to maintain a registry of the breeds it recognizes. Along with the studbooks that record the history of all breeding studs and bitches, the AKC keeps a list of all litters these dogs produce. Some purebred puppies go on to show and enter into breeding lines, but others receive what is known as limited registrations. This is usually given to puppies considered unsuitable for showing or breeding; progeny of a dog with a limited registration are not eligible for AKC registration of any kind. The AKC will also register dogs that belong to certain other recognized registries (usually those of other countries).

Indefinite Listing Privilege (ILP)

Should you get a puppy that belongs to a U.S. registry other than the AKC, you will not be able to show that puppy in AKC events without spaying or neutering and acquiring an indefinite listing privilege (ILP) number. No puppy registered under any other canine registry in the United States will be able to show in AKC conformation.

If you have a purebred boxer that cannot be registered with the AKC and want to compete with your boxer in AKC events other than conformation, the ILP number is the way you can do it. The ILP gives unregistered dogs and their owners a second chance to participate in AKC sports. There are several reasons that a pure-bred boxer might not be eligible for registration: he might have been a product of an unregistered litter or have unregistered parents, or his papers might have been withheld or lost by his owner. He might also have gone through a rescue program.

 **Alert!**

Most people underestimate how much time it will take to train their dogs to do anything. It generally takes about a year for a dog to be really solid and competitive in the obedience ring for each title; however, training for titles concurrently can save time. Often a dog's progress is directly connected to the human trainer's ability to communicate effectively with canines. It is not necessarily a deficiency in the canine's ability that slows the process.

Many dogs are enrolled in the ILP program after they have been surrendered or abandoned, then adopted by new owners from animal shelters or a boxer rescue groups. An ILP boxer can participate in the following AKC events:

- Obedience
- Tracking
- Agility
- Rally

To obtain an ILP number, you can download a form from the AKC Web site (online at *www.AKC.org*). ILP numbers can only be issued to AKC-registered breeds. Once enrolled in the ILP program, entering AKC events is as easy as with a registered dog. The only difference is that instead of an AKC registration number, you list the dog's ILP number on the entry form. Some clubs even offer trophies for the high-scoring ILP dog.

Titles

The purpose of the AKC continues to be the promotion of pure-bred dogs. Any club (such as a specialty, all-breed, obedience, or agility club) that wants to offer an AKC-sanctioned match, show, or trial must be a member of the AKC or affiliated with it through a member club. For instance, the American Boxer Club is a member of the AKC, and local boxer clubs that put on AKC events are members of the American Boxer Club. As dogs compete in and win various competitions, the AKC tracks and records their progress toward titles and championships. Chapters 18 and 19 describe the competitive events that the AKC sponsors and acknowledges, such as obedience, agility, and tracking.

 **Question?**

How can the AKC help new boxer owners?
The AKC provides a wealth of information for new puppy owners and new dog owners. The reason behind all the club's hard work is to improve the standard, look, temperament, working abilities, and health of a breed. Accordingly, all reputable breeders in the United States are affiliated with the AKC.

If you have any aspirations to show in conformation or to become a breeder, you need to start with AKC registered or registered boxers. The AKC regularly offers point shows, obedience trials, and other AKC events in all fifty states.

Judges' Education

The AKC also educates fanciers of the various breeds who are interested in becoming judges in conformation, obedience, agility, or tracking competitions. Potential AKC judges must meet a set of minimum requirements. They must be licensed by and in good standing with the AKC in order both to become a judge and to maintain a judging license. A judge must also keep up to date on the changes in AKC rules and in the breed standard.

Other Breed Registries

While the AKC is the oldest and best-known U.S. registry, there are other notable breed registries as well. For example, the United Kennel Club (UKC) is the second largest all-breed registry in the country, while the Canadian Kennel Club (CKC) is the primary dog registry in Canada.

 Essential

Most reputable breeders show their dogs to prove the worth of their lines. Most are also members of a local breed club, and probably an all-breed or obedience club or two. Additionally, most reputable breeders are supporters of their parent club (the American Boxer Club, for boxers), as well as the goals and objectives of the American Kennel Club.

The United Kennel Club (UKC)

The UKC has 250,000 registrations annually. Founded in 1898 by Chauncey Z. Bennett, the club has a long-standing history of supporting the total dog, or the notion that a dog should look and perform equally well. The UKC offers events including conformation shows, obedience and agility trials, field trials, bench shows, and hunting tests, all aimed at giving dogs a venue for proving their instincts and heritage. A pioneer in DNA testing to verify pedigrees, that club's code of ethics is intended to discourage retail sale of pups and to promote other pro-dog rules and guidelines.

The Canadian Kennel Club (CKC)

The CKC currently recognizes over 160 breeds. As a nonprofit organization, it is dedicated to encouraging, guiding, and advancing the interests of purebred dogs and their responsible owners in Canada, along with promoting the knowledge and the understanding of the benefits that dogs can bring to Canadian society.

A close relationship developed between the CKC and the AKC. The AKC agreed to allow dogs to be exhibited on both sides of the border without requiring registration in both national stud books. The AKC cancelled the first part of the arrangement in 1894, which stated that dogs could be shown on either side of the border without requiring registration in both national stud books, but both national clubs have maintained a close relationship.

 Fact

The Canadian Kennel Club (CKC) was founded in the 1880s. With the formation of the AKC in 1884, dog shows were held under AKC rules, and purebred dogs were registered with the AKC. By 1887, it was clear that a national Canadian club was needed. The following year, a general meeting was held in London, Ontario, and the CKC was formed.

What Is a Pedigree?

A dog's pedigree traces its ancestry. Preferably, the pedigree will show champions of record and obedience titles in your boxer's background, with dogs coming from recognized, reputable breeders and kennels. Any titles that a dog earns, whether in obedience, agility, tracking, or rally, become a permanent part of the dog's registered name.

What a Pedigree Looks Like

Pedigree for Jacquet's Heliocentric, CDX, bitch, brindle/white
DOB: 3/12/96 AKC Reg. #: WP698814/01

Generation 1	Generation 2	Generation 3	Generation 4
sire CH Jacquet's Greggson, SOM	sire ICH Jacquet's Novarese, SOM	sire ICH Jacquet's Agassiz	sire CH Merrilane's April Fashion, SOM
			dam Jacquet's Hot Summer
		dam Angel Angelli	sire Jacquet's Markham
			dam Bella Angelli
	dam ICH Jacquet's Aliage of Goldfield	sire ICH Jacquet's Urko, SOM	sire CH Happy Ours Fortune De Jacquet, SOM
			dam CH Jacquet's Candy Dancer
		dam CH Jacquet's Goldenfield Rubidoux, DOM	sire CH Merrilane's April Fashion, SOM
			dam Jacquet's Hot Summer
dam Jacquet's Mustang Sally	sire CH Goldfield's Eagle Dancer	sire Ch Marquam Hill's Traper of Turo, SOM	sire ICH Mephisto's Vendetta SOM
			dam Ch Turo's Whisper of 5-T's, DOM
		dam Ch Turo's Mirage	sire CH Mephisto's Warlock of Turo
			dam Obie One Knobe
	dam Jacquet's Hazel, CD	sire CH Goldfield's Dorian De Jacquet	sire CH Happy Ours Fortune de Jacquet, SOM
			dam CH Jacquet's Goldfield Rubidoux, DOM
		dam Jacquet's Diana	sire CH Jacquet's Winchester of BG
			dam CH Jacquet's Firesong

What a Pedigree Means

The following explanation of the pedigree for Jacquet's Heliocentric, CDX, will help you understand any pedigrees you read.

- Jacquet: Kennel name.
- Heliocentric: The part of Helio's registered name that differentiates her from any other boxer that the Jacquet kennel has registered with the AKC.
- DOB 3/12/96: Date that Helio was whelped.
- Reg. #: WP698814/01: Helio's registration number. The number "WP698814" is assigned to all puppies in Helio's litter. The digits "01" are particular to Helio and indicate that she was either the first puppy born or the first puppy in the litter to be registered.
- CDX: Abbreviation for the obedience title "Companion Dog Excellent." This indicates that Helio has earned not only her CDX but the preceding title of Companion Dog (abbreviated CD).

They are correct.

When two kennels or breeders become involved in partnership or cobreeding, the registered name might look something like this: Harpo's CertainCharm d'Jacquet, UD. In this case, the following explanations apply:

- Harpo: Primary kennel name.
- CertainCharm: The part of Charm's registered name that differentiates her from all the other boxers bred and registered by the Harpo kennel.
- d'Jacquet: Secondary kennel name. Usually, this indicates that the kennel doing the breeding (Harpo) either has an affiliation with the second kennel (Jacquet), or a requirement to include the Jacquet kennel name in the registered naming of the puppies. In this case, the Jacquet bitch owned by Harpo Boxers was bred to a Jacquet dog owned

by Jacquet Boxers. Whenever you see two kennels names, it usually indicates a positive relationship between breeders and is an interesting way to track the puppies.

- UD: Abbreviation for the obedience title "Utility Dog," signifying that Charm has earned first her CD, then her CDX, and finally the UD.

Registered Names

Naming a litter is a fun job that often takes much time and consideration. Registered names can be whimsical or formal or anything in between, usually reflecting some aspect of the breeder's or owner's personality. Some breeders choose the registered names of all their puppies. Some decide on the general theme that all names will follow and offer the puppy buyer a selection of names accordingly, and others allow buyers to choose any name they wish.

In the case of Jacquet's Heliocentric, CDX, heliocentric (meaning "sun-centered") describes the character of the boxer in question. Helio was a funny, good-natured, strong-minded bitch. She was sunny. Her name fit her perfectly.

Contracts

The most important piece of paper you will handle when buying a new boxer is the sales contract. Not all breeders use a contract; for those who do, the sales contract outlines their professional relationship with you. If you want a high-quality purebred dog, you may find that there are some strings attached. For instance, if you buy a show-quality bitch, the contract may stipulate that the kennel retains her breeding rights. If you buy a pet-quality puppy, the contract may require you to spay or neuter by a certain age. Often, though, the strings are in the best interests of the dog and the kennel, and they might also provide you with a safety net.

Spay/Neuter Contracts

A spay-neuter contract is one that requires you to have your puppy spayed or neutered by a certain age. If you purchase a pet-quality puppy from a reputable breeder, that breeder will not want that puppy to be bred. The puppy will have what is known as limited registration, meaning that any litters that puppy may eventually produce will not be eligible for AKC registration. Basically, the spay/neuter contract allows the breeder to decide what dogs will be bred from her lines.

Some people dislike spay/neuter contracts because they feel it should be their right to breed any dog they own. If you have done your homework and chosen a reputable breeder wisely, you would be well advised to heed the breeder's opinion. Reputable breeders only want the best specimens of the breed to reproduce. Any other breeding plan runs the risk of passing along undesirable traits. A boxer that is not a perfect conformation specimen can still be a wonderful family dog, so do not be discouraged on that account.

Other Contracts

A contract for a show-prospect puppy might define the minimum number of times the pup must be shown and who pays the show-related fees. If the puppy is a bitch, the contract might specify when she will be bred and who will choose the stud. A breeder who believes in the benefits of raw food may stipulate that only raw foods be fed to the pup. (In some cases, feeding food that the breeder feels is not optimal for the puppy may negate any health guarantees, so read your contracts carefully.) A sincere, reputable breeder will take the essence and specifics of the contract very seriously, and so should you.

Bringing Your Boxer Home

One of the most important aspects of boxer ownership is a well thought-out plan to bring your dog home. This cannot be emphasized enough, as the logistics of keeping your boxer will depend, in large part, on how well you have planned for your boxer's initial introduction to your life. This can make or break a boxer's experience in your home and potentially decide where the dog ends up—in your home or in rescue. This chapter thoroughly covers this crucial step.

How to Bring Your Puppy Home

You might develop a great relationship with a breeder who lives across the country, or you might find a faraway kennel that produces great champions or performance dogs with the perfect puppy for you. If the kennel you choose is literally across country, you may not be able to pick up your puppy by car. In that case, you can try to find someone else to drive the puppy cross-country; you can fly out yourself to pick up the puppy; or you can have the puppy shipped by air.

In order to travel with any dog, regardless of age, you should have a veterinarian sign a health certificate stating that the dog is healthy and fit to travel. (Health certification is necessary for travel by air.) If the dog is over six months of age, proof of rabies vaccination is also required.

If you are driving with a dog, it is still a good idea to get a health certificate that lists the vaccinations it has received. The dog should be current at least according to the laws of your home state. Some states require annual rabies vaccinations while others require them only every three years. It is also a good idea to know the law regarding canine vaccinations in any state that you plan to travel through. If your dog is not current on required vaccinations, he could be quarantined in that area until it is proven that he is not infectious.

Driving Cross-Country

Car travel with a puppy can be difficult. An eight-week-old puppy will need to potty almost every hour on the hour, effectively slowing you down. If you have a nice, comfy crate, the puppy may be able to hold it longer, but try not to push it too much. This is all brand new for the puppy, and you don't want to overwhelm him with challenges and too many new things right away.

 Fact

A young puppy between eight and ten weeks old should be given the chance to go out and potty at least once every hour it is awake, as well as immediately after every meal, nap, and play or training session. This is the easiest and most effective way to make sure the pup doesn't have accidents. Using this method also gives you ample opportunity to praise the pup for good potty behavior.

Flying with Your Puppy

Dogs can fly either in the cargo hold of airplanes or in the cabin. Either way, you will be charged an excess baggage fee. It is safer and less traumatic for the pup to fly in the cabin, as cargo holds are often noisy and extreme in temperature.

You can fly with your puppy inside of the cabin as long as his crate will fit under the seat in front of you. It is necessary to make reservations well in advance for this kind of travel, as most airlines place strict limits on the number of pets allowed in the cabin. You may want to put wee-wee pads in the crate so your pup can relieve himself during the flight. If you cannot fly out to pick up your pup yourself, you can make arrangements with the breeder to have the puppy shipped.

At the Airport

There is nothing more exciting than waiting to see your pup off-loaded from the hold of an airplane. The pup will probably have been on his own without other live contact for some considerable time, so he will probably be a bit shell-shocked by the time you see him. Some airlines will not release an animal shipped as cargo until you examine it and certify its safe and healthy arrival.

 **Fact**

Don't be disappointed if your pup relieved himself in his crate because of having to hold it too long or due to the stress of traveling. Clean him up and welcome him with all the enthusiasm and sympathy he deserves, then offer him a drink of water and a treat or two. Then take him home and let him check out his new surroundings. He has a lot of catching up to do in his new world.

When you're at the airport, keep your pup either in his crate or on leash. The sights and sounds of a busy airport could easily frighten him into running off. The best thing is to put him on leash and find a safe place where he can relieve himself. Then put him back in the crate and drive him home. You should take any new pup to your own vet within forty-eight hours of his arrival in order to make sure he's healthy.

New Puppy Basics

If you are getting a puppy, the breeder will tell you what kind of puppy food she uses. Many reputable breeders will provide you with a little going-home kit that includes food and toys or maybe a blanket that carries the scent of your puppy's litter. This can be a big help in easing your pup's transition into your family.

Alert!

Holidays and other special occasions are the worst times to bring home a new boxer. Unpredictable schedules and frequent visits from guests can create a chaotic environment for a new puppy or adult boxer. It is best to give your new boxer the benefit of your complete and total attention for a day or two (preferably a week) after he gets home. You may find that you, too, feel a little overwhelmed with your new dog.

Before you leave the breeder, be sure to ask about the puppy's housetraining experience, if any, as well as what kind of socialization he has had. In many cases, the dam will have begun to take the puppies out to train them to potty where she does, and they will have some rudimentary idea that a good, clean puppy does not potty in the area where it eats and sleeps. If the pup was raised in a cold climate, the breeder may have provided newspapers or wee-wee pads for the puppies to potty on. Just make sure you find out as much as you can about what the puppy knows about housetraining. It will help both of you in your continued education on this matter when you get the new puppy home.

Where Does the Puppy Sleep?

Before your puppy comes home, you should decide where he will sleep at night. The best option is a crate (wire or the plastic airline variety) that provides your new puppy with his own private space. People often buy the biggest crate that they can, thinking that the puppy will it need when he's an adult. If you do this, make sure that you can segment part of it off. Little puppies need littler spaces to feel comfortable.

 **Essential**

Since a crate is fairly cold and bare, you will need to make it nice and cushy by providing comfortable bedding—either a soft foam-filled pad or one made of fake sheepskin. The material should be something that your new puppy can snuggle into and that reminds him of the comfort of his pack. You can give him a few soft toys, too, and maybe a little hard plastic bone to chew on to reduce stress.

In addition, you will need a little collar, preferably cloth of some kind, and a leash, so that your puppy can be safe while learning what he needs to learn about limits in life. You'll need at least one small-to-medium bowl for food and one for water.

Crate Location

The best place for your new puppy to sleep is in your bedroom, where someone will hear him if he cries. If you leave your puppy alone at night, he will be slower to understand the importance of letting someone know when he needs to potty, and housetraining will be more difficult. By sleeping in your room, he is also less likely to feel overwhelmed by loneliness. He may still be frightened at being alone and may bark or whine somewhat at first. If he sleeps alone somewhere else in the house, he will be so excited when he does see you that he is likely to go potty on the spot, depriving you of the opportunity to show him the right place to go. Remember, the fewer mistakes your pup makes in the beginning, the more quickly and readily he will become housetrained.

What to Expect from Your Boxer Puppy

Your puppy has just made a huge life change, so he's likely to be unsure of how to behave in unfamiliar territory. He is certain to make mistakes; what you need is patience in clearly and kindly pointing out correct behaviors. You can start by teaching him to potty in a certain part of the yard, if that's what you want (a good way to save your landscaping from urine spots).

Basically, if you are kind and comforting, your pup should be happy and interested in his environment. He should investigate cautiously. Finding that he is safe and secure in his new surroundings, he will probably engage in boxer zoomies, running around as fast as those puppy paws will take him, tongue hanging out. Then he's likely to flop down near you to sleep the sleep of a contented puppy.

Naming Your Pup

If you get your new puppy from a reputable breeder, chances are that each member of the litter has already been given a registered name and maybe even a call name, too. Many reputable breeders name their entire litters to keep owners from choosing inappropriate names like _____'s Stupid Sally or _____'s Come Here Dammit. You are stuck with the registered name, but for an eight- to ten-week-old puppy, you shouldn't have much difficulty changing any call name that has been used.

 Fact

Your breeder might be willing to take your input and let you choose the name of your pup, as long as it fits within their chosen theme or method of naming puppies. If you are lucky enough to give your pup his registered name, try to think of something that will bring dignity and respect to the breed and to your dog when he is older.

Litters are often named according to variations on the theme of other names in the pedigree. The offspring of ____'s Jetbreaker might be _____'s Blazing Jet or _____'s Blazing Kisses. Themes are another common way to name litters. The litter theme might be anything from Olympic events (Ice Dancer, Beach Volleyball, Downhill Skier) to luck (Just for Luck, Lots of Luck, Kiss for Luck) to astronomy and space exploration themes (Hubble Telescope, Ursa Minor, Shooting Star). Litter theme names can be a lot of fun to think of, and they make for an entertaining way to follow the dogs of certain kennels in their show careers.

Litters can also be named by letter of the alphabet, starting with A (Artistry, Accolades, Anagram) for the first litter, B for the second, and continuing accordingly. This provides another way of tracking a kennel's pups through a show career.

Meeting Other Animals

You will hear a great deal of dissenting opinion among trainers and vets about when to introduce your puppy to other animals, especially other dogs. Your veterinarian is likely to say that your puppy should be protected from exposure to other dogs until six months of age, when his vaccinations will be complete. However, boxers that are not adequately socialized by the age of six months might never tolerate new dogs. The answer is to make sure your pup gets out as much as possible but only to places he is unlikely to encounter a lot of other dogs (or dog feces). Most infectious agents are transmitted through feces. Even if owners clean up frequently after their dogs, viruses and bacteria are still left behind that could infect your pup.

Classes Can Help

Do not walk your puppy on streets where a lot of other dogs are taken to go potty. Avoid dog play areas or public parks where you are likely to run into free-roaming dogs. An excellent solution to this early socializing dilemma is to find a puppy preschool or socialization class. Most classes require all canine attendees to be current on vaccinations, giving you some peace of mind and your puppy some valuable socialization. This is an excellent way for him to learn and play with other puppies among various distractions.

 **Essential**

A puppy socialization class or other training class is a good, safe bet because the puppy is unlikely to run into larger dogs off-leash who might not like puppies. Most of the dogs in a class setting are under control.

The last thing you want is for your puppy to have a bad experience with larger dogs. Classes are usually offered according to the dogs' ages, so this is a good way to avoid chance encounters with older dogs that may be hostile or aggressive to strange pups. Decline offers to introduce your puppy to larger dogs or to join doggie play groups unless you know from experience that all the others dogs are good with puppies. Your puppy will not be lonely or poorly socialized as long as you find a good puppy class for him to attend and you spend plenty of time on training and exercise. Chapter 16 provides detailed information on the process of socialization and the various periods of development of your boxer's development.

Other Pets in Your Home

You may be bringing your new boxer into a household full of other pets, such as other dogs, cats, birds, or even an iguana or two. If this is the case, you'll have to work out a method of safely introducing your boxer to your current pets (and vice versa).

If you have other dogs, arrange for them to meet the new pup (all on leash) at some neutral location, where no one will have territory to protect. Once they seem comfortable, you can let them sniff each other. However, should either one show aggression, it is best to separate them. If you can't do this, then make sure that the little newcomer has a crate or x-pen where it can watch the way your home is run. If you restrict your pup at first, your older dogs will not be as offended, since the newcomer will not have the full-run of "their" territory.

 **Alert!**

Do not assume that any other animals you already have in the house will share your enthusiasm for your adorable new boxer pup. Do not leave the puppy alone with any other animals or in any other situation where they might hurt him, even accidentally. Boxers have good memories. When yours grows up, you want him to have only good recollections of the other pets that share his home.

Before you bring the pup home, be sure you have a safe area set up where he can observe the household without getting in anyone's way. Check your pet store for a portable enclosure (called an exercise pen, or x-pen), or put the puppy in a large crate in a place that gives him a good view of all the action. This is the most effective way of ensuring peace in the house and assuring any other dogs that they still outrank the little interloper.

Your new boxer should spend his first month or so in the crate or x-pen. Doing this sort of slow, gradual introduction to the household, particularly if there are other dogs in the house, is one of the best ways to avoid canine altercations down the road. This gives the newcomer an opportunity to observe how the household is run from a more limited (neutral) perspective, and usually helps to diminish the drive in some young dogs to challenge the existing canines or humans in the new territory.

Even though the newcomer is crated or in an x-pen, he still needs adequate time to exercise and play and to work on lessons with you. Even if he seems trained, you should still go over all the basics so the two of you get to know each other. And if he doesn't know the basics, this is one of the best ways to quickly build a bond. Chapter 13 provides information on training basics for your new boxer.

When it is time to let your pup roam free with other dogs and cats in the house, it is best to closely supervise all play sessions. Do this until the pup is four to five months old and less likely to be injured in rough play.

Crate Training

In general, one of the safest places your boxer can be is in a crate, whether he's alone in the house, traveling with you in the car, or flying in an airplane. It's vital that your boxer doesn't consider the crate a frightening place, and it's up to you to make sure the pup learns early on in life that a crate is not only safe but also a good place to be.

 Fact

The protection of a crate has saved more than one dog's life in car accidents that have taken the lives of their owners. Crates can also save a lot of distress at the vet's office, especially if your dog has to stay. It really is a kindness to help your new boxer learn how to relax and enjoy his crate.

If you frequently take your dog in the car with you, he will need to be comfortable in the crate—for everyone's safety. Being restrained within the crate will keep your dog stationary instead of letting him fly around the car during sharp turns. However, if you are ever in a car accident or have to hit the brakes quickly, you don't want your boxer's crate (with him in it!) to fly forward and injure you. Crates should be secured in your vehicle as much as possible.

Size Matters

When it comes to crates, size matters a lot. When you get a new puppy, your tendency will most likely be to plan for the future and choose a crate he can grow into. But ideally, your dog's crate should be just big enough for him to stand up and turn around in. A crate that is too big can pose serious risks. On the other hand, you don't want a small, cramped crate to discourage your boxer from using it.

 **Fact**

Most boxer bitches will fit into a size 300 (22 inches wide by 32 long by 23 high) or 400 (24 inches wide by 36 long by 24 high) airline type crate as adults. Adult males will fit into a size 400 or 500 (27 inches wide by 40 long by 30 wide) crate. These crates will allow your boxer to move around comfortably, to stand up in the crate, and to turn around.

If the crate is too big, your boxer can be injured by being jostled around in it if you and your boxer are in a car accident. Any dog can more easily break out of a crate that is too big by pulling at the door with his teeth, and he can injure himself in doing this, especially as a puppy.

Boxer puppies, with their undershot jaws, are at risk of injuring their jaw joints and disfiguring the fronts of the jaw if they can get their teeth into the wire of the door and pull too much. An older boxer can do this as well, and being in a crate that is a bit too large enables him to do this much more readily than in one that is the correct size. To prevent injury to your pup's jaw, you need to train him not to do this, but the easiest thing is to ensure that it can't happen in the first place.

Making the Crate a Friendly Place

There are numerous dog products out there that serve as bedding and crate liners. You will find, after a little exploration, which types best suit you and your boxer. In any event, you'll want something that is soft and provides some cushioning from the hard surface of the crate. A few fun toys are also a must inside the crate, as is a coop cup or some kind of container that attaches on the inside to provide your dog with fresh, clean water.

If your young puppy finds the crate to be a scary or boring place, you can distract him with a sterilized shank bone or Kong-type toy stuffed with layers of peanut butter, yummy dog treats, and other goodies. Keep these on hand in your freezer for times when you need to leave your pup alone or as an incentive to be calm and quiet in his crate.

In fact, if your living space is limited, you can feed your pup his regular meals in his crate and avoid the disruption elsewhere. Anywhere a dog eats regularly will be considered a good place relatively quickly, and your pup will soon absolutely adore his crate. And soon he'll be quiet in there without food simply because the crate has many positive associations. Never leave your pup there too long that he becomes uncomfortable about needing to potty. Nothing makes any dog hate a crate more than that, and there is the risk that if he starts learning to potty in the crate, he will continue to soil in it.

 Fact

Dogs are hardwired to work their way up to the alpha dog position. What this means is that in absence of strong leadership, they will try to take command. It makes them feel more secure to know that someone is running the show, so to speak. This tendency is what can often lead to fights and agression in all dogs. To offset this possibility, it is recommended that you take a strong role in training your boxer.

Integrating a Boxer into Your Household

By the time you get your boxer home, you need to have decided where he will eat, sleep, play, and potty and who will feed, walk, train, and play with the dog and when. All of this should be well thought out in advance of the dog coming home, and the plan should be ready to be implemented the minute he comes through the door. This will include having purchased all supplies, equipment, and toys, and knowing how to use everything.

◀ **Do whatever it takes to ensure that your boxer is comfortable in his new home.**

Integrating the Older Boxer

Most of the discussion in this chapter has been about how to bring a new puppy into your home, but what if you decide that an older dog is best for you? Well, many of the same rules apply in bringing your new adult boxer home with you. You need all the same equipment, except, perhaps, on a larger scale.

If you get your new adult boxer from a boxer rescue organization, you want to make sure that you get as much information about the dog as possible. The organization should know something about the dog, even if he was an anonymous surrender. Your new boxer should have been tested with other dogs, cats, children, and so on. The rescue organization should also be able to tell you how he reacts to a variety of situations and if he has any significant quirks, such as a fear of thunderstorms or bicycles.

 **Essential**

> If you decide to get an adult rescue boxer, the rescue organization should also be able to tell you if your boxer is already crate trained. The same is true if you get a retired show dog or one that did not like to show. A show dog will likely be familiar with a crate, which makes your job easier from the start.

You need to ask as many questions as possible about your dog so that you know as much as you can about housetraining, food needs, known food allergies or intolerances, compatibility with other animals and children, and tolerance of new situations in general.

Yard Safety

It will be difficult to get a puppy from a reputable breeder or a dog from rescue if you do not have an adequately fenced yard. Boxers are, by and large, fabulous jumpers, and even many females can clear a five-foot fence from a sit with little or no difficulty. You therefore want a six-foot-high fence, minimum. You may also want to make sure that there is a barrier beneath the fence line to keep your boxer from digging his way out.

The fence needs to be strong and free of cracks, gaps, or exposed nails. A solid wood fence is preferable to chain link or any other type that passing people and dogs can see through. In general, you want your fence to serve as a visual barrier as much as a physical one, as other dogs may frequently pass by, possibly riling your dog into a frenzy.

 **Fact**

Invisible fencing consists of an underground barrier with a battery connection that the dog wears on a special collar. The collar gives the dog a shock as he crosses the barrier, reminding him of his boundaries. Invisible fencing is generally much cheaper than barrier fencing or hurricane fencing. However, boxers have a very high pain threshold, and they may not care that they are being shocked. Furthermore, while this method may keep your boxer in, it won't keep other dogs out.

Beyond putting an adequate fence system in place, you also need to make sure that your yard is free of any items that may harm your dog. This means that all potentially toxic plants (primarily flowering bulbs) must be removed from areas of the yard where the dog will be permitted. Grass is probably the best medium for most dogs, with a nice large tree or two for shade.

If you have decided that you want your boxer to potty in only one part of the yard, you should cordon that part off, or otherwise define it in some way. Cover this area with the kind of mulch or ground cover that is appropriate for your geographical area. To teach the dog that this is his potty space, march him out there as soon as he wakes up from a nap and periodically during play or lessons. When he does his duty in the right spot, be sure to give plenty of praise.

The First Few Nights

Hopefully, introducing your new boxer pup to your home will be a fairly simple process. You will have your crate ready for your new puppy, and he'll sleep in it at night. Keeping him in your bedroom with you during the night will help him feel more comfortable in his new surroundings. You might find that your puppy falls asleep with no protest and sleeps through most of the night. After all, he'll have his cushy new crate, toys, bed, and, if possible, something that smells like his littermates. That can be a toy that all the pups played with or a piece of bedding.

 **Alert!**

Don't expect the kids to take care of the boxer any more than you expect them to clean their rooms or take out the garbage. They will probably take care of the dog only when you stay after them to do it, and even then, they might not do a very thorough or careful job. This means that the dog's care will ultimately be your responsibility.

But what if it isn't so simple? If your pup has a real fit of homesickness for his dam, his littermates, and his breeder, it's okay to pet him in his crate and give him a few reassuring words. Just make sure he isn't protesting because he really has to potty. When you are sure that he does not, calmly and firmly tell him goodnight, and prepare to wait it out. Some puppies just need to fuss a little, but it is usually over in about ten minutes or less. Remember that the less you coddle him over this, the more quickly he'll get over it. Coddling him at this point will only set him up to think that if he protests enough, you'll give in, and you don't want that.

Finding a Veterinarian

Whether you have taken home a boxer puppy or an adult dog, you still need to choose a veterinarian. The best option is to find a vet who either has boxers herself or knows a great deal about the illnesses and congenital issues that boxers face. Of course, the most important thing is that the vet cares about your boxer. With any luck she'll also be someone you could enjoy taking your dog to see.

When take your new boxer to the vet for the first time, you might want to ask about how much exercise the dog needs. Get vaccinations schedules and an emergency vet referral if the vet isn't open around the clock, and ask whether she can recommend some basic training classes. Also check to see whether the clinic boards dogs in emergencies or if the vet can recommend someone else who does. Write down the vet's regular phone number, emergency contact number, address, and business hours. Keep this information accessible in multiple places in your home.

CHAPTER 6

Housetraining

Housetraining is one of the most important basic training lessons that you can give your dog. However, housetraining is more than just teaching your boxer to potty outside. It also makes your boxer feel comfortable in his surroundings and gets him used to different scenarios, whether it's the house, the yard, his crate, or the wider world. It's best to have the whole family get involved with housetraining.

Long-Term Confinement Areas

Many people work outside the home, and everyone needs to leave the house for extended periods of time for many different reasons. Just because you need to go out doesn't mean that your puppy doesn't need to potty as frequently. When you do need to leave for a bit, what should you do with your boxer?

Until your boxer is about a year old, if you need to be gone for an extended period of time, someone needs to come in and let him out of his crate to potty. He needs to stay in his crate because he doesn't know the rules yet. If you leave him alone and loose in the house, you will probably come back to little puppy puddles all over the house. You'll also probably find chewed up books, toys, and furniture, toilet paper rolls strewn around the house, and possibly worse. Also, your pup could injure himself on something that he chews or jumps on. So until he is well housetrained, and you have had the chance to test him with short periods of time, you are best advised not to leave him loose on his own.

Like the crate, you want to make the long-term confinement place as comfortable as possible with clean, fresh water available when the dog needs it, and toys and blankets that your boxer likes. Most people eventually find a space in the house that belongs to the dog. If you live in a part of the country that has basements, many dogs find their space there. If you are fortunate to have an extra room or room in the laundry area or garage, one of these spaces might be a good place for your dog.

 **Essential**

If you don't want your boxer to spend his day lounging on your bed or the furniture, you will need to get him his own bed. You can place this in a crate in your bedroom for now. Later, when he is older, you can let him loose in the house without being afraid that he'll cause all kinds of problems.

You can also buy attractive baby gates or barriers from many pet stores and pet catalogs. Put these up to block any areas of the house that you would prefer to be off-limits to your boxer while you are gone. Strategically placed, a few gates will prevent access to all parts of the house while you are gone. These are an effective and efficient solution if you live in a house or apartment that has a somewhat open plan type of arrangement. They're also helpful if you simply want to keep your dog in a kitchen or laundry area so that he doesn't roam the house while you are away.

Paper Training

Say you have the basic time and resources to get a boxer, but you do not have anyone to let the puppy out every four hours while

<u>you're at work.</u> Or maybe you live on the twentieth floor of an apartment building. Chances are, especially when your boxer puppy is little, you will find it very difficult to get the dog outside as readily and quickly as you might need to in order to avoid accidents. In either of these cases, paper training could be the solution.

In paper training, the dog learns to relieve himself on newspaper (or other special paper) in one very specific area of the house where the paper is always left on the floor for him. You place a large sheet of plastic under the paper, wrap up the whole bundle when the dog is done, and throw the whole thing away.

 Fact

There are two keys to making paper training a success. First of all, you must train your new boxer to potty on that area, and second, you must be sure to keep that area as scrupulously clean as possible. This will help encourage your pup to potty in that particular spot rather than relieving himself in an ever-larger area or throughout the house.

Originally, newspapers were used for paper training. These days, it is relatively inexpensive to buy paper or pads that have been impregnated with a smell that stimulates dogs to relieve themselves on that pad or paper. This also helps you avoid newsprint being spread all around the house via puppy paws. These specialty papers are also lined with plastic in many cases, eliminating the need for you to buy plastic sheets to put under the newspaper.

If you need to use the paper training technique, it is a good idea to place the papers in your long-term confinement area away from the kitchen and bedrooms for sanitary reasons.

Schedules and Routines

As a general rule of thumb, your puppy will need to potty every hour or so, including upon waking and after he eats, until about four months of age. Because puppies are small, their bladders and colons are simply not mature or strong enough to hold for more than relatively short periods of time. By taking your pup out every hour, in addition to after naps and meals, you won't have to clean up countless potty accidents. Your pup consequently won't be conditioned to potty in the wrong places. This routine also gives you ample opportunity to show the pup where you want him to potty on a regular basis.

Doggy Doors

If you have a doggy door, it will probably take relatively little time to train the pup how to get outside to relieve himself. If you don't have one, simply take him out hourly. The downside to doggy doors is that it is a bit harder to train your pup to potty only in one area of the yard because you are not always outside with him. (It would defeat the purpose of the doggy door if you were.) The upside is that if you can attach it to your long-term confinement area, making it easy for the dog to go outside whenever he needs to when you're away for extended periods of time.

✳ Ringing Bells

To use the bell ringing method, you simply hang a small bell on the door within the puppy's reach. In the early days of potty training, you ring the bell as you take the puppy outside. Eventually, the puppy becomes used to hearing the bell and associates it with going outside. When the pup is a little older, you can then encourage him to ring the bell before you go outside. When she learns to do this, praise mightily.

If you've been consistent in ringing the bell every time you've taken him out, it doesn't usually take too long for the pup to get the idea that he should ring the bell if he needs to go outside.

Generally speaking, the puppy will try to give you some kind of clue pretty quickly to let you know that he needs to go outside to potty. The problem is that what seems like clear communication to a boxer puppy, often a look or grimace at you, is not always clear or you are not looking at him at the right time to see it. The bell gives the puppy a better way to communicate his needs to you.

✳  **Alert!**

The downside of the bell-ringing method is that some playful boxer puppies just enjoy ringing the bell for fun, or they may not understand that it is meant only for one particular purpose. In this case, you need to take extra measures to teach the pup the bell's correct use, or give up and try a different method.

Dealing with Accidents

Chances are pretty good that, on at least one occasion, your pup will potty inside accidentally because he didn't know how to get out on his own, or he didn't know how to tell you he needed to get out.

When this happens, *do not* hit the puppy with a newspaper or rub the puppy's nose in it. These old-fashioned approaches eventually went out of favor because they failed to produce the desired results. These actions only put your relationship with your boxer at risk. After all, he's dependent upon you for everything; how secure can he feel if he is constantly being punished for something he can't help?

What should you do if your pup has an accident in the house? First, wipe up the urine or feces off the floor with a paper towel, placing it in a plastic bag that goes out with the trash. Then liberally douse the area with enzymatic cleaner and let the cleaner sit according to the manufacturer's instructions. Wipe up the cleaner with another paper towel, and rinse the area with a wet cloth rag or something else that you can launder completely.

 **Essential**

It seems excessive to some people to get out with their puppies every hour on the hour plus after every nap, meal, and play session. But if you can do it, housetraining will go very smoothly. After all, you are spending a great deal of time training your puppy and hence bonding with him. He will want to please you all the more for that reason. It is also the best time to train a pup to potty in a certain place on the yard, and you can reinforce the action positively every time you go out with your pup.

The point of this cleaning is to eliminate every trace of smell. Dog's noses have about 10,000 more scent receptors than we do. If even the tiniest little bit of scent remains, the pup, who is hard-wired to potty when he smells urine or feces, will potty there again—he can't help it. If he continues to potty there, it means you're not cleaning up well enough, and you need to get that puppy out more often!

Though punishment is pointless, you can give your pup some kind of negative verbal reinforcement, such as "Not in the house," "Ick," or "Phooey." This lets him know that while the accident is not his fault, messes do not belong in the house. Boxer puppies are smart. They can understand the tone of your voice and will try that much harder to hold it or to let you know when they need to go out.

Establishing a Potty Spot

Establishing a potty spot is easier in the beginning, so it's best to work on potty training and bonding early on. This method can be used to keep the majority of your yard from being soiled. If you're paper training, this lesson teaches the pup exactly where to relieve himself inside the house.

As noted earlier, all canines are hard-wired to relieve themselves where they can smell the scent left behind by other canines. Getting your puppy to potty in one place will make that spot smell like urine or feces. As you keep going out there when the puppy needs to potty, the smell will grow stronger. You must still pick up after your pup, of course, but that sensitive nose will help habituate him to potty in the spot you have chosen.

The same principles apply in the house if you need to paper train your pup. You need to get him to go on the papers in one spot in the house initially. After that, it's a little easier, and you can buy papers that are impregnated with the scent of urine. Of course, this scent won't be noticeable to you, but for a dog, it's all the persuasion needed.

 **Alert!**

If after several weeks or months of housetraining you are not seeing success most of the time, you may need to go back to square one. This likely means that your pup has gotten confused along the way and needs to be taught the basics once more. Don't get impatient with him—he'll get it right eventually.

How Long Does Housetraining Take?

As with all training, housetraining takes as long as it takes. There are so many variables in everyone's busy life that it is really hard to say. However, if you are able to spend the first few days or week with your new puppy, taking your new puppy out faithfully every hour on the hour without fail, after every nap, play session, and meal, you should begin to see some reliability. Your pup should be trying to let you know he needs to go out, which means that he is getting the idea that he needs to go out, and he wants to let you know so that you can help him.

By six months of age, you should see some reliability for periods of up to a few hours. The boxer is a slow-maturing breed, so, you may see accidents up until yours is a year old. However, along with the accidents, you should also be seeing major attempts to do the right thing as concerns potty training, and a minimum of accidents.

Housetraining the Adult Dog

Say you've fallen in love with an older boxer that you think would be your perfect dog, such as a retired show dog, or a rescue dog with a wonderful personality. You're all set to go ahead and take him home when you are informed that he is not housetrained. Should you still get the dog? If you have a bond with him, then the answer is yes.

Go back and reread all the information on housetraining a puppy, and apply this to your adult boxer accordingly, with one extra twist on the theme. For the first few days or a week (and you can actually do this with a puppy, too, to bond faster), you put the dog on a leash attached to your wrist or your belt, so the dog has to go everywhere in the house with you. You take the adult boxer out with you every hour on the hour, after every nap, after every meal. In addition, you should be taking your boxer for longer walks and training sessions.

The one thing to remember about potty training an adult boxer is that the dog is simply used to going wherever and whenever. You are likely to be faced with some pretty big accidents in the house at first. Just get out your enzymatic cleaners and clean, clean, clean. Use the negative verbal reinforcement as well. This is a dog that does not know these basic rules, and you need to communicate them—kindly.

 ▲ Adult dogs can be housetrained too. You can teach an old dog new tricks!

✳🐕 Fact

You may be temped to use ammonia to clean up any messes that your boxer makes inside the house. Don't! Ammonia resembles urine in smell—urine has ammonia in it, after all—so don't be tempted to get something cheaper than a good enzymatic cleaner. In the long run, it is cheaper to get the more expensive enzymatic cleaners. Bleach doesn't work either, and it can really mess up the finishes of your floors.

Obviously, you're going to praise your new adult boxer mightily when he does his stuff outside (or wherever you designate). It shouldn't take more than a month or so for him to have a pretty good idea about how this new aspect of his life works. Most importantly, after all the time you've spent hooked up to each other, you and he will have bonded. He wants you to be happy with him and will understand that by pottying where and when you say, he will be on the fast track to being your new best friend.

Relapses in Housetraining

Relapses in housetraining happen. You may notice these at particular times, such as when your puppy hits sexual maturity or goes through the growth and development stages in which he gains greater awareness of the genuine perils in the world (fear periods, as described in Chapter 16). Other times you might get caught in traffic and be unable to get home in time. Or there may simply be too many people in the house for your pup to discern his biological needs. Whatever the reason, you'll have accidents, and accidents usually lead to brief setbacks.

The best thing to do is to simply go back a step or two in housetraining. Put your outings back on a schedule, and you'll find in less than a week you can usually catch up on any time lost in the relapse. The same is true of an adult dog. However, try not to let these happen too often. Otherwise your new boxer, puppy or adult, might interpret your inattention to mean that potty training is not all that important to you and proceed to potty wherever he feels like it.

Basic Nutrition

There is a lot of controversy in the world of dog people as to what to feed your boxer. The dog-food industry is a multi-million-dollar one, packed with choices for your dog. From wet or dry commercial food to natural and raw foods, there are several decisions to make. There are other nutrition questions to answer: Is chocolate really toxic? And what's the truth about supplements and table scraps? This chapter covers all the bases to help you form a plan for your boxer's nutrition.

Essential Nutrients

It is generally agreed upon that there are basic vitamins and minerals that all dogs need. There is less agreement, however, on the amounts of those requirements. The vitamins that a dog needs are the following:

- Vitamin A
- Vitamin D
- Vitamin E
- Vitamin K
- Vitamin B1 (thiamin)
- Riboflavin
- Vitamin B6
- Niacin

- Pantothenic acid
- Vitamin B12
- Folic acid

Boxers especially need vitamin A for vision and growth and to support their immune systems. The minerals a dog needs are the following:

- Calcium
- Phosphorous
- Magnesium
- Sodium
- Potassium
- Chlorine
- Iron
- Copper
- Zinc
- Manganese
- Selenium
- Iodine

Commercial Foods

There is no doubt that the commercial dog-food industry is large. There are hundreds of different pet foods available all over the United States, but they're not all created equal. For example, price is a big indicator of quality. It seems unlikely that a company selling a forty-pound bag of generic dog food for $9.95 would be able to use a high-quality protein and grain in its food. The cost of the quality ingredients alone would generally be higher than this selling price.

Commercial dog-food supporters cite studies that suggest this food can provide the exact nutrients a dog needs because the vitamins and minerals are fixed in each batch, regardless of what individual ingredients are used. They maintain that this is a modern advantage of commercial dog foods.

At the other end of the spectrum, there are also veterinarians and some studies that suggest that modern canines are only about 1 to 3 percent removed in DNA from wild canines such as wolves and coyotes, and domestic dogs would therefore do better on a more natural, raw diet. These proponents suggest that dogs would live longer, healthier lives if they ate foods that were closer to what they would ideally have in the wild. They emphasize that it is unnatural to expect every single meal to be exactly balanced and that instead, the diet should be balanced over time. They also contend that additives and preservatives that are included in commercial dog foods are deleterious to canine health in the long term, as no one really knows the long-term effects of additives and preservatives on canine health. There is even some suggestion that an overdose of some vitamins and minerals can be as harmful to a dog as a deficiency.

Commercial Dog-Food Ingredients

The protein in dog food comes from a variety of sources. In the United States, cattle, swine, chickens, lambs, deer, and fish are commonly used. When animals are slaughtered for human consumption, only about 50 percent of the carcass is used for human food. The remaining parts are called by-products and include the bones, blood, intestines, lungs, and ligaments, and are used in pet or animal feed.

 Fact

Rendering is the process of extracting oil from fat or blubber, generally from animals that have already been dead for some time. Rendering separates fat-soluble materials from water-soluble and solid materials. It removes most of the water and kills bacterial contaminants. It may also destroy some of the natural enzymes and proteins found in the raw ingredients.

Commercial dog foods also commonly use by-product "meal." Meal is composed of by-products or other ingredients that are rendered rather than used fresh.

There is some question about how much of the nutrition in some of the less-expensive dog foods is available for the dog to process and digest. (The term for this is bioavailability.) The cooking or baking methods used to turn by-products and meal into kibble do not necessarily destroy any hormones or drugs that may be present in the animal carcass (such as the antibiotics or growth hormones used to fatten livestock or increase milk production). Even in small amounts, these compounds may have some negative long-term effects. For instance, some contend that the presence of hormones in protein sources cause secondary sexual characteristics to develop faster than normal.

 Question?

What does bioavailability mean?
The term "bioavailability" refers to how well the nutrients are used by the body. There is a growing body of evidence that nutrients from natural, nonsynthetic sources are absorbed and used most efficiently by the body.

Additionally, grains such as wheat, oats, and beans are generally difficult for dogs to digest. Many people wonder if the amount of grains used in some commercial dog foods exceed the amount a wild canine would normally eat. Nutrients in potatoes and corn are less available still to canines, and some ingredients, such as peanut hulls, have no significant nutritional value.

Preservatives

Since all commercial foods must be preserved to stay fresh and appealing to a dog from the top to the bottom of a forty-pound bag, suppliers add preservatives to the main ingredients or raw materials. These preservatives also ensure long shelf life. The preservatives may be natural or synthetic.

Synthetic preservatives include butylated hydroxanisole (BHA) and butylated hyroxytoluene (BHT), propyl fallate, propylene glycol (also used as a less-toxic version of antifreeze), and ethoxyquin. There is little information on the toxicity, safety, bioavailability, or effects of chronic use on pets. Natural preservatives such as vitamin C, vitamin E (mixed tocopherols) and oils of rosemary, clove, and other spices are used to preserve the fats in some products. Other ingredients, however, are also preserved individually.

Most fish meal and some prepared vitamin-mineral mixtures contain chemical preservatives. This means that along with some natural foods, your boxer might be eating several types of preservatives at once. There are no long-term studies on the effects of consuming multiple preservatives in combination over an extended amount of time.

What's the Answer?

If you decide to use commercial dog food, the best option would be to search for the highest-quality dog food available. Look for a product made of human-grade ingredients and the fewest, safest preservatives that you can find. There are some excellent choices out there. And remember that each dog is different. Some dogs live long, active lives no matter what they are fed, while others don't seem to do well on commercial dog foods. Gradually experiment with different options until you find what works best for both you and your boxer.

Natural and/or Raw Foods

Starting in the 1990s, a new wave of dog feeding began to sweep the nation. The BARF diet (standing for "bones and raw food" or "biologically appropriate food") grew in popularity, with the seminars of Ian Billinghurst, DVM, of Australia, being one of the most notable. His book, *Give Your Dog a Bone*, revolutionized how people fed their dogs, based upon his own personal observations as a vet and his own research over a thirty-year period. Another early pioneer in natural dog food revolution was Richard Pitcairn, D.V.M. His book, *Dr. Pitcairn's Complete Guide to Natural Health for Dogs and Cats*, provides recipes for cooked dog food and treats.

Early critics of the raw-food movement maintained that dogs would be malnourished unless they got their kibble regularly. But raw-food proponents argued back that the genuine bioavailability of highly processed kibbles was questionable in the first place, and the dangers of oversupplementation were as real as undersupplementation. Raw-food advocates maintain that using a natural approach, including various different meat and vegetable sources over time, more closely approximates how the dog would eat in the wild. This is more reminiscent of how humans tend to eat, which eventually provides a balanced consumption of readily bioavailable sources of vitamins and minerals.

 Essential

Proponents of the raw-food movement take the point of view that human-grade food (food fit for human consumption) is the only food that a dog should eat. They hold that biologically appropriate foods, or those that are closest to their natural states, will enhance your dog's health. The movement totally discourages the use of food by-products and rendered meat meals and preservatives as a source of food for your dog.

Most adult humans tend to remain generally healthy, even with extreme swings in diet and levels of consumption, such as what happens around the holidays and other celebrations. People commonly eat rich, high-calorie meals that are scarce in vitamins, but most of them survive just fine. Or they eat mostly junk for a few days, followed by organic produce only, or at least, balanced meals with vegetables. Some argue that dogs have the same ability to handle and even enjoy and benefit from a more widely varied diet.

Opposition to Raw/Natural Foods

At the advent of the raw and natural food movement, many vets and others felt that departing from the tradition of feeding commercial dog foods would be greatly detrimental to dogs. Others believed that a biologically appropriate diet, which includes raw meaty bones, would perforate the dog's intestines and produce bacterial infections through E. coli and other pathogens. However, many vets are currently moving in the direction of supporting the raw-food movement because they feel that they see an overall improvement in canine health.

Problems with Raw Foods

Some dogs have had difficulty with raw meaty bones or raw foods in general. But this usually happens when the dog's overall digestive system has been compromised to the point that he is not producing enough digestive enzymes to deal with the digestion of raw food or any pathogens that might occur in it. In the wild, canines often eat meat that is rancid without suffering any ill effects—not unlike those garbage-can raiders that can eat anything and never notice the difference. In general, domestic dogs do have the capability to digest foods that may be past their prime.

After a decade or more that has seen canines flourishing, for the most part, on raw food diets, more vets now support the choice to feed a raw or natural food diet as opposed to commercial dog food only.

Choosing the Right Food for Your Boxer

In general, you are better off feeding your new puppy what the breeder fed the litter, at least initially. If you feel you need to change, do so gradually. Watch for any signs that the pup is having difficulty in making the transition to another food source. These signs would include loose stools, increased gas, mucous in the stool, or vomiting. Any of those symptoms would suggest that the changes are not agreeing with the puppy.

Raw, Natural, or Commercial?

For some people, cooking for their dogs or preparing raw food diets is an overwhelming process. Other considerations are that if you have small children, there is a slightly greater risk of E. coli being spread around the house from the dog eating raw food. This risk is small if you take ordinary sanitary precautions. If you are not a great housekeeper, however, this might be an issue. On the other hand, if you have the time, you may want to either feed raw food or natural, home-cooked food.

 Alert!

The term "meat by-products" generally refers to the parts of the animal that humans will not or cannot eat. Meat meal generally refers to what has been boiled off a rendered carcass (dead by natural or accidental cause). These two items can include intestines, hair, feathers, and other items that are unfit for human consumption. It is also generally felt that the preservatives, BHA, BHT, propyl gallate, propylene glycol (also used as antifreeze), and ethoxyquin all have very questionable scientific documentation as to their safety.

There are some additives in processed commercial dog food that you might want to look out for, particularly in combination, as many are thought to be chemicals that can lead to cancer cell proliferation. Some additives to be wary of are these:

- Anticaking and antimicrobial agents
- Antioxidants

- Coloring, curing, drying, and firming agents
- Emulsifiers
- Flavor enhancers and flavoring agents
- Flour-treating and leavening agents
- Formulation aids
- Humectants
- Lubricants
- Nonnutritive and nutritive sweeteners
- Oxidizing and reducing agents
- PH control agents
- Processing aids
- Sequestrants
- Solvents
- Vehicles, including stabilizers, thickeners, surface active agents, surface finishing agents, synergists, and texturizers

Do Your Research

Before you start feeding a raw or natural food diet, you need to check your references, do your research, and make sure that you understand clearly what it will take to provide your boxer with a nutritionally balanced raw or natural diet over time. You can't just throw a raw frozen hamburger or a chicken wing at your boxer and expect that to be sufficient. There is some considerable research involved in providing the optimal diet for your dog.

If the time is takes to research and provide a raw or natural food diet is more than you have, then by all means go with a commercially prepared dog food. But do your research there as well, and try to find those that are prepared with human-grade foods and the fewest artificial preservatives.

How and When to Feed

Most breeders suggest that you feed your new boxer puppy at least four meals a day until he is about four to six months old. Then you can cut back to three meals a day, or two meals and a treat at lunch. Boxers are prone to a condition called bloat (described in Chapter 11), and it is therefore recommended that you feed yours at least twice a day. You should feed morning and evening, especially if you have a show dog or competition dog who may be working, at times, very intensely, or on the show grounds for long hours. Dogs can sometimes be low on energy due to low blood sugar is they are active and only eat once a day.

◄ Control your boxer's dining situation to be certain that it's peaceful and without distractions.

Where to Feed

Hopefully, you've decided on a nice quiet spot in a dog friendly part of your house or apartment, or in the crate where your boxer can eat in a leisurely, uninterrupted fashion. This is particularly important in the first few days or weeks when your new puppy comes home.

 **Essential**

> If you have parts of your house gated off for the pup, and you have to be gone all day, you can leave food out (free feed) if you feed commercial dog food. This is harder if you feed raw or home-cooked food. If you have a picky eater, try to leave a quality kibble out just to help ensure that your pup gets enough nutrition, and feed him his raw or home-cooked meals when you can be home with him and can supervise.

Puppies are very easily distracted, and you don't want yours getting off his feeding schedule for lack of a quiet place to eat and digest his meals. The same is true, however, of some older dogs, so finding a quiet spot for canine dining for your boxer is a must.

You Control the Food

You need to let your boxer know, in no uncertain terms, that you control the food. Make him sit and wait quietly while you get his food ready. He must wait to begin eating until you give the okay, even after you have set the bowl down. You should also be able to take his food away without any protest. If you do need to do this, reward his good behavior. This is a good way to build your leadership and teach a good "Wait" command. By letting him know that food is available in a calm environment, and that he will always get it back even with interruptions for safety or other reasons, you let your boxer know that he can trust you totally and relax about food in general. If you get an older boxer who seems inclined to guard his food, you will need to work on this as a separate training issue.

The Picky Eater

This may seem to be a contradiction in terms when we apply it to dogs. We assume that dogs will eat anything they can get their paws on, but with some young puppies, that may not be true.

Young puppies are sometimes stimulated to eat through competition with their littermates. Without that competition to encourage them, some pups don't eat much if they're not very hungry, or they might not understand that they should eat when food is available. If you have this type of puppy, simply to leave his food out for about ten minutes, then pick it up. The puppy will soon figure out that he'd better eat when dinner's on the table, so to speak.

Supplements and Table Scraps

Most vets recommend that you do not feed puppies under a year any supplements other than vitamin C unless specifically recommended or prescribed by your vet. Most vets feel that if you feed your boxer a high-quality dog food, he will receive all his vitamins that way. Other vets are beginning to carry vitamin/mineral formulas. Supplements such as glucosamine/chondroitin, MSM (methylsulfonylmethane, which supports the muscle and joint systems of the body), and mussel-shell capsules are often recommended for older, arthritic dogs, for instance.

 **Alert!**

It is generally not advised to overdose puppies on vitamins and minerals because it can cause bone overgrowth diseases like panosteitis. You are best off using supplements recommended by your vet or checking to see if she recommends anything at all. Do not just randomly supplement your puppy's food.

Most vets discourage owners from offering table scraps to their dogs. Most people think that they are doing their dogs a favor by giving them fat or other treats, but this is not a good idea. Many boxers are prone to pancreatitis (inflammation of the pancreas), which is very painful and can be life-threatening to your boxer, and concentrated cooked fat often causes the pancreas to become inflamed.

Furthermore, by giving table scraps, you could be creating a weight problem for your boxer. This won't be much of an issue while your boxer is a puppy, but it might become one as your boxer gets older. Under no circumstances should you let your boxer get fat. Many people love to indulge their boxers, but between bouts of pancreatitis, colitis, and the strain on your boxer's heart and joints from carrying excess weight, all you are doing by encouraging your boxer to be fat is shortening his or her life span. This is an active, naturally athletic, vigorous breed that should never be allowed to become overweight.

 **Fact**

Cooked bones become brittle and splinter. They can cause choking if they get stuck in your boxer's throat or mouth. If a broken bone lodges in your boxer's intestines, it may cause perforation, a serious condition that requires immediate veterinary care. Uncooked bones, such as chicken necks, wings, or backs, are much softer, and dogs can crunch them down and eat them safely. These are a good natural source of calcium.

✳Toxic Foods

Many ingredients that are perfectly safe for human beings are poisonous to dogs, sometimes in miniscule amounts. The following list includes items that your dog should never ingest:

- Chocolate contains a compound known as theobromine. This is present at higher concentrations in dark or baker's chocolate and is highly toxic to dogs.

- Grapes and raisins, even in small amounts, are capable of causing complete kidney failure in dogs. The reason for this is not understood, but the connection has been recently documented.
- Onions are toxic, raw or cooked, and foods containing onions should not be available to your dog.
- Caffeine is dangerous in even small amounts.
- Alcohol and recreational drugs are potentially lethal, in any amount.
- Animal fats, including oil, are difficult for your dog to digest and can cause pancreatitis, a very painful condition that can lead to death if not treated immediately.

The general rule is to avoid feeding your boxer anything other than his regular diet, whether you use commercial dog food or home-prepared foods. If you need to feed a treat, give you boxer something healthy, like a bit of raw carrot, apple, or plain cooked chicken breast, or a good quality dog biscuit.

Basic Health Care

Y ou are the first line of defense when it comes to your boxer's health. Bear this in mind in all your dealings concerning health and veterinary care pertaining to your boxer. Basic health care covers day-to-day issues, injuries, vaccinations, heartworm preventative medications, flea products, and monitoring for lumps and bumps. It might also include acupuncture, Chinese herbs, massage therapy, physical therapy, chiropractic, and even yoga for those boxers lucky enough to have these services available in their community.

Vaccinations

Like dog foods, vaccinations are yet another subject of controversy. On the one hand, vaccinations have virtually eliminated many lethal or severely debilitating communicable diseases of dogs. On the other hand, while the practice has been to inoculate dogs on an annual basis, some vets and researchers now believe this repeated practice unnecessarily provokes an immune response in pets that are vaccinated.

Some vets have embraced this philosophy on the basis of recent research. Dogs older than three or four years of age are likely to have developed lifelong immunity to the diseases for which they've been inoculated. Many vets now recommend against vaccinating dogs that suffer from immune-related diseases.

However, it is the law in many states to require vaccinations on an annual basis, especially for rabies, so there may be some conflict between growing research and local laws.

Immunization Timeline

If you bought your puppy from a reputable breeder, by eight weeks of age he had already received vaccinations for distemper, hepatitis, leptospirosis, parvovirus, and parainfluenza. This is usually administered in a combined shot called the DHLPP. There is some research that suggests that the combined shots may overstimulate the immune system in some breeds or individuals of some breeds. Overstimulation can lead to immune-mediated diseases in boxers, such as hypothyroidism, some types of digestive disorders, and pancreatitis.

Essential

While the puppy is developing in the uterus, antibodies to disease cross the placental barrier from the mother to the puppy. The puppy is thus naturally immune, at least for a short while, to any disease for which the mother has been inoculated or that she has contracted and survived. This is how early immunity is passed along to the puppy. The puppy gets more antibodies from the milk of the mother, and so the immunity continues at least until the puppy leaves his littermates and comes to your home.

The combination DHLPP vaccine is given at around twelve to fourteen weeks of age, and there is usually a parvovirus follow-up at sixteen to eighteen weeks. The reason for so many shots is that most of these diseases are fatal to puppies, and vaccinations are the best way known to prevent the puppy from contracting them. No one knows for certain when the puppy's antibodies from its mother are gone, although it is generally accepted that distemper antibodies are gone by twelve weeks.

There is some suggestion that the longer a puppy is allowed to nurse, the more antibodies he retains for a longer time. Your puppy can also develop immunity simply from being around other vaccinated dogs, which shed cells constantly that the puppy inhales or otherwise ingests.

∜ Different Diseases

Even though there is not complete agreement on immunization, it is generally considered sensible to err on the side of caution and to immunize anyway. The following diseases are easily preventable through immunizations, and many are fatal if they occur in the pup:

- **Distemper:** A virtually incurable virus, regardless of treatment, that attacks every tissue in the body. Unvaccinated puppies and canine senior citizens are the most susceptible. Symptoms resemble those of a bad cold, including runny nose and eyes and gastrointestinal problems. Dogs that do recover will probably be subject to severe neural disorders. Many wild animals and other dogs carry the virus.
- **Hepatitis:** Serious, especially in puppies. The disease is characterized by high fever, lethargy, and lack of appetite. The hepatitis virus in canines is much the same as in humans—it affects the liver and kidneys. Dogs that recover from hepatitis tend to have compromised immune systems and to be susceptible to other illnesses. It is usually spread by contact with an infected animal or its feces or urine.
- **Leptospirosis:** Before a vaccine was developed to prevent this disease, it was fatal. It produces extreme fevers, lethargy, jaundice, and internal bleeding. This is a bacterial disease transmitted by contact with the urine of rats, other wildlife, or affected dogs. Recovered dogs can be carriers, and leptospirosis can be transmitted from dogs to humans.

- **Parvovirus:** Parvo can be fatal if the dog has not been vaccinated for it; however, with vaccinations, early diagnosis, and prompt treatment, it is manageable. Symptoms include lethargy, loss of appetite, vomiting, and diarrhea that progresses to being bloody, leading eventually to collapse. Parvo attacks the bone marrow and intestinal tracts, particularly of young puppies, but it can occur in older dogs as well. Parvo tends to be transmitted most readily through urine or feces; however, it is also believed to be somewhat airborne.

- **Rabies:** Can be transmitted to people and is virtually always fatal. It attacks nerve tissue, resulting in paralysis and death. Many states require an annual vaccination for it. Rabies is spread in the saliva and is carried by skunks, raccoons, foxes, and other dogs and cats, although virtually any animal can carry it.

- **Bordatella (kennel cough):** Not usually life threatening, but in some cases it can lead to a serious bronchopneumonia. This ailment is highly contagious and characterized by sneezing, coughing, hacking, and retching. Nasal discharge may range from clear to lime green. Bordatella vaccine should be given every six to eight months to dogs that are in regular contact with other dogs. However, vaccines do not protect against all strains.

- **Coronavirus:** Corona, as its known, is usually self-limiting and not life threatening. It was first noted in the 1970's, just slightly earlier than Parvo. It produces a yellow/brown stool and is generally accompanied by lethargy, vomiting, and diarrhea. Like Parvo, corona is transmitted through contact of urine or feces of an affected dog, or again, it can be airborne. It is highly contagious.

- **Lyme disease:** First diagnosed in 1976 in Lyme, Connecticut. Symptoms tend to include sudden lameness, fever, swelling of the joints, and loss of appetite. This disease is more prevalent in some parts of the country than in others. It is transmitted by deer ticks that carry the disease.

▲ **Watch for lethargy in your boxer, as it is a sign of several different canine illnesses.**

If you look back at this list, you will notice that lethargy is a common symptom for most of these diseases. Since most boxers are rarely lethargic, you should get your dog to a vet as soon as you see this behavior. This is usually the very first symptom or indication that something is wrong, one that generally occurs well before vomiting, diarrhea, or other more serious symptoms are noticeable.

Most of the aforementioned diseases are deadly or severely debilitating, but they are also preventable. The wisest course of action is therefore to make sure your boxer gets at least the basic vaccinations. If you are concerned about the effects that vaccination is reputed to cause, you have one other option. You can have your vet take a blood sample and titre, or test, for the amount of antigen to any particular disease that your boxer has been vaccinated for in the past. The results of this test tell your vet whether your boxer has sufficient antigens to fight off various diseases.

 **fact**

Pet health care cost $18.2 billion in 2004, and the complexity of canine health care is a major reason that many boxers end up in rescue. Many owners cannot afford necessary veterinary care. It may be a luxury in your life to own a boxer, but at some point in time, your boxer will need veterinary care, so be sure that you have planned for it.

Spaying and Neutering

If you are not going to show your dog, or if you are not an informed breeder, you should absolutely spay (remove the uterus and ovaries of a female) or neuter (remove the testicles of a male) your boxer. Indeed, there are far too many boxers in rescue to risk an accidental mating. If your boxer has an hereditary illness or tendency to an illness, spaying or neutering eliminates the likelihood of that illness being passed along. This includes the inherited heart disease, hip dysplasia, and possibly, early onset of thyroid disease.

 **Essential**

Spaying and neutering are generally given as solutions to aggression and many other behavioral problems that they do not really address in all breeds. Regardless of whether you have your boxer pup spayed or neutered before sexual maturity, improper or insufficient training can still result in unacceptable behavior, including aggression. Don't use spaying or neutering as a substitute for training and behavioral management.

Spay/Neuter As Cancer Prevention

If you spay or neuter your boxer before sexual maturity, it is believed that you are reducing the risk of some kinds of cancers, particularly breast cancers in females. Studies also suggest that you are reducing the overall likelihood of cancer if you spay or neuter your boxer before sexual maturity. However, current research also suggests that if you spay or neuter your boxer before sexual maturity that they tend to grow taller, and may have some kind of joint problems later in life.

Probably the best time to spay a female if you do not wish to show her is before she has time to come into her first heat. Her breeder should be able to approximate the time when your bitch will come into heat. The best time to neuter a young male is probably after he is about 8 or 9 months old. He will have reached sexual maturity physically but not really had time to develop bad habits about it.

Later in life, intact females are more prone to developing pyometra (a hormonally induced infection of the uterus), a life-threatening condition. So again, you may want to spay your female boxer puppy before her first heat. Spaying a female while she is in her hormonal cycle is very hard on her, as the uterus and surrounding tissue is engorged with blood awaiting fertilization. Many reputable vets will not spay a bitch within sixty days of estrus in order to allow her glands and organs to go back to a normal size.

Spay/Neuter Surgery

Spaying and neutering are surgical procedures that must be performed by a board-licensed veterinarian. These procedures are done under a general anesthetic. Spaying is easier on a younger female, but it is still a good idea for older females in order to prevent pyometra. Technically called an ovariohysterectomy, spaying is considered major surgery regardless of when it is done.

The neuter, which removes the testicles, especially if there is a retained testicle, such as in a monorchid or cryptorchid, is technically surgical castration.

Lumps and Bumps

Compared to humans, dogs in general are thirty-five times more likely to develop skin cancer, four times as likely to develop a breast tumor, eight times as likely to suffer from bone cancer, and twice as likely to develop leukemia. Given that boxers are prone to a variety of cancers and other tumors, it is best to start to examine your boxer early for lumps and bumps, preferably while he's a puppy.

Examining Your Boxer

It's a good idea to get your pup used to being massaged by making it a common practice to run your hands over every square inch of his body. He should learn to stand perfectly still during the exam and to accept handling so you can incorporate this health prevention with basic training. If you do feel a bump, take him to your veterinarian as soon as possible. It is entirely possible that the bump will be a benign histiocytoma, to which boxers are very prone, especially as youngsters, but you want to be certain.

If it is not a benign tumor or a grade one mast cell tumor, your vet is likely to refer you to a veterinary oncologist. Mast cell tumors in dogs occur primarily as either skin tumors or subcutaneous masses. It is important to remember that mast cell tumors are extremely variable in their clinical presentation. They can resemble any other type of skin or subcutaneous tumor, both benign (i.e., lipoma) and malignant. Mast cell tumors are highly aggressive and unpredictable in terms of treatment.

The oncologist will be able to tell you exactly what kind of cancer your boxer has and what treatment options are available. Chemotherapy and radiation are available options for dogs, and there are many ways to ease a dog's discomfort during treatment. Still, the recovery rate is not good for dogs with cancer.

The most common fatal cancers for boxers are lymphoma, fibrosarcoma, and undifferentiated mast cell cancer. When cancer is detected at the lower grades and the surgeon is able to remove all cancerous tissue, boxers recover from mast cell cancer better than many other breeds. However, the number and types of cancers and tumors that can befall your boxer is great. The best prevention is to keep a constant lookout for lumps and bumps.

 **Alert!**

An early symptom of cancer in dogs is excessive water drinking. While this may also indicate diabetes or Cushing's syndrome, if those two illnesses are ruled out, cancer is likely to be behind the excessive consumption of water. Other signs of cancer are lumps and bumps, bleeding or discharge from any orifice or sore, persistent stiffness or lameness, unusual lack of appetite, breathing difficulties, sudden, unexplained weight loss, body odors, black stools or urine, and difficulty urinating or defecating.

Gingival Hyperplasia

Gingival hyperplasia is a form of benign tumor that boxers and other bracycephalic dogs are prone to developing. The condition makes the gums of the boxer's mouth appear to be growing over his teeth. This is a common tumor that is relatively easily removed under general anesthesia. If these tumors are not removed, the teeth under them become useless, and eating can become painful. In addition, the teeth underneath the epulis, as the tumors are called, can rot. This gives harmful bacteria a means of getting into the blood stream and traveling to the heart, where they create problems.

Boxers routinely get gingival hyperplasia as early as two years of age, although they may get it at a much older age. Even if removed, these tumors can continue to recur. It is very important to routinely check your boxer's teeth and gums and to brush his teeth. Checking for plaque on the teeth or gingival hyperplasia is a good way of maintaining good dental health.

If Your Boxer Needs Medication

Your boxer is most likely to need medication for a thyroid condition. Thyroid problems generally do not appear until your boxer is at least eight, or middle-aged in human terms. Even before that, however, it is not unlikely that your boxer will need something at some time.

 Fact

Canines do not have as many taste receptors as humans do (one explanation for how they can eat things like garbage and feces). It isn't the taste of a pill so much as the change in texture that bothers most dogs. Some boxers don't mind taking pills, but some do. Crushing the pills into food is probably the most successful way to get your dog to ingest his medication.

There are a variety of ways to give your boxer medications. You can buy dispensers made for administering liquid treatments to dogs. Pills can be crushed into your dog's food (assuming, of course, that the medication can be taken with food). If your boxer needs medication at a time when he would not be eating his regular meals, it is quite effective to glue the pill to a slice of soft cheese or luncheon meat with a little peanut butter or cream cheese. Otherwise, you must force feed the medication. Hold the dog's jaws open with one hand and with the other place the pill as far back on the tongue as you can. Hold the muzzle closed, and stroke the dog's neck to encourage swallowing.

Parasite Prevention

Parasites are a big issue in the basic health care arena, probably accounting for the majority of treatments that your boxer will receive in his life. There are a great many things that you can do to prevent parasites, and since some of these parasites can be transmitted to humans, you are wise to do whatever you can to prevent them.

External Parasites

External parasites live on the outside of your dog's body and use your boxer as their host. These include fleas, ticks, and mites.

Fleas

Fleas are probably the first thing that many people think of when they think of dogs—that's how common they are. The good news is that fleas are relatively easy to get rid of; the bad news is that they're difficult to prevent.

The life cycle of a flea includes four stages—eggs, larvae, pupae or nymphs, and adults. The adult stage is most visible and irritating to the dog in the life of the flea. Most flea-control products concentrate on this cycle of the flea's life. The itchy truth of the matter is that while you can see adult fleas, what you don't see is the twenty to thirty batches of eggs that those fleas lay every day, most of which fall off as your boxer travels through the park, over your furniture, all around the house, and up and down the yard.

 **Essential**

One of the easiest ways to decrease the probability of health problems in your dog is to keep him clean in all respects. Bathing him regularly and keeping his nails short and neat is a great start. Also be on the alert for any strange odors or signs of discomfort, as these may indicate infection, injury, or illness. Consult your vet if you notice any such symptoms.

Once these eggs have fallen off your boxer, they hatch into larvae in one to ten days. The larvae don't travel except to move away from bright lights. They feed on dead organic matter, including adult flea feces, for about seven days. Around this time, the larvae pupate into protective pupae and change into adult fleas. This takes only a few days, but an unhatched flea can wait inside the pupae for up to two years. Once hatched, the adult fleas must eat within a few days, so they find your boxer. A flea will not leave a host voluntarily. Grooming or bathing is the only way to dislodge it.

Treating fleas takes a multipronged approach. First, the environment needs to be treated as much as the dog. Vacuuming the area daily for about three weeks is a good idea, as is washing the dog's bedding and sleeping area. The most effective thing to do for the areas that cannot be washed or vacuumed is to spray with an insect growth regulator (IGR) and an insecticide to kill the adult fleas. Most IGRs are also effective against eggs and larvae. They mimic the flea's own hormones and stop the eggs from developing into larvae and then into pupae and fleas. While IGRs are generally effective for a few months, most insecticides are only effective for a few days, and they can be very toxic.

 **Fact**

Additional things that you can do to repel fleas is to add a few drops (but a few drops only, as this can be toxic in excess) of pennyroyal, eucalyptus, or oil of rosemary to your boxer's bath. You can also supplement your boxer's food with raw, fresh garlic (minced or grated) and brewer's yeast, which will make his blood taste bad to a flea. You can confine your boxer to just one part of the house to limit the spread of fleas, and you can vacuum daily, putting insecticide in the vacuum cleaner bag to kill the fleas as soon as they are sucked up.

Be aware that flea collars and many flea bombs, while toxic to fleas, are also highly toxic to boxer puppies. So tread lightly with the chemicals. Remember, too, that if you've had an infestation of fleas, you will also probably have worms, as the two tend to go together.

— Ticks

While not as common as fleas, ticks are still everywhere in nature. They are most efficient at drinking the blood of their host, and they give dogs diseases like Lyme disease, Rocky Mountain spotted fever, tick bite paralysis, and sometimes just a nasty infection from the bite site. They are controlled in much the same way as fleas, and many of the same products, insect growth regulators and insecticides, will work on both or either.

Ticks are most often found in wild areas, especially those that are hot and humid. They have a life expectancy of a week to about six months. They can't jump or fly, but they do crawl slowly. They usually get onto you or your boxer by pure luck—your boxer brushes up against something that they were on, and they latch on to the unsuspecting host.

— Mites

Mites are microscopic little insects that take up permanent residence whenever they can. There are several different kinds of mites that the dog owner should be aware of, including Demodex mites, Cheyletiellosis mites, Sarcoptes mites, and ear mites (*Otodectes cynotis*).

- **Demodex mites:** These are probably the most common mites found in dogs. They cause problems when present in larger than normal amounts. After they take up residence in the dog's hair follicles and sebaceous glands, the dog's hair falls out and leaves behind large unsightly patches of red skin. Sometimes called red or demodectic mange, this is generally a sign of a somewhat compromised immune system in the dog. It tends to be an inherited problem.
- **Cheyletiellosis mites:** Also known as hook-mouthed mites, these are responsible for the walking dandruff kind of con-

dition that affects dogs, cats, and rabbits. If the scaly, oily skin is left untreated, the mites are easily transmitted to other animals as well as to humans.

- **Sarcoptes mites:** These cause the highly contagious sarcoptic mange, which is characterized by intense itching. In humans, they can result in scabies. The cycle of the Sarcoptes mite is about three weeks. Scabies is highly contagious and is readily transmitted to humans.
- **Ear mites (Otodectes cynotis):** These affect the outer ear canal of your boxer, although they can affect other areas as well. Boxers with ear mites tend to shake their heads a lot or scratch at their ears. A dark-brown to black waxy discharge confirms the diagnosis of ear mites.

Infestation with any of these mites requires veterinary care. Treatment may also be necessary for any member of the family who has come in contact with the mites.

Internal Parasites

No discussion of dog health would be complete without a discussion of worms, the internal parasites that can infest dogs. Most worm infestations are relatively easy to control. If they are not controlled, they can weaken the dog, and other medical problems can occur. The following sections describe the worms that have the most serious effects. Many types of worms can be transmitted to humans.

Roundworms

These worms live in the dog's intestines and shed eggs continuously. The eggs are everywhere, and can affect humans, so it is generally advised to keep your house and any areas of the house your boxer has access to clean and sanitary. Get your boxer tested for worms regularly. In puppies, roundworms cause bloated bellies, diarrhea, coughing, and vomiting and are passed from the dam (through blood or milk) to the puppies. Affected puppies are more lethargic than normal. The worms look like spaghetti and can be as long as six inches. Since roundworms can kill puppies and severely affect adults if the infestation is bad enough, it is important to regularly examine your boxer's stool and keep an eye out for them.

Hookworms

Hookworm infestations include dark stools, weight loss, general weakness, pale coloration, and anemia, as well as some skin problems. Hookworms can also be passed to humans, so it is important to maintain sanitary conditions around your boxer and your children. Most heartworm preventatives also prevent hookworms, so discuss this with your vet. Hookworms are usually passed through exposure to feces, so be very careful how you dispose of your boxer's feces to avoid the possibility of a hookworm infestation.

Tapeworms

There are many species of tapeworms, which can also affect humans. The most common way that dogs get tapeworms is by eating the fleas that are biting them. The best way for humans to avoid tapeworms is to keep dogs and the house free of fleas (and to refrain from eating any fleas!). While tapeworm infestations are not life threatening to dogs, they can cause serious liver disease in humans.

✳ 🐕 Alert!

Be aware that fleas can travel easily from dog to dog, as they are adept jumpers. If your dog is greeting the neighbor's dog, playing with others in the park, or even visiting another dog's home, that dog's fleas can be transferred to your pet. Therefore, be sure to ask other owners about their dogs' flea status before you introduce your dog to a play session. Once your dog has fleas, they'll be all over your house in no time.

Whipworms

Common in North America, these worms attach themselves to the dog's lower intestines, where they feed. They may only cause anything from an upset tummy to colic and diarrhea. These worms can live for months or years in the dog with little or no other evidence. Treatment is tricky due to their odd life cycles, and whipworm eggs can live as long as five years in the environment, which makes cleaning up your dog's feces essential. If your dog has occasional bouts of diarrhea that you can't explain by any other means, he may have whipworms.

 **Essential**

Don't let the idea of all these alternative treatments for dogs overwhelm you. The best way to maintain your boxer's health is to keep him and his environment as clean and parasite-free as possible. An annual physical, where your vet can go over your boxer, listen to his heart, lungs, and breathing, do routine blood work, and check for lumps you may have missed will help maintain your boxer's quality of life and well-being. Alternative treatments can be sought if a particular need is discovered.

Heartworms

Heartworms are long thin worms that can grow up to twelve inches in length. They live in the dog's heart and the major blood vessels surrounding the heart. Symptoms of heartworms may be lethargy, loss of appetite, coughing, the development of a potbelly, and anemia. The dog gets heartworms from being stung by a mosquito that has the microfilarie of heartworms in it. Mosquitoes pass the heartworm from dog to dog. However, whether or not your dog gets heartworms also depends upon his own state of health and immune system. Not every dog bitten by a mosquito carrying heartworm develops the disease. And not every mosquito carries the heartworm, even in climates where heartworm is prevalent, such as the South and parts of the Midwest. However, mosquitos carrying heartworms can be found almost anywhere in the United States.

Holistic Care or Complementary Medicine

In the world of veterinary medicine, there are now more alternative treatment options available than ever, including vitamins, minerals, herbs, acupuncture, homeopathy, and chiropractic care.

Many traditional veterinarians use complementary medicine because they are not happy with the results of conventional treatments alone, and many pets do improve with alternative therapies. Additionally, in the world of complementary medicines, there are herbs and homeopathic treatments that can do what no conventional drugs can, including heal the liver, calm the spirit without causing drowsiness, and reduce reaction times, just for example. Homeopathy and herbs have been notable in treating anxiety and aggression in dogs. Complementary medicine, in the world of veterinary care, is here to stay.

Common Illnesses and Injuries In Boxers

As a first-time boxer owner, you may find it rather difficult to determine if your dog is ill or injured. Boxers are very stoic, so they do not want to show you that they are hurt or uncomfortable. Therefore it is up to you to be observant and to know what is normal for your boxer and what is not. Even if there is an injury and your boxer is bearing it quietly, don't assume she doesn't need veterinary care.

When to Take Your Boxer to the Vet

Cuts, scratches, or punctures of any depth, sore limbs, unexplained vomiting, persistent itches, hives, and swollen or red eyes necessitate immediate veterinary care. Loud or unusual stomach noises with swelling or distension also need to be immediately addressed by a vet. Generally, any condition that you have a question about or that makes you feel uneasy requires veterinary care, if for no other reason than to put your mind at ease.

As a general rule of thumb, if you even suspect or feel that something is off with your boxer, a trip to the vet might be in order. Your instincts are often a good indicator that something may be wrong even if it isn't really evident on the surface. Many a serious illness has been prevented in boxers through their owners' preventive instincts. You'll know your boxer better than anyone else, so you will pick up on the subtleties of a disease or injury before it becomes chronic or needs intensive care.

 **Fact**

Healthy in a boxer means a bright, shiny coat and eyes, a high level of energy, enormous curiosity, enthusiasm, a general alert demeanor, a humorous good nature, fresh breath, and urine and feces that are not malodorous. Teeth should be clean, with no tissue overgrowing the teeth (gingival hyperplasia). Nails should be short and close to the pad. Ears should be clean with no waxy discharges.

Allergies

People wonder what possible difference allergies could make to a dog. After all, people with allergies get along just fine in life. But people are also in a position to observe any ill or annoying effects that an allergen may have on them. Their reactions might be as extreme as becoming physically ill and suffering anaphylactic shock to a mild case of hives or jitters, or sneezing, depending upon how reactive their bodies are to a particular allergen.

The same is true for dogs, and just as in humans, most reactions to food allergies tend to be on the mild side. Still, allergies, even subtle ones, can impact your boxer's behavior, health, longevity, and overall well-being. It is therefore wise to pay attention to what you feed your boxer and to notice how he reacts.

According to Dr. Alfred Plechner, researcher and expert in the field of allergies in animals and author of *Pet Allergies: Remedies for an Epidemic*, allergies are often a form of unrecognized deficiency disease. Recognizing that pet allergies signal a nutritional deficiency can help you to make the necessary adjustments to your dog's diet.

How can you tell if your dog has allergies? Hives, gunky ears, redness in the haws of the eyes, or a lackluster coat with dandruff or other related symptoms are early warning signs. Here is a checklist of other things to watch for:

- Lack of appetite
- Large, smelly stools
- Excessive gas
- Dirty teeth with brown spots
- Bad breath
- Excessive shedding
- Dull coat
- Ear and/or skin infection
- Lack of energy, or hyperactivity
- Need for frequent worming

All of these conditions can happen with any boxer, but they should only happen occasionally. If one or more of them is occurring frequently, or continuously, it is time to have your vet do an allergy test on your boxer to find out what is causing the condition or conditions.

✘ Ear Infections and Eye Injuries

Chronic ear infections can signal the fact that your boxer has an allergy to something he is eating on a regular basis. However, an ear infection might also be caused by mites. In both cases, your vet can provide you with treatment. In any event, if your boxer has chronic or recurring ear infections, or if your boxer is scratching at his ears or shaking his head, or if the ear seems red and hot or has a smelly discharge of any kind, it is time to see the vet.

Like many other breeds that have large, slightly protruding eyes, boxers get their fair share of eye injuries. Most boxer owners have at least one dog who has scratched the cornea of his eye at least once. Sometimes the scratch will be related to something specific, such as being scratched by a cat or by jumping into a tree after a squirrel. Just as often, you will not have any idea how the injury occurred.

 **Fact**

If you find your boxer getting most of his ear infections during the summer months, you may have a boxer who likes to play in water. Many like to bite the water coming out of a hose or sprinkler head or stick their heads under running water. As innocuous as this may sound, getting water in their ears can be a cause of ongoing, chronic ear infections for many boxers. If you notice that your boxer's ear infections correspond with warmer weather, you may need to restrict his water playtime.

Signs of a scratched cornea are as follows:

- Your boxer squints on one side of his or her face.
- Your boxer has one eye that is suddenly pointed in a different direction.
- Your boxer has bloody tears dripping out of his eye.

You need to get to your vet immediately to be sure that no infection sets in and for antibiotics and an ophthalmic ointment to make sure the scratch on the cornea does not need stitching. If the cornea is abraded over a large area, or if the cornea is having difficulty healing, your boxer may need his eyelid sewn shut to enable the eye to heal. He may also need a partial grid keratotomy, a procedure in which a canine ophthalmologist cuts a small grid over the damaged area with a laser to get the body to send more blood to the area and heal the cornea. Boxers over the age of about seven seem to have a harder time healing eye injuries. If you wait too long before getting attention for this emergency, the cornea can become necrotic, and your boxer may lose his sight or even his eye. Never delay getting treatment for your boxer if you suspect an eye injury.

◀ Making sure your boxer never wanders too far out of sight is one way to prevent injuries.

Cuts and Scrapes

It is important to have any cut, scrape, or puncture that bleeds freely and is anything other than tiny looked at by your vet to be sure that it doesn't need to be stitched or have other treatment applied to it. Since dogs lick their wounds, and they can lick their stitches out, it is sometimes necessary to put on an Elizabethan collar that prevents them from reaching the injured part of their body. An Elizabethan collar is not a fashion statement for dogs, but a device that vets recommend you use (and can furnish to you) that prevents your boxer from licking a wound that needs to heal. It fits around the neck like a funnel restricting your boxer's ability to reach wounds. Without restrictions, dogs will at times, lick stitches out of wounds and re-open them.

Cuts and punctures, especially, need to be looked at by a vet. Sometimes these wounds heal on the outside while the inside becomes infected and abscessed. Be on the safe side, and get injuries checked out by your veterinarian.

Puncture Wounds

Most boxer owners are bound to experience at least one situation in their boxer's life where the boxer experiences a puncture wound—especially the males. The puncture wound might be administered by another dog or cat during play or a fight, or your boxer might run into a nail or fence and puncture himself that way. The danger in puncture wounds is that they close up and begin to heal quickly on the top, often hiding a deeper wound that can abscess if left untreated.

Most puncture wounds are treated by putting an antiseptic and antibiotic ointment deep into the recesses of the wound so that infection cannot develop. Sometimes, the vet will also administer an oral antibiotic along with the topical treatment.

Foxtails

If your boxer never gets out of the city, you may not have to worry about foxtails. Throughout most of the continental United States, however, there are types of grass that spread their seeds by throwing a type of head called a foxtail. These seed heads are slightly barbed, allowing them to move easily in one direction and making it difficult to pull them back out again. A nosy, enthusiastic boxer can unwittingly inhale the foxtail way up into the nasal passages, where it gets stuck. Your boxer will sneeze and scrunch up the side of the face that has the foxtail but will be unable to expel the foxtail because of the way it spreads and imbeds itself once exposed to moisture from the boxer's nasal passages. As your boxer is trying to sneeze the foxtail out, the foxtail is planting itself. If the foxtail is not taken out, it can migrate further. Dogs have been known to have them end up in their brain from either ear or nose, and they invariably will cause an infection if left inside any dog too long. This can cause chronic illness from infection or worse. So if you see your boxer scrunching up one side of his face and sneezing that seems very loud and violent, take your boxer to your vet immediately.

Stomach Problems

One of the things that every new boxer owner eventually finds out is that boxers can often have funny tummies, or a tendency toward upset or delicate stomachs. They generally vomit a lot, and their stomachs gurgle. Many owners find themselves juggling different dog foods or eating programs to try to find something that will suit their boxer. This is actually a good idea, especially if the problem is an undiagnosed allergy.

Boxers are prone to colitis and ileitis, both disorders of the digestive tract. They are also prone to pancreatic exocrine insufficiency. If your vet finds that your boxer has any of these conditions, your boxer may need to be on a very specific diet for life.

 Alert!

If you have a new puppy that is finding it hard to eat and to put on weight, the pup should see a vet. The same is true of an adult dog. If your boxer has had a stable period of digestion in which he has been eating but then develops problems, you need to take note. An upset stomach could be a sign of poisoning or illness.

Pancreatitis or pancreatic insufficiency is an inability of the boxer's pancreas to produce sufficient amounts of digestive enzymes. In some boxers, this appears to be an inherited condition. In other cases, it is linked to the damage sustained by chronic inflammation of the pancreas. Contributing factors to the latter form of pancreatitis are specific diseases of other organs, such as liver problems, Cushing's disease, chronic bowel disease in the form of colitis or ileitis, and allergies. A lot of veterinary literature points to the following factors in the development of pancreatitis:

- Diets high in fat content
- Obesity
- Cushing's disease
- Use of prescription corticosteroids
- Any sort of unusual diet, such as one that includes lots of fatty treats

One of the most common times of the year for veterinary emergencies is the Thanksgiving holiday. People share the fat and skin of their turkey dinners with their dogs, which provokes an attack of pancreatitis. Pancreatitis is a very painful condition. You are doing your boxer no favors by sharing your rich food and treats with him, and you may create a chronically painful physical disorder for him by doing so.

Diarrhea

Anytime your boxer has really loose stools (diarrhea), he needs to see a vet. Many if not most canine diseases are capable of causing diarrhea in an affected boxer, so you need to know what condition your boxer has to treat it accordingly. Also, if your boxer has eaten something that has not agreed with him, or if he has been poisoned, diarrhea is likely to result. The cause should be determined for your boxer's safety and well-being. Any condition causing severe diarrhea can be fatal if not addressed, especially in young puppies.

 **Alert!**

If you are a gardener, you need to be aware that cocoa mulch is toxic to dogs in much the same way as chocolate, as are hanging baskets that are made of cocoa mulch. If you use this type of mulch, make sure that it is in an area where your boxer has no access. Don't use it at all if you can't keep your boxer away from it.

If your dog is suffering from diarrhea, it could mean that he has ingested some kind of poison. The most common way that dogs get poisoned is by eating rat or gopher bait. If you suspect that your boxer has eaten some of this poison, or eaten a poisoned gopher or rat, you should get him to your vet's office as quickly as possible. Most common rat and gopher poisons rely on anti-coagulants to kill the rodents. These are toxic and often fatal to dogs as well. So if you suspect your boxer of being poisoned, your vet needs to know in order to administer the correct antidote. Be aware, too, that snail and slug baits are poisonous to dogs and usually very attractive to them.

 **Fact**

A lesser known but equally potent form of poison for many dogs is any form of diet pill. Herbal diet formulas that contain ephedra and guarana can be equally lethal. The canine metabolism works quite differently from the human metabolism, and diet pills can affect your boxer's heart, kidneys, liver, and brain.

Another common source of poisoning for most dogs is chocolate. Chocolate contains a compound called theobromine, which is toxic to dogs in general. However, the toxicity for any particular dog is very hard to predict. Some dogs (including some boxers) have eaten large amounts of chocolate with no ill effects, yet others die from just a few bites. In general, the darker the chocolate, the greater the risk of poisoning to dogs.

Emergency Veterinary Care

Now that you know a bit about your boxer's basic care, including what common injuries and illnesses to be watchful for, there is still the category of veterinary care that every boxer owner needs to know about and fears the most: emergency veterinary care. An emergency can take any of numerous forms, so you need to be familiar with basic preparations and procedures in case you and your boxer are ever caught in such a situation.

What Constitutes an Emergency?

As you've already read, many conditions require a trip to a vet. So how does an emergency differ? An emergency is any situation that is immediately life threatening to your boxer, such as being hit by a car, having seizures, being injured in a bad fight, being bitten by a poisonous snake, collapsing, or any number of other things. As with common injuries and illnesses, if you have any questions, you are best advised to get your boxer to a vet immediately.

What to Do in an Emergency

If your boxer has experienced serious trauma, you need to determine the following:

- Are there any broken bones, severe contusions, or a blocked airway?
- Is your boxer bleeding profusely? If so, is it from one localized cut, a scrape, or has a major artery or blood vessel been punctured?
- Are the gums pale, possibly indicating severe shock or internal bleeding?

If any of these conditions is evident, call your vet with an explanation. Calling ahead will alert them to be ready for your emergency, which will save time once you arrive.

 **Alert!**

If you have any questions concerning a possible emergency situation, you can check your boxer's heart rate. Normal for an adult is between seventy and 160 beats per minute at rest, slightly faster for puppies. An adult's normal rectal temperature is between 100.5 and 102.5 degrees Fahrenheit, and slightly higher for puppies. If either measurement is too high or too low, a visit to the vet is in order.

Natural Disaster Emergencies

Natural disasters can cause a difficult situation for both you and your boxer. Are you in an earthquake zone, a wildfire zone, tornado alley, or a hurricane zone? If so, take extra precautions to prepare food and veterinary supplies in case you are evacuated from your home for any reason. If you are separated from your boxer during a natural disaster, you will want to search for him as soon as you safely can. Animal shelters and boxer rescue groups are good places to start.

Although it is a good idea to have a license and tag on your boxer that lists your name, and the name of your vet as contacts should your boxer be lost or separated from you at any time, having your boxer microchipped is also a good idea since collars can be lost or removed. Microchips are tiny pieces of traceable material including numbers that can be registered with a number of different national registries. This is proof of your boxer's connection to you.

If Something Happens to You

The final emergency to prepare for is the one that includes something happening to you. What becomes of your beloved boxer? Be certain that you either have a will or a trust that will tell your estate what is to be come of your beloved boxer. This may seem extreme, but of all the boxers that go into rescue each year, the saddest are those that have lost a loving family or home through the death of an owner.

Some boxer owners arrange trusts for their boxers to ensure that their dog's health, home, and well-being will continue and will be honored until the boxer is no longer living. Then and only then can the estate be distributed to human inheritors. More and more attorneys and estate planners are willing and capable of preparing such a legal trust for your boxer.

You can arrange for a perpetual trust that takes care of your boxer until he dies. Alternately, you can will your boxer to a loving friend or relative who will care for him, or you can designate that he go to a rescue where you know a wonderful home will be found for it. Some reputable breeders insist that the boxer be returned to them if anything happens to you, so you need to make those wishes known to your estate as well. The executor of the estate, which could possibly end up being someone you do not know, can then make arrangements for your boxer to go back to the breeder or elsewhere.

▲ Since your boxer cannot take care of himself, you must take proper precautions in the event of an emergency.

Being Prepared

If you are fortunate, you will never have a real veterinary emergency with your boxer. However, it is best to be prepared for an emergency just in case you do. The primary way to be prepared for an emergency is to have a regular vet with whom you have a good relationship. Ideally, this should be the person who regularly sees your boxer for check-ups and vaccinations.

Unless your veterinarian works with a large hospital that has weekend and night hours, she will probably refer you to an emergency veterinary practice for nights and weekends. Be sure that you have this number handy right under your regular vet's number. Tape this on your refrigerator or put it in a file where you can find it easily. You will also want to include in this file any medications that your boxer might be taking, and an up-to-date record of vaccinations. Make sure you know where the emergency vet is located and how to get there quickly but safely.

Emergency Checklist

Elsewhere in your box of veterinary emergency supplies you should keep the following:

☐ A digital thermometer (faster and easier to use)

☐ A muzzle designed for the boxer snout. Several companies that make humane muzzles to fit the boxer—the type made for scissor-bite breeds will not work.

☐ Some long, thin pieces of wood (yardsticks work well for this), just in case you need to make a splint or tourniquet.

☐ Several blankets, so you can carry your boxer without unnecessary joint movement

☐ Several rolls of vet wrap, a stretchy, first-aid wrap that sticks to itself. This can be a lifesaver for your boxer.

☐ Basic first-aid items, including tweezers, adhesive tape, an antiseptic/antibiotic ointment, ipecac (to induce vomiting), cotton balls, a germicidal soap or wash, and rubbing alcohol.

☐ An extra collar and leash. These can be invaluable in an emergency where you do not have access to your normal equipment or home.

If you have all these items in a veterinary emergency kit, you are prepared for almost any emergency likely to come your boxer's way. It is also a good idea to keep duplicates of your boxer's veterinary records at your office or with a friend or family member who does not live with you.

Bleeding

Probably one of the biggest, most immediate emergencies you will need to deal with is bleeding. If blood is spurting from the boxer in what seem to be rhythmic outbursts, an artery has been cut or punctured. You must act quickly or your boxer will bleed to death. If the bleeding is coming from a limb you may be able to apply a tourniquet from the supplies in your veterinary emergency kit. If the wound is on your boxer's body, you will need to apply a pressure bandage or your hand, depending upon what is available.

If you do not have your veterinary emergency kit available, and the puncture or cut is on a limb, tear off a strip of your clothing to create a tourniquet. Place the tourniquet above the wound and find an emergency vet as quickly as you can. Be very careful that you only tighten this to the point where the bleeding lessens dramatically. You don't want to entirely cut off the circulation to your boxer's limb.

Poisoning

Unfortunately, there are many ways your boxer can be poisoned. Many household items, from lawn chemicals to rodent poisons to chocolate, can poison a curious boxer. The symptoms of poisoning are as varied as the poisons. They can include nausea, vomiting, diarrhea, bleeding from bodily orifices, seizures, convulsions, rapid pulse, weak pulse, excess salivation, labored breathing, and collapse. No matter what time of the day or night the poisoning occurs, contact your emergency vet immediately, even if you do not know what the poison might have been. If you see any of these symptoms and know of no other cause, you can assume that somehow, your boxer had access to a poison or to a poisoned rodent.

If Your Dog Has Been Poisoned

In the case of poisoning, your vet may tell you to induce vomiting, which is why you should keep ipecac handy. However, should you find yourself without it, a teaspoon or so of hydrogen peroxide per ten pounds of body weight (about a quarter of a cup for an adult male boxer) will do the job. Certain types of poison, such as caustic materials like lye or petroleum products, will contraindicate treatment by vomiting. Contact your veterinarian first.

Not many adult boxers will ingest caustic substances or petroleum voluntarily. Your boxer is more likely to be poisoned by something that either tastes good or is fun to play with. Puppies, on the other hand, do not always have good enough judgment to avoid things that taste bad, so you must be more careful that they are not exposed to poisonous substances.

Snakebite

There are poisonous varieties of snakes throughout the continental United States and Alaska. That said, it is the West and Southwest that has the most snake bites, although poisonous snakes are also common in the South.

Any time a snake bites, it is probably poisonous. Nonpoisonous snakes are generally less aggressive and do not bite as often. It is important to know what your local poisonous snakes look like. Rattlesnakes are probably the most common threat to all dogs. Not all dogs die from snakebites, but some succumb to unattended secondary infections.

 Alert!

The most poisonous of all snakes are the babies; they have more poison per square inch, so to speak, than the adults, and they can bring it to their fangs and the surface of what they have struck more quickly. Be especially careful around immature rattlesnakes. Do not think they are less dangerous or toxic because they are small as just the opposite is true.

If you suspect that a rattlesnake or other poisonous snake has struck your boxer, call your vet so she can acquire the antivenom needed to treat your boxer. In addition, your boxer will also probably be treated with antibiotics and an anti-inflammatory drug of some kind. If you see two holes or puncture wounds anywhere on your boxer's body, very symmetrical and about an inch apart, you can assume that your boxer has been struck by a rattlesnake even if you have not seen it. However, sometimes a snake will strike and only get one fang in the dog. If you live in rattlesnake country and you know your boxer has not been in a fight, one puncture hole on a paw or lower extremity accompanied by swelling is a good sign that your boxer has been stuck by a rattlesnake. You need to see the vet as soon as possible. The effect of rattlesnake venom in the blood stream causes extreme thirst and irritability.

 Fact

In some of the Western and Southwestern states, there are trainers who will snakeproof your dog to reduce the likelihood that your boxer will be struck by a rattlesnake. Many of these options use extreme aversive methods like a shock collar, so it might be worthwhile to put your nosy boxer through some snake avoidance training. However, before you undertake this, make sure your trainer thoroughly explains what the training will entail.

Shock

Shock is a generalized reduction in the function of the circulatory system, including drop in blood pressure. Shock may set in after an injury, trauma, serious infection, or emotional upset. Common signs of shock are pale gums, labored breathing, weak, rapid pulse, cold extremities, and eventually, if not treated, a lapse of consciousness into coma.

 **Esseñtial**

> Anytime your boxer has suffered an extreme trauma, he should be seen by a vet immediately even if you don't see any other symptoms of injury. Sometimes shock can prove fatal even if the initial injury is not, so it is very important that your boxer be seen by a vet after any trauma.

If the shock state has not been precipitated by trauma, you must suspect an insect bite or an irregular heartbeat. Get your boxer to the vet as soon as possible. Be sure to keep your boxer warm but do not use a muzzle, as his breathing may already be restricted.

Heat Exhaustion

The short, bracycephalic nose of the boxer has as many obstructive folds inside as outside. This renders the boxer particularly susceptible to heat stroke and heat exhaustion. The distinctive boxer head can work against the boxer's well-being. In hot, humid weather they simply cannot breathe well enough to cool themselves off as efficiently as many other breeds.

Precautions
You must never leave your boxer in a closed car in hot or even warm weather. The interior of a car heats up quickly if left in direct sunlight. Even in a ventilated car, never leave your boxer for long without water. Accordingly, you must never leave your boxer in a back yard without shade and access to fresh water in hot climates or in warm weather (or cold, for that matter!). You must also monitor physical activity on hot days to make sure that your boxer is not overheating. Most adult boxers will know when they are getting too hot, but young puppies that love to play often will not and are at risk of overheating.

 Alert!

Signs of heat stroke or overheating include a temperature that may rise as high as 109 degrees Fahrenheit; a weak and rapid pulse; gums and tongue that are sometimes swollen and almost fiery red; extreme rapid panting; an inability to walk and move; and sometimes vomiting and diarrhea. If you see any of these signs alone or in combination on a hot humid day, you need to take measures to cool your boxer down quickly.

Once overheating has occurred—and symptoms of overheating can occur long before an internal temperature of 109 occurs— the only way to save your boxer is to cool him off. If you have a pool to put him in, by all means do, or hose him down as much as possible with cool water. If you have access to ice cubes, press ice to the pads of his paws, his ears, and private parts. All dogs perspire through the pads of their paws, and applying ice or cool clothes to their paws is one way to cool them off as well.

Finally, you need to get your boxer to a vet immediately, as he may need other veterinary treatment as well, such as help in restoring fluids and electrolytes.

Solutions to Overheating

Boxers that are regularly exposed to heat can usually tolerate it. However, even those in the Southern and Southwestern states are at risk when the heat changes from cool or cold to hot suddenly. Just as humans need to time to acclimate, so do boxers. So when you've had a sudden increase in temperature in spring or fall, keep a close eye on your boxer for a week or so until he has acclimated.

If you take your boxer hiking or like to play fetch or other active games, there are still things that you can do to stay active in hot weather. One is to dress your boxer in a wet coat. Popular in the Southwest, these dog garments are made of materials that retain water, such as chamois or terry cloth. You soak the wet coat, and as the water evaporates it keeps your boxer cool. You can also get wet mats for your boxer's crate, which work on the same principle. Other solutions are to keep a spray bottle handy and frequently spray the pads of his feet, his underarms, ears, and genitals, where the blood vessels are closer to the surface. Some people think that spraying a dog's coat will cool him off, but the sunlight on the water usually only makes him hotter.

 **Fact**

Some breeders suggest that you keep a squeeze bottle of honey handy for your boxer in hot weather. Honey contains a lot of electrolytes as well as vitamins and minerals, and the sugar gives instant energy, all of which helps to offset heat stress. As a preventive measure in the really hot months, some vets recommend that you crush a vitamin B tablet (twenty-five to fifty milligrams) into your boxer's food once a day or every other day. Vitamin B helps in preventing and recovering from overheating.

How to Muzzle

If your boxer is ever hurt or becomes very ill, he may bite if you try to move him or examine. This doesn't mean that he wants to hurt you; he's just frightened and in pain. A muzzle makes an emergency situation easier for everyone. You should invest in a muzzle that has been specially designed for the boxer snout. These muzzles allow your boxer to breathe, eat, drink water, and pant, although they do not to let him extend his teeth to bite.

If you do not have a muzzle, you can use vet wrap or other strips of cloth. Wind the cloth around your boxer's muzzle and then wrap and tie it up around the head behind the ears. Wrap relatively loosely, only to keep your boxer's jaws from opening enough to bite, being careful not to cover his nostrils or to catch his tongue between his teeth. Monitor your boxer closely the whole time he is muzzled to be sure he can breathe and pant. Otherwise, he is at risk of overheating or suffocating if he becomes sick to his stomach.

Performing CPR

If you ever find that your boxer is silent and not breathing, it could mean that his heart has stopped beating. Doing CPR could help to restart his heart. Alternatively, if your boxer has inhaled water, his heart and breathing may also have stopped. In either case you must perform cardiopulmonary resuscitation (CPR). If your boxer has been in the water, you must first lift him by the hindquarters and attempt to let the water drain out of his lungs. If you can't lift him, put his head and neck slightly lower than his body in order to drain the fluids.

 Fact

The easiest way to find your boxer's pulse is to feel for the femoral artery, located on the inside of his thigh. Move your index finger down the femur (the thigh bone), and apply slight pressure. If you cannot get to his rear legs, check the carotid artery on your boxer's throat— just below and to the left of the jaw joint. It's a good idea to practice finding your boxer's pulse long before any emergency occurs.

To begin performing CPR, open your dog's mouth and pull his tongue forward or to one side. Look to see whether anything is blocking his airway, and use your fingers to clear his mouth and upper throat of any mucous or blockages. Put your hands, one on top of the other, over the region of the heart, and compress the chest with strong downward thrusts. You will need to do about 100 compressions per minute, checking every thirty seconds or so for a heartbeat. If you get nothing, hold your boxer's mouth closed, put your mouth around his nose, and breath directly into his nasal passages for four beats ("one and two and three and four and"). Compress the chest again for about fifty compressions, check for a pulse, and breathe again into the nostrils. Hopefully, you will get your boxer back to breathing again.

 **Alert!**

Never leave your boxer unsupervised with rawhide chews. Boxers tend to create a lot of saliva, which can melt the chew into a soft rubbery mass. Your boxer may inhale this mass and get it stuck in his airway. In this event, you'll have to reach down your boxer's throat to remove the obstruction.

If your boxer is not breathing for reasons other than drowning, or if your boxer is choking or suffocating, you must immediately pry open his jaws, put something between the back canine teeth to prop the jaws open, and reach down the throat to clear the obstruction. If you cannot remove the obstruction, and if after several attempts to cough it out, your boxer cannot breathe, you must attempt a canine equivalent of the Heimlich maneuver.

To do that, you must place your boxer on his side. Put your hands palms down, one on top of the other, right below the rib cage near the loin, and administer a sharp, upward thrust. Repeat until the object is expelled or pushed far enough up into the throat so that you can grasp it and pull it out. If these efforts fail, resume CPR in hopes of moving the object one way or another. If you have a friend or family member handy, have them drive you to your veterinarian while you continue CPR on the way.

Restraining an Injured Boxer

If your boxer has been hit by a car, the first thing that you must do is to restrain him so that he doesn't follow his instincts to run and hide in a quiet, safe place. It is best to wrap him in a blanket, which puts no pressure on his injuries but will help to keep him from flailing about and injuring himself more. This is what the blankets in your veterinary emergency kits are for—that and to move your boxer with the least amount of pressure on the injured area as possible. If you can get someone to drive you to the vet, you can hold your boxer down gently. It is very important to avoid putting pressure on the injuries unless you are attempting to prevent your boxer from bleeding to death.

 Fact

During your boxer's recovery phase, you will find the best way to help your boxer to heal is to keep him in his crate. Crating a hurt dog is a very common thing to do, especially during recovery from surgery or from extensive soft-tissue injuries. With many types of traumas, it is almost certain that crate rest will be prescribed.

When moving an injured dog, you need to take special precautions. It is best to fashion a stretcher from any available materials, such as a board, piece of plywood, or a blanket. Move your boxer as gently as possible, without allowing any injured limbs to dangle or be jostled too much. The most important thing is to get your boxer to a vet as quickly as you safely can. Have a friend or family member drive while you comfort your boxer and prevent him from moving.

CHAPTER  11

Hereditary Diseases

Boxers are prone to various inherited conditions and diseases, in which a genetic abnormality plays a major role in causing a disease or condition. Some disorders can occur as a result of spontaneous mutations of cells, but most genetic conditions or diseases are inherited. Although there are several serious health problems common among boxers, breeders can avoid many of them by performing screening tests on their breeding stock. Some lines are healthier than others, and have greater longevity.

Boxer Cardiomyopathy (BCM)

One of the most important discoveries of the past several decades in terms of boxer health has been the identification of a heart condition usually known as boxer cardiomyopathy (BCM). It is also called boxer familial disease, familial ventricular arrhythmia in boxers (FVA), boxer electrical conductivity disease, and right ventricular arrhythmia cardiomyopathy. When present, BCM can significantly reduce an individual's life. It is not uncommon for affected boxers to die suddenly while still young, at age six or so. BCM can be expensive and is best treated under the supervision of a canine cardiologist.

History of the Condition

References to sudden deaths in boxers go all the way back to Frau Stockmann in Germany. As chronicled by Dr. Kathryn Meurs of Ohio State University, in a study commissioned by the American Boxer Club into the causes and etiology of boxer cardiomyopathy, the recent chronology of studies into BCM reads as follows:

1980: Dr. Neil Harpster of Angell Memorial Hospital in Boston characterizes a heart disease he was seeing in some of his boxer patients as boxer cardiomyopathy (BCM). He outlined the progression of the disease in three stages:

- **Type I:** Irregular heartbeats, no symptoms
- **Type II:** Irregular heartbeats, fainting spells (syncope)
- **Type III:** Dilated, flabby heart, congestive heart failure, coughing, breathing difficulties

1991: Dr. Bruce Keene identifies a family of boxers with dilated cardiomyopathy, which responds favorably to L-carnitine supplements.
1993: Dr. John-Karl Goodwin identifies a family of boxers with ventricular premature contractions (VPCs).
1997: Dr. Kate Meurs's study on boxer cardiomyopathy for the American Boxer Club begins.

These studies have shown that BCM differs from other forms of cardiomyopathy found in other breeds (which boxers can also display). It consists primarily of an electrical conduction disorder that causes the heart to beat erratically, or to have an arrhythmia in the form of a ventricular premature contraction, some of the time. If the erratic beats occur in sequence for too long a period of time, weakness, collapse, or sudden death can occur. The only treatments available are prescription heart medications from your vet, and even most of those do not greatly enhance the quality of life for the severely affected dog.

On the other hand, some boxers with BCM live a normal life and die of old age or other unrelated causes. Most affected boxers have normal echocardiograms and no measurable symptoms. Owners often have no idea that their boxers have this condition until the dog suddenly dies. By then, of course, it is too late to perform any treatment. If your boxer has experienced any fainting spells, BCM might be the reason. You are advised to take him to a canine cardiologist.

 **Fact**

In cases of BCM, if the boxer's heart can correct itself during the irregular beating sequences, the boxer recovers from such an episode. Episodes tend to get worse over time, so treatment is usually required. There are drugs for this disease.

One of the best indicators of BCM is the twenty-four-hour Holter monitor report, which measures ventricular premature contractions (VPCs).

Of the 188 mature boxers that Dr. Meurs studied, thirty-one had been observed to suffer from fainting spells. The remaining 157 had normal echocardiograms and no other observable sign of boxer cardiomyopathy. The Holter monitor reports produced the following measurements over a twenty-four-hour period:

- 81 percent of dogs had at least one VPC
- 50 percent had more than 10 VPCs
- 36 percent had more than 50 VPCs
- 31 percent had more than 100 VPCs
- 22 percent had more than 500 VPCs
- 0.4 percent had more than 3000 VPCs

It's more likely that the ones with the higher VPCs will die early or at an earlier age of the complications without medication. However, a confusing aspect is that there is the occasional boxer with fairly significant VPCs who makes it to a relatively old age. This is one of the problems with this disease. There have been only about 10 years of real research, and the results are not as clear as one might like for indications of exactly what to do. Still, the general assumption is that the fewer VPCs, the better off the dog is in life and in breeding.

It is suggested that no breeder breed a boxer with over fifty VPCs. If there is some pressing reason to do so, such as to save a line of boxers from extinction, the more affected boxer should only be bred to a boxer whose line and family routinely has fewer than fifty VPCs and no BCM deaths in recent generations. As Dr. Meurs states, "The likelihood that FVA is inherited . . . justifies recommending careful screening of breeding animals of a mature age and consideration of removal of affected dogs from breeding programs."

Mode of Inheritance

Dr. Meurs's findings suggest that boxer cardiomyopathy has equal occurrence in both sexes and that it has a male-to-male-transmission pattern. Two affected parents are capable of producing offspring that do not display the disease. However, the offspring will definitely carry the genes for the disease. Unfortunately, two *unaffected* parents can also produce affected offspring if one carries the genetic pattern (is double dominant) for the disease. There is no way of testing for genetic double dominance at this time.

For this reason, it is important to ask about your puppy's lines before you buy. A reputable breeder should have Holter statistics on all her breeding stock. Have other members of the line been measured with more than fifty VPCs? Have any died from boxer cardiomyopathy? What relation did those dogs have to your puppy—grandparents, uncles, aunts, siblings? This is important, as heart problems tend to run in families.

Subaortic Stenosis

While BCM tends to be the cause of death in dogs that die unexpectedly at around age six, subaortic stenosis is responsible for the death of many younger boxers, sometimes as early as two years of age.

Subaortic stenosis is a heart disease that occurs when two of the three flaps that comprise the aortic valve fuse together. This fusion narrows the opening to the aorta, which in turn restricts the blood flow out of the left ventricle into the aorta. Symptoms of this condition include exercise intolerance, fainting, and a systolic murmur (a murmur or slight noise that is heard when the heart contracts). Reduced blood flow can result in sudden death. A definitive diagnosis must be made by a canine cardiologist after detection of a heart murmur. It is known that this is an inherited disease, although the mode of inheritance is not known at this time. However, affected dogs should not be bred for any reason.

Subaortic stenosis can be fairly expensive and should be treated under the supervision of a canine cardiologist.

Hypothyroidism

Of all the diseases that boxers can get, hypothyroidism is the easiest to treat. Hypothyroidism is the most common endocrine disease in all dogs. The thyroid gland controls the speed of metabolism of almost all body cells. When the thyroid produces lower-than-normal levels of hormones, many bodily systems can be affected.

The typical clinical symptoms of hypothyroidism include weight gain, sluggishness, ear inflammation, weakness, cold intolerance, and infertility. Skin and coat problems are also common, including hair loss, thickening of the skin, pruritus (itchy skin), pyoderma (inflammation of skin with pus-filled lesions), hyperpigmentation (skin turns very dark), and crusty, flaky skin.

 Essential

Many boxer owners have found that sudden displays of aggression are an early sign of thyroid disease. In performance dogs, thyroid disease is often marked by sudden confusion when asked to perform well-known tasks.

Through a number of studies, Michigan State University has developed a thyroid panel to determine whether the body chemistry of an individual dog has the major elements associated with thyroid disease, specifically with the form known as autoimmune thyroiditis. This makes it important to test breeding dogs in order to reduce the incidence of thyroid disease. If you suspect that your boxer is suffering from thyroid problems, be sure you ask your veterinarian to perform the comprehensive Michigan State University thyroid panel. A less extensive panel is likely to miss important warning signs.

 Alert!

Because hypothyroidism affects the body's metabolism and all internal organs, leaving the condition untreated means sentencing your boxer to a substandard level of existence. Autoimmune thyroiditis generally responds well to Soloxine, which your regular veterinarian can prescribe for your boxer.

The best way to prevent this disease is to remove affected dogs from the breeding program, although their tendency to infertility may be nature's way of doing just that.

Hip Dysplasia

Conventional veterinary medicine regards hip dysplasia as a genetic disease. The malformation of the hip joint leads to osteoarthritis, which can eventually lead to pain and debilitation. The hip is a ball-and-socket joint, where the top of the femur fits into the socket of the pelvis. Tendons and ligaments hold this joint together.

Hip dysplasia occurs when the socket is poorly formed or the ligaments are loose, enabling the ball of the femur to slide out of the socket. This causes cartilage damage in the joint. The cartilage loses its thickness and elasticity, which are important in absorbing the effects of weight and stress on the joint during movement. Eventually, through normal wear and tear, the hip becomes extremely painful, and range of motion may be decreased.

 Fact

No one knows when or if a dysplastic dog will start showing clinical signs of lameness due to pain. Long before actual limping occurs, the stoic boxer may swing his legs out slightly to avoid bending the hip in a normal gait. Boxers may also become somewhat sullen or surly. It is difficult to assess how much hip dysplasia affects a boxer's life span, but it definitely affects his quality of life.

There appears to be no rhyme or reason to the severity of changes that occur in the hip when X-rayed. Plenty of dysplastic dogs with severe arthritis and hip dysplasia can run, jump, and play as if nothing was wrong with them. Some dogs with barely any arthritic radiographic changes are severely lame.

The following factors can worsen the effects of hip dysplasia:

- **Excess weight:** Extra body weight puts extra pressure on the hips.
- **Excess or prolonged exercise before maturity:** Among the larger of the medium-sized breeds, boxers tend not to have bone maturity (when the growth plates of the bones close, and growth is finished) until between eighteen months to two years of age.
- **A fast growth rate in a puppy:** This may actually be a bone overgrowth disease, such as panosteitis or osteochondritis, which may be the result of a high-calorie or over-supplemented diet, or even injury.

The raw-food movement takes the position that feeding a raw diet supplemented with vitamin C helps eliminate the effects and even the genetic tendency toward hip dysplasia. While long-term studies have not been done on this, many breeders recommend that you add additional vitamin C to a puppy's food to aid in the development of good ligaments, tendons, and cartilage.

▲ Watch for decreased range of motion in your boxer's hips, as this could indicate hip dysplasia.

Because of the risk to the pups' bones in terms of bone overgrowth diseases (panosteitis and osteochondritis) and a tendency to hip dysplasia, it is critically important to not overexercise your young puppy. Dogs, especially males, should not jog or run long distances regularly before eighteen months to two years. Males seem to be more prone to bone overgrowth diseases and mature later than females.

Boxer Colitis

Boxers can have very delicate tummies, and most of their admirers accept that about them. They should be fed a consistent diet on a regular schedule. In general, there is some evidence to suggest that some stomach disturbances may be the result of elevated autoimmune antibodies. The full Michigan Statue University thyroid panel, normally performed to detect thyroid problems, can detect those elevated levels.

If you have a picky eater whose back is frequently hunched up like a horseshoe, you probably have a boxer with colitis. This disorder is so common in boxers that vets tend to refer to it as boxer colitis. Symptoms can vary from an occasionally upset stomach, which you can manage by not changing foods on your boxer and feeding at precisely the same time each day, to constant bloody diarrhea and vomiting. If your boxer's stomach upsets are boxer colitis, keeping to a set schedule along with bland foods and digestive enzymes will probably solve your (and his!) problems.

Pancreatic Exocrine Insufficiency

If the stomach upsets come with great hunger, your boxer has full-blown pancreatic exocrine insufficiency (PEI), the inability to produce sufficient digestive enzymes.

In some cases, this appears to be an inherited condition. Signs of PEI include chronic diarrhea and weight loss despite a good, even ravenous appetite. The hearty appetite is due to the fact that nutrients are poorly absorbed. The appetite center in the brain is never really satisfied, leaving the dog chronically hungry. These dogs may also experience malabsorption problems, inflammatory bowel disease, or colitis, worsened by the presence of undigested foods.

Pancreatitis

Symptoms of chronic pancreatitis include diarrhea and roaching (back hunched up like a horseshoe). Pancreatitis is the result of inflammation of the pancreas due to overwork or irritation. The adrenal glands may release cortisol to help reduce the inflammation. If this does not solve the problem, the tissues of the pancreas swell and obstruct the pancreatic duct. The pancreas produces enzymes that aid in the digestion of food. If these enzymes become active while still in the pancreas, the boxer's body literally begins to digest itself. Scarring and further inflammation are the results.

Pancreatic inflammation can result in varying degrees of pain. This can range from mild discomfort to severe enough pain to require a pain medication. Because digestive enzymes cannot reach the small intestine, foods are poorly digested. The dog's body may begin to consider these incompletely digested molecules to be toxins or irritants, which can initiate an immune system response.

 Fact

When inflammation of the pancreas occurs gradually and over time, it is termed chronic. This is the most common form of pancreatitis in boxers. Many with this form can go for years at a time without an episode of sudden and severe pancreas inflammation. Sudden and severe inflammation of the pancreas is acute pancreatitis, which does not last as long as chronic pancreatitis. This is the form that is most commonly found in dogs that have been given large amounts of cooked fats, such as during Thanksgiving.

Digestion of dietary fats (lipids) can be particularly compromised in cases of pancreatitis. The close proximity of the pancreas to the liver can result in inflammation of the liver and the bile duct. This can interfere with both formation and secretion of bile. If this happens, then the lipids will be insufficiently digested, and the boxer absorbs the undigested lipids into the lymphatic system, which will also set off an immune response. The body will try to rid itself of these irritants by vomiting or diarrhea. In severe cases, the boxer will develop inflammatory bowel disease or malabsorption conditions in conjunction with bouts of pancreatitis.

 **Essential**

Many proponents of raw-food feel that feeding a dog with a compromised digestive system a raw food diet is an obvious choice, since the raw food contains enzymes and is easier to digest. Boxers with chronic pancreatitis and mild boxer colitis and inflammatory bowel disease have done very well on a raw diet.

Complications of chronic or acute pancreatitis can include liver problems leading to a serious blood-clotting abnormality. Inflammation can compromise the liver's ability to process bilirubin, which results in jaundice.

To fully diagnose your boxer's condition, there are several blood tests that veterinarians use. These tests generally measure levels of enzymes present in the bloodstream, which will determine the exact type of problem he has.

Bloat

Bloat, or gastric dilatation-volvulus (GDV), is a serious condition that could threaten the life of your boxer. While the diagnosis of bloat is simple, the pathological changes in the dog's body make treatment complicated, expensive, and not always successful. Breeds that are typically affected are the large to giant breeds or breeds with deep chests.

Simple gastric distention can occur in any breed or age of dog, and it's common in young puppies or dogs that overeat. Belching of gas, vomiting, or simple digestion usually relieves the problem of discomfort.

Since boxers are somewhat predisposed to simple gastric distention and bloat, your breeder will probably recommend ways to prevent bloat, such as feeding smaller, more frequent meals or giving digestive enzymes that help your boxer digest food more efficiently.

In severe cases of gastric distention, or after a gastric torsion (twisted gut), your vet might suggest surgery to anchor the stomach in place so that twisting cannot occur or cannot occur again. When torsion occurs, the esophagus is closed off, limiting or stopping the dog's ability to relieve distention by vomiting or belching. Often the spleen becomes entrapped as well, and its blood supply is cut off.

Here are a few symptoms of gastric torsion:

- Unsuccessful attempts at vomiting
- Restlessness
- Roached back
- Bloated abdomen that may feel tight
- Pale or off-color gums
- Licking air
- Seeking a hiding place
- Drinking water excessively
- Heavy or rapid panting
- Accelerated heartbeat
- Weak pulse
- Collapse

If you see any of these signs in combination, you will want to get your boxer to a vet as soon as safely possible.

 **Alert!**

Some people feel that putting a dog's bowl on an elevated platform increases the likelihood of bloating. However, many boxer owners have found out the hard way that boxers gulp too much air when eating off the ground, so raising the food bowls may solve some problems with boxers. Many boxer owners have also found that feeding at least two meals, with a biscuit for lunch in between or before bedtime, reduces the likelihood of bloat. Another solution is to have adequate fresh water readily available.

There are as many theories about the cause of bloating as there are dog breeds. The first major physiological cause is deep chest. Other causes include stress; fasting, then eating a great deal of food; activities that result in gulping air; eating too fast; drinking too much water before and after eating; eating gas-producing foods; exercise immediately before or after eating; heredity—especially having a first-degree relative who bloated.

Cancers

Boxers are very prone to a whole host of cancers. One of the most common is mast cell cancer. Boxers frequently recover from this form at a greater rate than many breeds. Many boxers that get benign tumors like fatty lipomas and histiocytomas will never get a more malignant form of cancer.

The bad news is that boxers do get lymphoma, fibrosarcoma, osteosarcoma, mast cell cancer, and virtually every other cancer known to the canine world. Boxers also get a brain tumor that seems to be specific to the breed. Breeders of many of the longer-lived lines often say that their boxers live until a certain age, then die of a brain tumor or some other fast-acting cancer. Many, if not most, boxers go out of this world because of cancer.

Spaying or neutering your boxer will help reduce the incidence of cancer if done while your boxer is quite young. All male dogs with one undescended testicle (monorchids) or whose testicles never descended at all (cryptorchids) should be neutered shortly after six months. The undescended testicle is at a great risk of becoming cancerous. A male with one or more undescended testicles should never be bred.

Gliomas

Boxers and other bracycephalic, or short-nosed, breeds have the highest incidence of a type of brain tumor known as gliomas. These tumors start in the glial cells (supporting cells) within the brain. As they grow, they cause compression and death of the surrounding brain tissue. The tumors can vary in malignancy from slow-growing, relatively benign tumors to high-grade, aggressive tumors known as globastoma multiforme. These latter tumors are resistant to current forms of treatment. They tend to occur in older boxers.

Symptoms of glioma include seizures, behavioral changes (including sudden unprovoked aggression), circling, and general clumsiness, an indication of damage to the forebrain. A tumor in the brain stem could trigger head titling, nystagmus (rapid flicking of the eyes), difficulty swallowing, and unsteady walking.

Cancer Treatments

There are almost as many options for cancer treatment these days for dogs as for people, including surgery, tumor-inhibiting drugs, and radiation. There are holistic approaches to feeding. You can attempt to avoid lines of boxers that displayed a tendency to develop cancer in them. Unfortunately, cancer is kind of a wild card in life. While you can take all sensible precautions, there may be nothing you can do to avoid it.

Spondylosis

Spondylosis or spondylosis deformans, as it is technically known, is a condition of the spine in which bridges, or spurs, are formed along the bottom of the vertebrae, in essence fusing it. Spondylosis has been diagnosed in humans, bovines, and even whales. Boxers are well represented in spondylosis studies.

 Fact

A collapse of the hind end, known as going down in the rear, is a common occurrence in many older boxers, and there seems to be no one cause. Probable causes are advanced spondylosis, advanced arthritis due to hip dysplasia, and degenerative myelopathy.

Although spondylosis is considered to be a generalized disease of aging, European boxer breeders have noted some genetic tendencies toward the disease. If a boxer's spine shows signs of spondylosis at the age of two, the dog should be removed from any breeding program. A later onset of spondylosis due to age or spondylosis due to injury is not as problematic as the early-onset type of spondylosis.

A lack of flexibility is also commonly in evidence, including another condition common to boxers. This is known as going down in the rear, or being unable to stabilize and get up from a prone position and to walk.

Degenerative Myelopathy

Degenerative myelopathy (DM) is a potentially debilitating neurological condition that can eventually paralyze its victims. The cause of DM is unknown, although there is some suggestion that it is not dissimilar to multiple sclerosis in humans. While DM is described as a degenerative neurological condition, there is no screening test for the disease. A definitive identification of it can therefore be made only in autopsy.

 **Fact**

There is some suggestion among those vets and researchers interested in alternative approaches to veterinary care that over vaccination may be a contributor to degenerative myelopathy. The suggestion is that vaccination protocols should change so that young animals are not vaccinated as frequently or as early.

Signs of DM usually appear between ages of five and nine years of age. It begins with loss of coordination in the hind legs. The boxer may wobble or drag its feet, wearing the hair off the tops of its toes on his hind legs. The condition progresses to paralysis in approximately three to six months, although a focused effort at rebuilding the rear leg muscles early in the diagnosis may forestall the paralysis somewhat. Swimming has been found to be a good way to build muscles in a failing rear end of a boxer.

No pain appears to be associated with the paralysis. The dog, which may be perfectly healthy in every other way, wants to continue its life as usual. Many boxers with this condition do very well on a cart that supports their rear end and allows them at least some mobility. Most veterinary care is aimed at slowing the progression of the disease and doing as much rehabilitation as possible. In early-identified cases, the effective rate of early intervention has been as high as 80 percent.

Future research on this debilitating illness will look at a combination of genetic, environmental, and toxic factors likely to lead to DM. Other research suggests that there is overwhelming evidence that DM is an autoimmune disease attacking the nervous system leading to progressive damage of the nervous system involved.

CHAPTER 12

Grooming Basics

An ungroomed or dirty boxer is like an unkempt beauty queen: You know she's lovely underneath and deserves every chance to be looking her best! A well-groomed boxer is clean and free of fleas, with short nails and trimmed whiskers, tail hair, and ear hair. These simple maintenance tasks are not difficult, and they all contribute to maintaining an overall good quality of life for your boxer.

Grooming Considerations for Boxers

Boxers, being a short-coated breed, need relatively little grooming to make them look great. Grooming isn't just for looks but to maintain the health of the skin and to keep the coat shiny. In addition, grooming is a chance to go over every square inch of your boxer to check for lumps and bumps. It gives you a chance to check for sore muscles and tight joints. Grooming can and should be more than a cleaning and sprucing up of your boxer; it should be a weekly checkup of his health and well-being.

Grooming basics include brushing, bathing, maintaining toe nails, trimming whiskers and extraneous hair, dental hygiene, and checking for fleas and other pests. This is the minimum amount of grooming that you should do. An added massage is even nicer for your boxer.

Alert!

Fleas are nasty for dogs and humans, and they carry disease. However, it is best not to use a commercial flea collar, as the chemicals that permeate those collars are sometimes toxic to dogs, especially young puppies. If you have a flea problem, get a topical flea product from your vet that has the chemical to kill the fleas calibrated for the weight of your boxer. Also, get a flea comb, which not only takes out fleas, but also flea eggs, dirt, dander and dead hair. It's a cheap investment in good grooming.

Professional Versus Home Grooming

Although we live in a busy world where many professional dog groomers abound, there are some good reasons why you might want to do your boxer's grooming yourself. First of all, it keeps you in touch with your boxer and thus aware of any lumps and bumps that might come up on your boxer's body. The importance of this cannot be overemphasized in maintaining an early warning system to maintain health for your boxer.

Grooming your boxer yourself also gives you a chance to check on sore muscles and joints. It gives you a chance to massage the occiput, the jaw line underneath the jowls, the neck, down the spine, then the front legs, bending them to see the range of motion in the limbs. The front leg should come slightly forward then bend at the elbow joint if the range of motion is normal—the movement should be smooth and fluid, and your boxer should show no signs of pain. To check the back leg, push the knee and stifle forward, then stretch the leg back and extend gently, only as far as your boxer will let you, to see the range of motion there. The motion should be smooth and fluid.

◄ Frequent, consistent grooming helps contribute to your boxer's overall well-being.

Though doing the grooming yourself is ideal, some people have difficulty fitting this routine into their schedules. If you find that you cannot do at least a biweekly grooming session, you might want to engage the services of a professional groomer. While professionals will not be as attuned to physical changes in your boxer, if you are having a flea problem or are too busy or too physically incapacitated to groom your boxer, hiring a professional groomer to bathe, groom and to trim his nails is a good idea.

Bathing

Generally, dogs do not need to be bathed as often as humans. Brushing can rid the coat of dirt, dander, and dead hair, so your boxer needs to be bathed on average of about once per month, depending on how dirty he is getting. Certainly, he should be bathed if he gets mud, dust, or anything noxious on his coat. Bathing is essential for healthy skin and the shiny coat that is the boxer's hallmark.

To ensure that your boxer is good about being bathed, you need to start with him when he is just a little pup. If all he knows is a nice warm bath with soapy water and a shower or bath surface that has secure footing, your little boxer will grow up thinking that baths are okay experiences—or even fun ones! On the other hand, if you take your boxer out to the back yard and hose him down with cold water, he will probably come to hate being bathed, and you will struggle with him every time he needs a bath.

To bathe your boxer, first make sure he is completely wet. Then apply a thin line of shampoo along his spine and a dollop on the front of his chest. Then add a little more water, and lather his entire body. Work it in well, lightly scratching your fingers through the coat and massaging as you go so that every square inch of his body is soapy.

 **Essential**

Never use human soap products on your boxer. These products can be damaging to your boxer's coat, removing the protective oils. Only use shampoos or products made especially for dogs. There is such a wide variety of these products that you are sure to find something that will meet your boxer's needs. There is everything from medicated shampoos to shampoos with oatmeal conditioners, extra shine, and flea repellents.

When you are done with that, you might want to squirt some soap on your boxer's paws and take a brush to the pads of his feet. Dogs' feet get even dirtier than yours do when you walk around barefoot. Additionally, all dogs sweat through the pads on their feet. Thoroughly cleaning the paws will help your dog perspire more efficiently.

When you are done with his paws, while the suds are still standing on his coat, wash your boxer's head and face. You don't want shampoo dripping into your boxer's eyes while you shampoo the rest of him. Gently wash his head, flews, the folds under his eyes, and the areas above his snout and under her chin. Be sure to take a warm cloth and gently rub his nose to clean off any leftover food residue. Remember that bathing is a great opportunity to check for lumps and bumps, so don't ignore that opportunity. When you are done lathering your boxer's head, check his ears, and wash them out with a cloth as well.

Once your boxer has been thoroughly washed, he needs an equally thorough rinse. Shampoo left on the coat can be irritating to his skin, so be very sure that his entire body, feet, head, and ears have been thoroughly rinsed before you dry him off.

Healthy Ears

Bath time is a good chance to check your boxer's ears for mites and black waxy residue that might suggest an allergy or some kind of illness. Dogs' ears tend to be an early warning system on health. If they are clean and fresh, your dog's health is probably fine. If you notice that waxy stuff tends to build up in the ears, you want your vet to take a closer look. If your boxer has been shaking his head or scratching at his ears recently, he has a problem. If the discharge in his ears has an unusual odor, it usually a sign of mites or an infection. Go see your vet right away.

The ears should be kept clean and free of hair. It makes it easier to keep the ears clean if they are shaved. After you have washed the overall ear inside and out with a cloth during your boxer's bath, you can take a cotton ball and a special ear cleaner and wipe down farther into the ear canal.

Brushing

Boxers do not need excessive grooming, but a good brushing at least once a week is in order. It is also a good idea to brush your boxer before you bathe him to remove all dead hair and dander. In nice weather, it is best to do this outside. Even boxers can shed quite a bit during changes in seasons, when other breeds normally shed their coats. Regular brushing for your boxer is like a combination sponge bath and massage—it takes the dirt and dander out of his coat, along with the dead hair, and distributes his own body oils that make his coat shine.

 **fact**

Wire brushes that are used on longer-haired dogs and terriers are not good for boxers. The wire brushes are too harsh for the softer coat of the boxer and may scratch his skin. A better choice is a natural bristle brush or one with rubber nubs, or both. While the first will take out more dirt, dander, and dead hair, the second gives the surface of the skin a good massage.

Normally, a natural bristle brush, a slicker brush, or a glove with a brush in it will be enough to keep his coat shiny. However, if your boxer is a woolly boxer, or one with a heavier, slightly longer coat, you may need a coat stripper (a comb-like tool with slightly serrated edges and a handle) to get out the excess hair. If you find your boxer shedding too much hair, you might want to have his thyroid checked, or add omega-3 and omega-6 fatty acids to his food, or both. When boxers shed excessively, it usually means they need some kind of adjustment to their diet. Alternatively, they may be developing thyroiditis.

Trimming Nails

This task may seem daunting to a new boxer owner, but it is imperative to ensure your dog's health. A dog with long nails that spread their feet is at risk of his joints being misaligned because he cannot stand squarely on his paws. Long toenails are at risk of being torn out of the pads of the paws, and repair to this might require surgery or cauterization. Because the nails hit the ground, there is risk of infection to a torn nail. A good rule of thumb is that if you can hear your boxer's nails tapping on the floor as he walks, the nails are too long.

Before you start to trim your boxer's nails, you must know where the quick or the living portion of the nail is. On light-colored nails, this is pretty easy to see. On dark nails, this is harder, so you need to proceed more cautiously and take smaller snips of the nail with your nail trimmer. If you accidentally hit the quick of the nail, and your boxer yelps and bleeds, don't panic. A styptic pencil will stop the bleeding, as will cornmeal.

 Question?

What is the quick in a dog's toenail?
The quick is the blood vessel that supports the nail, and it runs past the pad of the paw through the nail almost to the end of the nail. If you cut it, it will bleed, and your boxer will yelp and pull his foot back. The quick contains nerve endings for the nail, so cutting it is painful. You will need to keep something on hand to stop the bleeding, such as a styptic pencil or powder in case you miscalculate and cut into the quick accidentally.

One of the best nail trimmers is the guillotine type. It is easy to handle and easier to control exactly where it cuts the nail. All pet stores and pet supply catalogs carry this type of nail trimmer.

For a boxer, you will probably need a large one, especially if your boxer is a male.

Another good option is to get an electric- or battery-powered hand grinder. This is the piece of equipment used by carpenters to reach difficult corners of wood-trimmed cabinets or similar projects. These grinders come with little sandpaper belts that fit around the grinder head, or you can buy a stone head that will probably never need to be replaced.

One advantage of the grinder is that you are less likely to cut the quick and make it bleed. If you reach the quick with a grinder, it will bleed much less than if it has been cut. Another advantage of the grinder is that you can take the discoloration off the outside of the nails. People who show dogs do this routinely, although it isn't a necessary element of grooming your boxer if he is not a show dog.

A disadvantage of a grinder is that it is loud, which may frighten a puppy, and many dogs do not like the feel of the grinder grinding their nails down. You also have to be careful that you don't let the nail get too hot as it grinds. Even with the disadvantages, the grinder is a fast, safe way to quickly trim your boxer's nails.

Dental Hygiene

Many dog owners are unaware they need to clean their dog's teeth. In fact, it is important to brush your boxer's teeth at least once a week. This addresses the plaque and tartar that builds up on their teeth, and it keeps you abreast of what is going on inside your boxer's mouth. Ideally, you should start looking at your boxer's mouth as a puppy, so he gets used to having you handle his mouth, especially to open it. If you have a show-prospect puppy, you will need to teach him to have his mouth examined regularly in the show ring. This is a good thing to teach any puppy, and it will make your vet's life much easier in giving good care to your boxer.

Dental Hygiene Guidelines

In terms of overall health care, it is particularly important to stay on top of the dental health of your boxer. Brushing his teeth regularly will help keep plaque and tartar at bay. Rather than human toothpaste, use a particularly tasty liver- or chicken-flavored one made especially for dogs.

If you find that your boxer's teeth are brown and dirty, and his breath is smelly, you will need to take him into your vet for a teeth cleaning under anesthesia to get rid of the plaque and to freshen his breath.

 Fact

The raw-food movement input is that the teeth of dogs that eat raw, meaty bones, or even just raw food with naturally occurring enzymes, are often as clean as teeth coming out of your vet's office after a cleaning. Raw-food advocates use this as one more reason to feed raw food—dental health.

In addition, if you want to get your dog a chew, get one that has nubs on it made specifically for cleaning canine teeth.

Gingival Hyperplasia

One big reason to brush your boxer's teeth at least once a week is that you will then be more aware of a condition that boxer's and other bracycephalic breeds are prone to getting. This is a type of benign tumor called gingival hyperplasia. It is usually found through grooming procedures in taking care of your boxer's teeth. Gingival hyperplasia is sometimes referred to as a gum disease, but gums only become diseased if food and other particles get trapped between the teeth and the tumorous tissue.

⚐ Alert!

One of the first noticeable effects of gingival hyperplasia is that it seems like your boxer's teeth are disappearing. The second is that you may notice your boxer eating more slowly or not eating at all. This is because, once the tissue has grown over the teeth, it hurts to eat. A third effect is that your boxer's breath begins to smell really bad, and this is a result of food and other particles trapped beneath the tumors in the gums. If you notice any of these things, take your boxer to a vet right away.

The bad news is that gingival hyperplasia is a type of tumor that grows over teeth, eventually killing the teeth if the tissue is not removed. Of course, a vet must remove this tissue under anesthesia. If this condition is not addressed, the plaque under the tumors, which is called epulis, can become infected. This, in turn, can affect the heart.

CHAPTER 13

Training Basics

As people have moved from the smaller, more rural areas into sprawling cities, the need for dogs and for jobs that dogs performed in rural life has diminished. Thanks to the rapid advancement of technology in our world, we have become accustomed to being able to program things instantly. Dog training is not like that. It takes more time and effort than many people realize. And despite the changing times, a dog still instinctively wants a job.

Why Train?

While it's true that there are more people who have assistance dogs, therapy dogs, police and military dogs, or simply companion dogs, the notion of the noble dog that runs wild and free no longer exists in most parts of the United States. Almost every city and county in the country has leash laws, vaccination requirements for dangerous and communicable diseases, and rules about where dogs are and are not welcome, unless they have specialized training that would allow them access to more places, such as police dogs, assistance dogs, and therapy dogs.

Along with that shift in why we have dogs, society has, in general, become less tolerant of dogs being dogs. If your dog barks too much, growls at someone, or bites, you will probably receive a visit from an animal control agency or worse. Oddly enough, in these more restrictive times, *fewer* trainers genuinely understand how to teach dogs what they need to know to be good dogs. Fewer people know how to productively channel those drives which still exist in dogs that were bred for a specific purpose or purposes, such as boxers.

 **Fact**

Boxers are often called the gentle guard dog, or a hearing guard dog. But like any dog of any breed, they can be provoked, or if allowed to remain untrained and unchecked in their destructive puppy behavior, they can grow up thinking that any and all behavior is allowed. Without sufficient socialization and training to know that aggressive, or even just rough tendencies are not permissible, a young boxer can make any number of mistakes that can prove fatal to him.

When dogs attack people, there is a situation in which a dog with a particular drive was not protected from the downsides of its own drive. In other words, there were no other reasonable and appropriate outlets for that dog's energy and intelligence other than attacking, and the dog was allowed to do so. This is a very negative event for dogs overall. We live in litigious times, and training is our best defense against someone who wants to sue us for a mistake that our dog might possibly make.

Alert!

If you do no formal training, you are still training your boxer. Lack of training is training. By lack of formal training, you may be teaching your boxer that it is all right to bark too much, to menace people, and possibly to bite those that disagree with him. All these behaviors constitute a risk to the owner of any dog who does them.

Boxers are not generally on dangerous dog lists across America at this time, but a slip up on the part of just a few, and they could be—which is why you need to train your boxer. Boxers are candidates for the dangerous dog lists not because they are generally dangerous or aggressive but because they are a powerful dog with lots of energy.

Bear in mind that the majority of the sins that get boxers put onto individual dangerous dog lists are errors in owner management and not innately dangerous characteristics of the breed that are always a risk to society. Train your boxer so he does not make the kind of errors in judgment that will result in making him and the rest of his breed known as a potentially dangerous dog to officials and others looking for reasons to ban dogs.

 **Essential**

If your boxer is in a dog fight or in any incident where a human or animal is bitten or injured and in need of medical treatment, if you have proof that your boxer has an AKC title, a CGC (Canine Good Citizenship certificate), or even proof of regular obedience training, your boxer is not likely to be written up as the problem. Evidence of showing and training can reduce your liability insurance should you choose to carry it for owning dogs.

Even more important than reducing your risk in owning a powerful, good-sized canine is that through training, you have the opportunity to build a wonderful relationship with your boxer. You will learn more about your boxer through training than through almost anything else you do. And he will learn about you.

How to Train

There are many good training methods available to you in training your boxer. Most good dog trainers and behaviorists agree that the best way to train is to be fair, clear, and concise. Many methods can help you to do this. If you are new to dog ownership and training, how do you decide what is fair, clear, and concise? Here is a situation where you must put your gut level instincts on the line. If you do not understand the methods, or you are uncomfortable applying them, then those methods are wrong for you and your boxer.

The following sections focus on some training methods now considered to be outmoded or not particularly useful in training any dog, including alpha rolling to establish dominance, tricking a dog to leave it, and using physical force to train a puppy.

 **Fact**

Dogs are very clear with each other in body language and other subtleties of communication that people do not always understand. As a boxer owner, you need to be as clear and fair as you can in communicating for the best results in dealing with your boxer if you want to have a good working relationship with him.

Alpha Rolling to Establish Dominance

When one dog rolls another onto its back, the dominant dog has compliance from the one being rolled. It is not a fight in a real sense, and both are very clear on why the rolling is occurring. The canine being rolled onto its back is agreeing that it did something wrong.

When you do this to your boxer, especially if it is an adult or young adult, unless the reason for doing this is totally clear to your boxer (unlikely if your instructor uses this as a dominance tool), then you and your boxer will just end up tired, frustrated, and out of sorts with each other from the scuffle that is required to achieve this.

The best way of establishing dominance over your dog is to train him in the basic obedience commands of sit, come, down, leave it, and stay. Do this methodically when the pup is young. If you do have a problem when your boxer is in adolescence or any other time, you can put him on the NILIF program. An acronym for "nothing in life is free", this technique requires your boxer to work for all food, love, and privileges by waiting for you say when he can eat, go through a doorway, or wait in a sit or down. You choose when and how long to play ball, and you choose the time to go in and leave the game.

Tricking the Dog to Leave It

Probably one of the most potentially damaging exercises for a young puppy is this one, which is often used in puppy classes. The exercise goes like this. An attractive object such as a toy or food is put in front of the puppy. The puppy goes to investigate, and is corrected for it. Basically, this just teaches the pup that you are not always to be trusted. This is not the kind of lesson you want to be teaching your boxer.

Instead, give the command "Leave it" and substitute a toy for the forbidden object. Give much praise for leaving it. If this training is done patiently, kindly, and consistently at home, you will teach your boxer puppy that yes, indeed, there are some things that are not available for his perusal and also that there are many rewards for not investigating without your permission.

Using Physical Force to Train Your Puppy

Dog training has come a long way in the last decade and a half in that many more humane, motivational methods are now known to be very effective in training all dogs. From clicker training to the use of food and toys as inducements to learn new behaviors, dog training has come into the twenty-first century with a lot of positives.

An old-fashioned, less-effective method of training was to force the puppy into the position that you wanted him to be in and then praise. For instance, pushing a puppy into a sit was the common way to teach it. There are a number of problems with this approach. First of all, by forcing your puppy to do anything, you are making the experience of training unpleasant. Secondly, by forcing him to sit physically, you are putting a lot of strain and pressure on young, unformed joints, thus risking joint problems later in life. But third, you are depriving him of the joy of learning to learn with you as the leader. Part of what makes for that wonderful boxer/human bond is that you know and trust each other to be consistent and respectful of each other's status.

Choosing a Trainer

The ideal trainer for you and your boxer is someone you like. Your chosen trainer should have a proven track record of training dogs, should use modern, motivational methods (though not necessarily exclusively), and should genuinely like boxers.

This last point is important because there are some ways in which the learning curve of boxers tends to vary a bit from the sporting and herding breeds, which generally produce most of the canine trainers nationally. Don't be concerned if your boxer does not learn as quickly as the sporting and herding dogs. Also, don't be surprised if he does better, or if his learning curve appears to take longer only to end up doing better than many of his herding and hunting classmates. Boxers, like other members of the AKC's Working Group, are a little different in how they process things.

 Fact

If you come across a trainer who uses force only and says no to using food in training a puppy, pass until you can find someone who is more in tune with the times. This is not the best use of training time for either you or your boxer.

Some trainers just assume that boxers are stubborn and stupid because they are very careful in how they approach doing new things. Remember, the working dog was bred to watch carefully and to figure out what to do after much careful observation. This tendency has come down to us today in the form, at times, of what seems to be a flat-line, then spiking kind of learning curve in boxers. Often, you will see no gradual improvement. Then when you're ready to give up, your boxer will be doing things perfectly! On the other hand, sometimes he'll be the first one to get it exactly right.

Should You Train Your Boxer by Yourself?

In general, your boxer puppy (and you!) will benefit greatly from training with a class. Classes provide opportunities for socialization skills, working with distractions, and camaraderie for you in wading through the difficulty of learning the skills you need to train your boxer while learning all about him and how to communicate with a canine, while he learns about you.

If you live in a part of the country where there are no humane training classes, you might find that you are on your own for training. If that's the case, then by all means, train on your own. You will need to train on your in any event to help thoroughly instill the basics.

It is very difficult for many pups to be able to learn well with distractions initially, and you will find that what your pup has learned at home will be harder to repeat in a class with the excitement of having other puppies or dogs around as well. This is common and part of the canine learning curve. With practice, patience, and persistence, your boxer will soon be able to do all the things he knows in a new and distracting environment.

Modern Training Methods

Since the 1990s, the dog world has seen many changes in how to train dogs of all breeds. One of the biggest influences on canine training methods came from knowledge gained in training sea mammals such as dolphins and killer whales. After all, the trainers could not force or compel certain behaviors out of mammals as large as whales, so they had to figure out how to get the whales to perform voluntarily. The most effective methods used rewards.

The trainers would reward the whales or dolphins for doing certain things by feeding them fish.

The big sea mammals did what they were asked and got paid in food. Behaviors could be shaped or induced, by using food as a lure. Once trained, the whale or porpoise could then perform for audiences of hundreds—jumping through hoops, playing basketball, and all kinds of behaviors that had previously not been associated with marine mammals.

The implications of this type of training for dogs was profound. It changed training dogs from pop-and-jerk or force to systems of an inducement and reward. The result was that many dogs were far happier to perform when given the option to learn in a clear and humane way than when they were physically forced into behavior they didn't understand.

 Essential

Clicker training, or the method of clicking and treating when a dog does a correct or desirable behavior, became popular in training for obedience and agility competition. In clicker training, the absence of a click and treat was the correction to the dog that meant that he had made an error, or had failed to do what was required correctly. This and other inducive methods produced dogs that worked more happily and, in many cases, more confidently, and with more problem-solving ability.

Many people who do compete in obedience are hesitant to put a spirited young show-prospect boxer through obedience training. They remember when the old methods of harsh corrections were the only way to correct or to train a dog, especially for obedience competition. Many young boxers who were corrected too harshly came to dislike and fear anything to do with training, including leashes and dog shows in general.

This was a result of being corrected in harsh ways when the dog had no understanding that a particular behavior was wrong. A prime example of this, for instance, is the forced sit or down. Many dogs, and especially boxers, will struggle mightily against the force of being pushed into a sit or down, while they will comply readily when induced with a treat or toy and praise with clear direction. Many boxers learned to hate obedience training because it seemed unjust and unclear. As a breed, boxers are quite sensitive, especially to what they perceive as injustices.

▲ **Once you find a training regimen that works for you and your boxer, stick to it, and keep him out of mischief!**

Consider this example. Say that while learning to play the piano, you hit the wrong notes. A good piano teacher will not hit you for your error and yell, "Wrong!" or call you bad names. If this did happen, you'd probably begin to hate the piano very quickly. It's much the same for dogs and some of the old training methods. If you gave a dog a harsh collar correction for making an honest, untrained mistake, it would not be surprising if he never wanted to do that activity again.

✳ Training Classes ⼊

Now that you know what you don't want out of training or a training class, what is it that you should be looking for?

First of all, again, you want to find a trainer who has experience with and compassion for dogs and who likes boxers, if not all breeds of dogs. Second, the class should be conducted in such as way that you and your pup should progress from not knowing how to do a particular skill, to knowing what is required of you, and to knowing how the skill should at least look once fully trained.

The instructor should have an objective for each week of either introducing you and your pup to a new skill or moving to a more refined level of an old skill. A basic puppy class should take you through teaching your puppy basic good behavior, such as walking on leash without pulling as well as a good puppy sit, down, come, and leave it. Your puppy should become familiar with walking in strange places and on strange surfaces and with approaching other puppies and other people. The class might also include an introduction to AKC dog sports you can do with your puppy when he is old enough.

A basic class for an adult boxer should do much the same, especially if your boxer has never had other training, and it should prepare the boxer to pass the AKC's Canine Good Citizen test. You should get information on how to go further in dog sports with your boxer.

However, the outcome is dependent upon you and the time you put in working with your boxer to refine his skills as a good, polite dog, and yours as a trainer. To continue to make progress, you need to work at least one or two ten- to fifteen-minute training sessions each day working on old and new skills. Fifteen minutes is not much time, but it will bring you the reward of getting to know your boxer better, perhaps, than any dog you've ever known. You don't want to skimp on the time you put into basic training your boxer.

CHAPTER 14

⚡ Teaching Commands

Awell-trained boxer is a joy to be around. He is welcome anyplace that accepts dogs because he knows how to behave around people and other dogs. He comes when called, and he knows how to stay when required. He can be taken on trips and family outings and is a polite hotel or houseguest. The basic commands are the building blocks of what makes for such a good, well-behaved dog.

⚡Basic Guidelines

The most important thing a boxer needs to know is how to avoid being a danger to himself. This includes not running off to chase a cat or a ball into the street, not getting into fights with other dogs, and greeting people sensibly and nicely. A well-trained boxer rarely gets into trouble because he knows the rules. He has the freedom to be a dog, but he's a dog that is safe and secure in knowing what he knows, which includes his place in the pack and in larger society.

The untrained boxer, by contrast, has few privileges because he is too unruly. He runs away instead of coming on recall, risking his life and inconveniencing the people trying to catch him. He is put away when guests come because he jumps on people too much or may be aggressive. He may be locked away for the family meals because he either begs or jumps on the table, assuming he is welcome to do so. He isn't taken for walks because he pulls so hard that no one wants to walk him, and he can't go on family outings because he is generally a nuisance.

Two Types of Behavior

First, you want to teach your boxer to perform ordinary behaviors (things that he does on his own, whether or not you command him) on your command. Examples of this are sit, stay, down, and come—all things that your boxer would do whether you taught him or not. This type of training puts those behaviors that he already does on command. Once he's learned the command, he will produce the desired behavior in distracting situations simply because he has been trained to do so.

 Fact

When a dog is not trained, he is often banished to the back yard, garage, or some other place where he is not an immediate nuisance or problem to the family. Boxers are social animals. One of the cruelest forms of punishment is to isolate them from their human pack and the society of other living beings. Spending quality time with your boxer by training him to be the informed dog he needs to be to live in society today will make him the good, beloved boxer he deserves to be.

The second type of behavior you want your boxer to learn is not to do things you don't want him to do. Examples of this are jumping on you or others (which he is well capable of) chasing the cats, chewing the furniture, or any other natural behavior that you consider undesirable. This type of behavior is something that you will want to inhibit or extinguish. You will want to use the "Leave it" command to stop a variety of undesirable behaviors, from chasing the cat, chewing the furniture, or counter-surfing. Jumping on you will require an "Off" command, and not pulling on the leash will require your boxer to learn to walk nicely on a loose leash.

For the first type of behaviors, you will generally use inducements for the boxer to do the behavior, then positive reinforcements via treats and praise to establish the behavior that you want to see. Any behavior that has the focus and gets a reward is likely to occur again. For example, if you call your dog, and when he comes to you he gets praise and a treat, he is likely to come to you willingly and readily the next time you call him. The more that you get positive responses from him, which you reward accordingly, the more you are building the response as a habit. When he can do a behavior on command consistently, we considered him trained, at least with respect to that command.

Alert!

How quickly a dog learns a particular skill or a particular command depends upon the extent to which the behavior you are trying to instill is in line with the purpose for which he was bred. Since boxers were originally a multifunctional breed, they should be able to learn most things with relative ease.

The second type of training is known as deterrent training, and there are a number of ways to approach this. When the pup is small, you substitute a toy or approved chew when your boxer puppy is chewing on furniture, a shoe, or anything that is not a dog toy. When the pup is engaged in pursuing the cat, you step in and offer the pup something more interesting to do. In both cases, you say "No" to the offending behavior, and you praise mightily when your boxer accepts the other toy or another activity in lieu of chasing the cat.

◄ When training or playing with your boxer, always stay away from streets and other dangerous locations.

–   You are offering a negative reinforcement for the bad behavior and a positive reinforcement for accepting the correction and taking the alternative that is offered. As your boxer gets older, you may need to simply offer a negative reinforcement. For instance, when he pulls on the leash, you will begin your deterrent training by simply stopping. When the pup hits the end of the leash, he self-corrects with a collar correction. He may also find the lack of forward motion unrewarding and boring, so he stops pulling. You move forward, and if he pulls again, you stop again. Eventually, he gives it up, realizing that if he pulls, the walk stops, and it's no fun. If he pulls when he is older, heavier, and more powerful, you may give him a collar pop as a correction to remind him of the unpleasant consequences of continuing to pull on leash.

How to Train Behaviors

The primary key in training any behavior is consistency. First of all, you must be clear that you understand what it is that you are trying to teach your boxer. Next, you must think like a dog. For instance, your boxer might chase a cat across a busy street and refuse to listen when you try to stop him. If you are angry and upset when he gets back, and you scold him, you will have been inconsistent in your training.

> Consistency is extremely important when training your boxer. If you roughhouse with your boxer and he jumps all over someone else to roughhouse, he may frighten or hurt the person. If you then yell at him for jumping up, you've really confused him. In his mind, roughhousing and jumping on people are his ways of showing affection. Consistency is training your boxer in such a way that he is predictable in life.

Look at the job of training from a dog's point of view. Chasing the cat is fun, and running is fun; but coming back to you is unpleasant because you were angry. You've taught him to avoid you after he chases cats. You've done nothing to inhibit his cat-chasing tendencies, but you may have taught him that returning to you is not always rewarding, so you may have eroded what has previously been a fairly consistent habit of coming when called.

This doesn't mean that you can never roughhouse with your boxer or that he can never jump up to kiss you. However, to make his behavior predictable to the outside world and controllable to you, you must be able to put a command name to those activities so that he jumps up on command and will roughhouse or play on command or by invitation only. Once those activities are on command, they are easier to stop. He can jump up and roughhouse with you, but he will also know commands that restrict the behavior.

Come

Perhaps the most useful command you can teach your boxer is to come when called. A good recall, as its known, can be a lifesaver. It is no substitute for a leash or fenced yard, but it is vitally important that your boxer know what the command means and that he understands how to perform it. Therefore, it's vitally important to motivate your boxer to want to come to you rather than relying on threats. Most boxers are smart, and yours will learn very quickly that if he is not on a leash, you are in no position to enforce the recall, and threats won't work. He knows you're not able to carry them out.

 Essential

In training your recall, it is essential to remember two points. For one, never use your recall command (usually "Come") unless you're sure your boxer will come. This means you're either a psychic or your boxer is on leash, and you can haul him in. Also, never call your boxer away from something fun into a negative situation. What this means is that you never call your boxer to correct him for anything.

One assumption that we can make from these two essential points is that you should never recall your boxer to something negative, and that you should never recall your boxer unless you're sure he'll come or you can reinforce it.

— If you feed your boxer twice a day, you have two really good motivational times that he will really *want* to come and is likely to––mealtimes. Even if you are too busy to train, you're never too busy to feed your boxer, so take advantage of meals as a time when you can work on a recall. If he's right there as you prepare his food, take a few steps back with his bowl and say, "Come!" Your boxer will follow you to his food, and when he does, you can praise him greatly with a "Yes!," "Good come," or whatever you choose. Generally, training is a matter of saying and reinforcing the right things at the right time.

A significant proportion of boxers tend to get the zoomies. That is, they run off joyfully and will not come back. These boxers are hard to train to recall, but it is imperative to get a good reliable recall on this type of boxer.

The Recall Game

Let's say your young boxer has just played keep-away for two solid hours. You are angry, frustrated, possibly humiliated, and you probably feel hurt that the dog you lavish so much attention on has taken off. Yes, your boxer should come on recall, but if he doesn't, you need to do something about it. One thing that works well with boxers is an exercise called the recall game. To play, you need one boxer, one or more family members, and two to four slapsticks. (Refer to the sidebar for instructions on making a slapstick.)

 Essential

To make a slapstick, take some soft nylon clothesline and duct tape. Cut the line into sections about ten to twelve inches long, and use the duct tape to tape them in the middle. Keep wrapping until the bundle is about an inch or so wide to fit comfortably in the palm of your hand and has some heft to it.

If you have a bolter or a zoomer, you probably also have a boxer with fairly high prey and play drive. The slapstick, when you hold it in the middle and slap it from side to side, will move in a way that is intended to stimulate your boxer's prey drive, and excite him into chasing it. The fact that it is in your hand is the good news. It means you now have a tool that will probably induce your boxer to want to return to you.

Rules of the Game

With a puppy, you have all family members stand in a fairly large circle in an enclosed area and slap the sticks on the ground between their feet while calling the pup's name. The pup runs for that person. When he gets to the slapstick, the person throws it behind him. Then the next person calls the puppy. The game goes round and round, with your puppy running for the new, exciting movement of the slapstick. Every time the puppy approaches the next person, he is greatly praised.

If you are all alone, you can still play this with your pup. You will need to keep a few slapsticks in your pocket. When your puppy goes to one through your legs, you throw the other and call him back. You can also throw these straight out from side to side if you wish. Your puppy will go for each slapstick in turn, picking up the one he's just left to find the other.

The point of this game is to make the recall so much fun that it's simply irresistible to your boxer. You will need to take a slapstick with you everywhere until your boxer develops the habit of returning to you on recall. Your slapstick is your trump card in calling him back under even extreme circumstances. The point is to always make the recall more fun than not coming when you call.

Sit

Obviously, your puppy or adult boxer knows how to sit. He just doesn't know that the command for resting on his haunches is "Sit," and he can't know how to respond to your command without training. Trainers in the good old days used to push on a pup's haunches to get him to sit. However, trainers today know that if you control the head, you control the dog, so inducing your pup to sit is probably the most effective thing you can do.

You need to begin your training session when your puppy is alert, but not too bouncy or too inclined to want to take a nap. You need your pup to be able to concentrate. You will need several pieces of a particularly tasty treat, something that he wouldn't ordinarily be eating—maybe last night's leftover steak.

Have several pieces of the treat in your hand, and use one to get your pup's attention. When he is focusing on the food, draw your hand back over his head between his ears. His nose should follow the treat like a homing device. As your pup's head follows the treat, his rear should suddenly shift and drop to a sitting position. Praise immediately and say, "Good sit!," offering the treat as a reward for sitting.

If he doesn't sit, don't worry. Keep at it until he does, then give the treat with lots of praise. Your boxer will quickly figure out that sitting is good. Practice this several times until you think that your pup knows what the command means. Then say the word "Sit" along with drawing the treat back over his head. When he does, praise mightily, and let it go until tomorrow.

At your next training session, you will pick up where you left off, and by progressing in small increments, you'll find that in just a few days, your boxer puppy will sit at any time. That's when you start to stop moving your hand over his head and start to randomize the rewards. As you randomize by occasionally not giving treats, be sure that you still praise enthusiastically. Only use food as a lure and as a way to help clarify any exercise for your pup. The truth is that he will work for praise. But don't fall into the bad habit of expecting your boxer to continue to want to work without at least his payment of praise. By not continuing to praise, you risk losing his interest in interacting in this way with you. After all, what's in it for him?

Down

Once you have firmed up your recall, and your sit is solid and fast, you are ready for training your boxer the down. Down is a good control exercise as well as a way to express your dominance over your boxer, which is the main reason that teaching it has resulted in so many human/canine wrestling matches.

To prepare for teaching the down, your pup needs to be in training mode—alert, but not too bouncy or too tired. Have him sit in front of you, with the good bait ready in your right hand, then suddenly drop your right hand to a point below his chest. Many times, the pup will simply get down on his stomach to figure out how to get that good bait out of your hand. If he does not, you can use the rung of a chair to get him to lie down by putting your bait hand under the chair. Once your boxer's front legs and elbows are on the ground, you can also push gently backward on his shoulders. This action will gently fold him the rest of the way into a down. It is not a force move. Once he is down, whatever way it happened, you give him the treat and praise him with a "Good down!"

  **Alert!**

Don't confuse your boxer by saying "Down" when what you really mean is "Off," such as off the couch or off the counter. "Down" means "Lie down with all four feet out and your tummy on the floor." "Off" means "Get off whatever or whomever you have parked yourself on at the moment."

Because the down is a vulnerable position, fearful boxers may worry about it, and dominant boxers may dislike it. Don't put your boxer in a vulnerable position while he is learning this exercise. For instance, don't put him in a down position in an area where he might be uncomfortable while he's learning, such as at a busy dog park or other areas where there are loose dogs.

When your boxer is down, praise him and help him to stay down for a few moments. Do this by petting him and saying "Stay, good stay." By now he should know what "good" means. He is also beginning to distinguish the different sounds that go with different activities or positions. Don't allow him to get up until you say,

"Okay," or another release word. This is an important exercise to help him build self-control, so don't skimp on training it.

⌐Off

"Off" should be an all-purpose command with a variety of meanings, as in "Get off Grandma, the couch, the counter, the cat, the chandelier," or whatever is inappropriate.

To teach off, your boxer has to be on something that is inappropriate at some point in time. The very first time you find your boxer on the couch or the counter, you very gently take him by his collar and help him off, saying, "Off." When he is off, you say "Good off." The same goes for the first time he jumps on someone (even you).

In the beginning, it is a good idea to offer him a chew or something else to do so that he doesn't think too much about doing the inappropriate behavior again. If he jumps on someone, wanting to be petted, have him sit nicely and be petted that way. This way he doesn't feel he is losing out on potentially rewarding situations.

⌐ Stay/Wait

As you are training the sit and down, you slowly extend the time that you expect your boxer to hold the desired positions. You are helping him to learn through gentle repetition and through helping him to hold his position for longer and longer periods of time.

The extended stay should be in a down. That way, if your boxer gets bored or tired while concentrating on his stay, he can fall asleep and still be a good dog. If you put him on a sit and he goes down without your telling him to, he is not doing the exercise that you asked for even if he holds his stay.

Once the down is fairly solid, ask your boxer to stay for a short period of time and extend it to as much as five minutes. You can make the down/stay exercise easy if you pick a time that your boxer would normally be snoozing. Your eventual goal is a thirty-minute down, or enough time to comfortably eat dinner without interruption. Pick a place in the house where your boxer is not isolated but can still be part of the family's activities although on a down. This is important, especially if he tends to be a worrier.

If you find that your boxer is having trouble staying, don't fight with him to keep him down. If he gets up, keep asking him to do a down until he complies. Don't make this a wrestling match but instead be firm and consistent. You will find that your boxer will resign himself to going down and staying because of your consistency in giving the command. He eventually figures he might as well give up and stay there.

 **Fact**

If your boxer really has a problem getting past just a few minutes of staying down, you can offer him a tummy rub once he is down. Don't physically roll your boxer over, but offer him a treat from the front to lure his head over his right shoulder. In order to follow what is undoubtedly a good treat, he will have to roll over on his left hip a bit, thus exposing his tummy. If you spend a few minutes rubbing his tummy, you are rewarding him for staying down.

You will want to begin to extend the sit to a stay as well, asking for more and more time. If your boxer gets up before you release him, patiently and consistently put him back in his sit. However, if you want your boxer to stay anywhere for a very extended amount of time, for instance thirty minutes, you are best to put him on a down first. If he has to stay and wait, he might as well be comfortable.

Walkies

"Walkies" is the command that signals a nice, peaceful walk. This isn't formal heeling—just a casual walk for both of you. Boxers, left to their own devices, tend to pull like sled dogs, so you want to start the basics of this early in your pup's life. Boxers are energetic, enthusiastic dogs who usually need to burn off energy with a walk, but they often get walked the least because energetic, enthusiastic dogs are also the worst pullers. It's too difficult and not much fun for the owners to walk while their boxer is pulling them down the street.

When your boxer is young, and therefore the lightest that he will ever be, it is the time to really instill this command and behavior. Start out with puppy on the leash, and say "Walkies." If he forges ahead and hits the end of the leash, stop. Wait until the leash is loose again before you repeat the command and start again. It shouldn't take him too long to realize that he isn't going anywhere unless the leash is loose. However, it might take several training sessions.

Some boxers will give up with pulling on the leash fairly quickly, but the really enthusiastic energetic ones may not. They may stop, turn around to look at what the problem is—you. Hopefully, you have your slapstick with you, and you bring that to your boxer's attention. (See page 185 for an explanation of the slapstick.) If you have played the recall game, this will be a source of great excitement and joy to your boxer, so he'll come back. Use the slapstick as a lure to get a loose leash, and then you can say "Good walkies!" in all truthfulness. You and your boxer will be walking down the street, and he will not be pulling. This serves two functions. One is that you have now become a source of great interest and excitement because in addition to initiating the walk you have the slapstick, and you have greatly praised your boxer for not pulling.

Continue on your walk in a happy, upbeat way, and as long as your boxer is not pulling, keep praising. You might even want to bring some treats along for when he is not pulling, just to emphasize your point even more. Walking nicely on leash without pulling is a real skill, but with time and effort, your boxer can readily master it.

CHAPTER 15

Basic Manners

Basic manners are an extension of basic training and essential to the development of every good boxer, the key behavioral elements that make our boxers safe and easy to live with in today's society. They are not only part of what every good boxer needs to know but also what every good boxer owner needs to know to help his or her boxer to be a canine good citizen who will be welcomed in most, if not all, places.

Ground Rules

Basic manners are literally a must for every good dog in today's society. There is too great a risk of liability for you as a dog owner if your boxer makes a big mistake and injures another person or animal. And with animal rights activists questioning whether people should own any companion animal, it is important that you know how to navigate today's society safely with your boxer. Your boxer doesn't have to be perfect all the time, but very good much of the time, and basic manners will help defuse any behavioral questions or issues that might arise.

The first ground rule is that you must be a thoughtful dog and boxer owner. If you don't like to hear a dog bark at all times of the day and night, then you must teach your boxer not to bark. Furthermore, if you don't like aggressive, dangerous dogs, then you must make sure that yours is not. If you don't like pushy, rambunctious dogs, then your boxer must learn to contain himself. Finally, if you want to be able to take your boxer to public places, then your boxer must be a model canine citizen when he is in those situations.

 **Essential**

> As gross as this subject is, a basic ground rule of being a good boxer owner is that you must scoop your boxer's poop. Scooping needn't be expensive or obvious, and you don't have to carry a pooper scooper around with you to be prepared. Be ecologically minded and recycle used plastic grocery and produce bags. Turn the bag inside out like a glove with your hand in the middle. Grab the poop, pull the plastic around it, and deposit in the nearest garbage can.

You must be prepared to scoop poop from any and all situations (it is the law in most places), and you must be prepared to politely apologize for any transgressions your boxer commits. This is a sort of noblesse oblige. After all, you own a boxer, so you can afford to be gracious and polite and to go the extra mile to be a good dog owner. This also means that you obey the law concerning dog ownership, and you are prepared to accept the consequences if you don't. After all, all dog owners suffer for the behavior of bad dog owners, not just you.

The best way to avoid problems is to have a long-term goal of owning a good dog and taking the steps you need to take to have one. The first step in that plan is to teach the basics: come, sit, down, off, and stay. But the second is to know and to accept your responsibility as the leader.

 ## Being the Leader

In any canine pack there is a leader. This is the highest-ranking member of the pack, known as the alpha, who basically runs things, whether that leadership appears obvious or not. In many canine packs, it sometimes seems like the alpha is not doing anything. In fact, he doesn't have to. He is the leader, so the other members of the pack do everything for him, or appear to, and that's because the other members of the pack are well-trained in their roles.

Many people find the notion of having power over their dogs a difficult or even offensive concept. There are movements afoot today to make canine ownership a guardianship. But guardianship really has no place in a canine pack structure. Dogs are hardwired in the wild and in your house to respect the leader and to understand that not everyone has equal power. Canine behaviorists used to believe that there was a big difference between how domestic and wild dogs behaved because of the changes introduced by selective breeding by humans. In 2002, however, a study of wild versus domestic canines discovered that only 2 percent of their genetic material was different. That's not a lot, and to many trainers and behaviorists, this discovery suggested that appropriate training is that in which the leader decides and enforces the rules. The more clearly they are defined and enforced, the better the pack functions, and the less inappropriate behavior develops.

 Fact

Some people struggle with the notion of leadership, perhaps finding the idea that they have control over the dog or any living being repugnant. It is also those people who won't exert their leadership who produce the most dogs with the most and biggest problems in behavior. But clear rules clearly enforced are what make for the happiest and safest boxer.

Dogs don't think like people. For instance, if you were able to talk to your boxer puppy, you would probably find that he is a great studier of life, and an almost unerring statistician (as are puppies of other breeds). He studies you and your family to understand how the pack is run and who is really in charge in just the same way a little wolf cub observes the other wolves in his pack.

Dogs are fundamentally opportunists who will take advantage of a situation when they can. If you fail to enforce clear, consistent rules of dominant behavior, your boxer will decide to rise in the pack structure, intimidating the lesser members in what ways he can. This is how problem dogs are created and why it is so important to train your boxer. Further, since dogs crave a pack order, they will feel compelled to enforce their order if no one else is doing the job.

How Problems Develop

Very few problems that you will run into are the result of there being something fundamentally wrong with your boxer's temperament. Most problem dogs are normal dogs doing normal things at the wrong time or place for the owner's lifestyle. Problems come about because dogs learn undesirable behavior through cause and effect.

In the early 1900s, a branch of behavioral science researched the principles of learning and behavior. What they found was that if an action is followed by a satisfying state of affairs, it is likely that that action will be repeated. The more often that action gets a satisfying response, the more likely that action or behavior is to be repeated. This concept came to be known as operant conditioning, and many of the more modern training techniques are based upon its principles.

Operant Conditioning

Operant conditioning takes place all the time, even when we don't intend it. A good example is dogs that love to raid the trash. While you are gone, your boxer smells something good in the trash, gets into the trash can, and finds last night's leftovers. The leftovers are a very potent positive reinforcer or reward for your boxer, virtually guaranteeing that he will try raiding the trash again. He still has enough of the wild hunter in him to think that scavenging is a good thing, and the trash provides the perfect opportunity and reinforcer for him to do so.

Let's say, however, that he tries the trash at a later time. This time, he accidentally tips the can over or something near to it in his efforts to get the trash can lid off. The result is a loud crash and bang, which scares him, and he runs off without the reward of the leftovers from last night's dinner. In this case, he's had a negative reinforcement and will be less likely to try the trash again soon. This time he learned that trash, no matter how good it smells, can be scary.

 **Essential**

> The main theme to present in training basic manners is to give negative reinforcements to those behaviors that you don't want to see continue, and positive ones to those behaviors that you do want to see continue. Keeping that in mind, you can address or approach any potential problems in owning your boxer.

You will face a myriad of good and bad advice in training, so you need to keep the most salient information in mind. All dogs learn by cause and effect, so you will need to understand what causes are getting which effects. You then direct your knowledge so that you get the effects you want out of your boxers.

On or Off Furniture?

Some people will tell you that you can never let your boxer on your bed or furniture, or he will think he's in charge. This, like everything else in training, has a caveat. Yes, if you let your boxer do everything his way, with no corrections or ramifications, he could think that he is in charge and that the furniture is his. However, if you train a good off, have plenty of nice, cushy beds for him to lie on, and if you plan for quality time on your couch, favorite chair, or bed, then routinely tell him to get off, the chances are that he will see the situation for what it is—a special time together where he has access to you and your undivided attention and affection. If you let him be on the bed or furniture all the time, you diminish that sense of specialness, and you increase his sense of entitlement and territoriality. Similarly, if you rarely ask him to do anything for you (such as sit, stay, down, off and come), he may have a different attitude toward you when you tell him to get off your favorite chair or bed.

If you never ask him to learn the things that every good boxer should know, then you may be risking bad behavior if you let your boxer on the bed. If you do teach him these basic things, sharing this kind of quality time with you on furniture will only enhance your relationship. The decision that you make about this should be based upon what you have taught your boxer and the amount of control you have over him in your human/canine relationship.

On or Off People?

One of the most disruptive things about having dogs in public is that they sometimes jump on people, which is an especially big problem when they jump on people who are afraid of dogs.

At dog shows, there are many people who find dogs jumping on them a perfectly normal part of what dog shows are about. After all, in that busy setting, how are dogs going to get to know people but to jump up and introduce themselves? So, many otherwise well-trained and well-behaved dogs may appear to be not so well trained or well behaved.

In fact, there are many competitive-obedience training methods that encourage having the dog jump on the trainer to encourage bonding, and to make some kinds of exercises easier. So there may be some reasons to encourage your boxer to jump on you. However, if you do train this, it must be under your control, not his. So instead of discouraging all jumping up on you when he is a pup, you need to get control of the behavior so he can still do it at your invitation. That is the way you gain control of most behaviors. If you can train the opposite of a behavior you don't want along with what you do want, you can usually put both on command readily.

▲ Getting along with other dogs is a major part of good boxer manners.

 Leave It

Because dogs do not understand English as such, it is important to establish very strong connections to the commands that they do understand and that you will need to use the most often. That is why you worked early and often on the "Come," "Sit," "Down," "Off," and "Stay" commands. But "Leave it" or an equivalent command can be a life-saving basic, too.

Leadership in the leave-it department is vital. If you do not have your boxer's trust in you as the leader, you may have no way to enforce the command. You need to start this when your boxer is a puppy and makes his first attempt at chewing anything he shouldn't. Since you are strictly supervising your new pup, you will know the first instant it happens. Swoop right in there and say very firmly, "Leave it!" Quickly substitute an approved chew or toy for the forbidden item. Once those sharp little puppy teeth are firmly planted on the approved item, follow up by saying, "Good leave it!"

 **Essential**

"Leave it" should mean "Leave what you're doing any time, any place and under any circumstances." This command can encompass not chasing the cat, not eating the Sunday dinner pot roast, or not picking up a poisonous toad or snake. "Leave it" is important.

In this way, your puppy learns that "leave it" is important, but that leave it also may have an important and positive upside. Leave it does not make him lose his pleasurable activity. It only replaces one with another. It he executes "leave it" correctly, you will be pleased with him, and other privileges may appear. So "leave it" is stern and firm, but good consequences come from leaving it.

No Bad Looks

If you've never owned a dog before, or a boxer, you may not be aware that as the young males, and sometimes females, come into late adolescence/early adulthood, they will decide that they need to stand their ground territorially, which tends to extend to wherever they are. In these situations, they will often assume a particular stance and stare out at the world. This is an invitation to mayhem in dog language, or at least to a challenge from other equally immature young males (for the most part). Your job, as the owner, is to be aware of this type of look and to nip it in the bud.

Rather than let your boxer get the adrenaline rush of skirmish, which can be quite addictive, you can, when you identify that look and posture, correct him, distract him from staring at the other dog, and say, "No bad looks." Obviously, you want to distract him in every way possible, and you might want to move out of the other dog's line of sight altogether, if possible. And obviously, you want to reward him when he breaks off a bad look!

Alert!

Don't let another dog lock eyes with your boxer or vice versa. Boxers are notorious not for starting fights, but for finishing them. The best way to avoid the negative ramifications that go with a skirmish is to block eye contact. Most dogs will give up the bad impulses once eye contact is broken. If another dog does engage your boxer in a skirmish, if you can throw a jacket or towel over their eyes so they can't see each other, you have a good chance of extinguishing the problem.

You can start this training when he is a puppy if he occasionally gets to be too stern or rough or dominant with other puppies and dogs. No one likes a boxer that is a bully, and the "No bad looks" command, incorporated with "Leave it," is probably the best possible guarantee you will ever have to help ensure that your boxer will never be involved in a fight.

Barking

Nothing will alienate your neighbors faster than an inappropriately barking dog or one that barks at all hours of the day and night. On the other hand, it is comforting to know that your boxer could sound an alarm if needed. So, barking, as such, is not so bad, but excess, incessant barking is very bad.

The first way to address excess barking is to train your boxer to bark on command. After all, if he can bark on command, he can stop on command too, since he knows from other training what commands and their opposites mean (remember the on-and-off the furniture rules, jumping up on people and not jumping up on people?). If you train this, you have the added advantage to allowing your boxer to bark at strangers you don't know or in other situations where you might like to have a barking dog.

 **Fact**

Barking is traditionally understood to occur for the following reasons: anxiety, boredom, and attention-seeking due to loneliness. In boxers, there may be one more category: barking out of sheer joy. The happy barker is not anxious, bored, or lonely but just overjoyed with life and wants to tell the world.

Barking Commands

There are a number of ways to teach your dog to bark and not bark on command. The first is pretty direct. When your boxer barks, you say, "Good bark." He will be very surprised and not understand what you are saying at first. Just like every other situation, if you are consistent with your praise, he will come to understand what "Good bark" means. And once he does, then you can tell him to bark, and he should bark. Once he will bark on command, you now have the option of saying, "No bark," when he does bark. If you have trained your other alternative behaviors correctly and your boxer understands the command, your boxer should know what this means and stop barking.

A second way to train your boxer to bark on command is to make silly sounds yourself, including barking like a dog. Your boxer will look at you like you have lost your mind, but he generally gets the idea pretty quickly, and will make some kind of sound. When he does, praise him excitedly. If you do this several times a day for a week or so, your boxer should be able to bark on command pretty easily. Then, of course, once he can bark on command, you

can also stop him more readily. Combining the two methods usually helps to get barking on command the fastest.

Problem Barking

While putting barking on command while you are around can
be an effective way to stop excess barking, if your boxer barks
while you are not around, training him to bark on command may
or may not help.

Since excess barking is usually a stress release of some kind,
it is what as known as a self-rewarding behavior. In other words, it
is worth it for him to bark because it helps to diffuse any negative
emotions he might be feeling. This is the kind of barking that is
harder to break. In these cases, especially since most people are
out of their homes eight or more hours a day to work, barking can
be a hard problem to address.

Most dogs that are tired are not inclined to bark. If you can get
up an hour or so earlier to take your boxer for a long walk or run,
you will do much to prevent problem barking. Or get up an hour
earlier just to train him. Anything that tires him out will help to
prevent barking. This helps especially if he is an anxious or bored
barker. Another thing that can help is to hire a dog walker to take
him for an additional walk during the day, or you can take him to
doggy day care.

But what if you don't live in an area where dog walkers or
doggy day care are available, and you commute so much that you
don't have an extra hour in the morning to walk or train? Well, if
you have still decided that a boxer does fit your lifestyle choices,
you may need to get a bark collar.

Bark Collars

The most humane bark collar is one that is instructional in that
it emits a sound that is audible to humans before it emits a high-
pitched sound audible only to dogs. The warning sound helps the
dog to understand that if they do not stop barking, an unpleasant

consequence, the high-pitched sound, will occur. This collar runs on batteries.

Another collar that has gained in popularity is a citronella collar. It releases citronella, a natural strong-smelling substance (not unpleasant to humans), if the dog barks. Dogs do not like the smell of citronella, so they will tend to stop barking when the collar releases the smell. This type of collar gives no other warning to alert the dog to the coming correction. Some citronella collars need batteries and vials of citronella to work. Some just need citronella.

The final collar is the original bark collar, which gives the dog a mild to strong shock if he barks. This collar is also battery operated and also gives no warning sound to let the dog know that a correction is coming.

Socialization Is a Must

Canine behaviorists, trainers, and breeders all agree that socialization is a must. The puppy should meet a wide range of dogs, including other puppies and adults, so that he learns how to behave and to interact with them every time he sees one. Socialization also includes walking on new surfaces, riding in the car, and attending puppy classes where he can learn to concentrate when surrounded by distractions. You need to provide your boxer with these life lessons early on.

Socialization at Home

One of the first and most important things that a puppy learns is who lives in his home and how he should behave around these people. The pup must learn how to respect the other pack members. Socialization should begin in a safe and familiar environment, so what place is better than in the puppy's new home?

As the owner, you must make sure that everyone in the family knows that the puppy should be treated like a puppy and not a little human in furry clothes. Further, everyone needs to know how to train in the same way. Everyone needs to learn how to teach the basic commands correctly. This is where the recall game (described on page 185) and other dog-related activities can become a family affair. Training is a very essential part of your puppy's early socialization, which includes learning how to learn and learning how to work well with each family member.

Family Socialization Basics

The issue of a dog not coming when called is a huge problem for many dog owners. Many dogs don't come when they are called because they don't get enough exercise, and the freedom of being off-leash is just too enticing. Without enough exercise and training, your boxer could take off for hours at a time. If you have a large enough and protected back yard, this may not be a problem, but most people do not have this luxury. Walks and training help to expend the energy that the puppy has, so start little walks with your pup, even if just in the backyard, and start to play the recall game as soon as the walk is over.

Having the ability to come when called (recall) is a very important part of socialization, and it can be critical in an emergency situation. By playing the recall game, you help expend puppy energy and build a very positive reaction in your pup to what it means to come.

Praise for Coming When Called

The point that your boxer should be praised for coming when called cannot be overemphasized. Furthermore, not being pleasant to your boxer when he comes on recall is one of the biggest mistakes inexperienced dog owners make.

Going to the park to play, then calling him when it's time to go home is almost guaranteed to make your boxer not want to come on recall. Why? It won't take him long to realize that when you call him at the park, the fun is over, and he might not be ready to end the fun. You can circumvent this problem by calling him to you and other family members several times during the outing, sometimes giving him a treat, or sometimes just to play with the slapstick. Then let him go have fun again.

The solution to not making the recall a sour exercise is for you to go get him for anything unpleasant, such as having his nails done or leaving the park, and making certain that the recall itself is always positive.

 **Fact**

One of the quickest ways to kill a potential recall or, sometimes even to undo a good one is to do something that your boxer sees as unpleasant when you call him. This could be something like clipping nails, being put in his crate, taking a bath, or anything else that he doesn't like (although you should be working to make all these things as pleasant as possible). Of course, punishing him when he finally returns is a virtual guarantee that he will be unlikely to return to you on recall for some time!

When in Doubt, Keep Your Boxer on a Leash

Regardless of when you get your boxer—as a small puppy or as a larger dog—there will be some point in time when he is likely to test his mettle, or he is not yet proofed or mature enough to be off-leash in certain situations. Between four and eight months, he will decide there's a big, wide world out there that he is entitled to see, and he could run off to check it out.

 **Essential**

Have your boxer's collar in hand before you offer the treat or toy when he comes on recall. Young children often have a hard time with this one. They simply want to give him the treat, but if he is rewarded first, then runs off, he has been rewarded for running off instead of coming. This can also have some unfortunate consequences and is not a behavior that you want to reinforce.

Even when older, your boxer might simply not be "proofed" enough (has not learned a recall in enough circumstances) not to chase a cat, a dog, a bicyclist, or anything else that grabs his attention. Letting your boxer off-leash in the wrong circumstances can have terrible outcomes. And he could learn only too well that you can't catch him if he runs away, and this seriously damages his recall.

Entering and Exiting Rules

Teaching your boxer when and how to pass through doorways is an important part of his in-home socialization and training. If he goes through the door first, he might have the impression he outranks human members of the pack, and you don't want that possibility to develop.

Secondly, if your boxer goes through doors first, he might assume that it is okay for him to do so any old time, and he might bolt out of a door or open gate into a street and get lost or worse. Make sure not only that your boxer does not go through a door or gate first but that he learns not to go through one at all unless someone in the family gives him an "Okay" command. This way, if someone accidentally leaves a gate open, your boxer may well stay safely in the yard. A sit/stay is a good thing to learn by doors, and a down/stay is handy for gates. Training and socialization merge at this point to create a dog that is very aware of the rules and is a canine good citizen as a result. A loose, running dog is generally not perceived as one that is well socialized.

Table Manners

Technically your boxer will never be eating at the table with you, so this refers to his manners *around* the dinner table, and specifically, around food. For starters, it is a good idea for children in the family to feed your boxer. It elevates them above the puppy's status if they control when, where, and how much he eats. In the beginning, it is a good idea for your pup to learn to sit and wait while his food is prepared.

While the adults in the family prepare the food, the children can supervise the puppy sitting and learning the sit/stay. When the food is ready, the children can give the pup his dinner. They should always make him wait for an okay before he starts to eat. Everyone in the family should practice taking the pup's food away for short amounts of time (seconds, at most), with a wait (sit/stay) before giving it back. This exercise is not done to tease him. Instead, when performed in a very matter-of-fact way, it tells him that the benevolent pack leaders will keep him fed. This makes him learn that humans control food but that they are fair with it, and he will always get it back if he patiently does what is asked of him—to sit and wait.

 **Alert!**

To contribute to your boxer's good manners, never, ever feed him from the table. This rule is very hard for small children to follow. After all, here is their beloved boxer waiting patiently for a tidbit. And he'll probably even eat their unwanted vegetables. What more could a child ask for?

Here's the cardinal rule: Do not feed your boxer from the table. If you're having trouble keeping small children from feeding the dog from the table, it might be a good idea to put the boxer in a sit/stay a short distance away from the family dinner table while the family eats. This will go far toward solving the problem of bad table manners in the boxer, and is an essential part of his learning and socialization if you have friends and family over for dinner. This training will reduce his expectation of food from people around the dinner table and tend to instill in him a respect for guests in the house because they get to eat, and he does not—a simple reinforcement of good manners around humans not in his family or pack.

Puppy Socialization

Because dogs grow up so much more quickly than humans, their life lessons are much condensed. Up until about day forty-nine of a puppy's life, his mother and his pack are the most important things in his life. Hopefully, a good, conscientious breeder is providing stimuli over and above just his pack involvement. Even if the breeder is not, it is not until about day forty-nine that the pup's brain is neurologically complete.

It was once thought that staying with the pack and dam past that time made it harder for a pup to bond with people. There is some evidence a pup needs to learn some important social lessons between weeks seven to nine, so more breeders are leaving the pups with the mother and pack longer for the additional value of canine socialization.

Three to Seven Weeks

It used to be that a pup would be weaned from between three to seven weeks, but more recent research suggests that the pup's stomach is still permeable to undigested proteins before the age of six weeks. If the breeder wants to diminish the likelihood of allergies, it might be better to wait until after six weeks to start introducing foods to the pups. Most responsible breeders do not wean before six weeks, when the puppy's teeth are getting sharper and mom is more reluctant to continue to feed the puppies. From week three to seven, the mother is teaching her pups how to nurse gently, and they are learning from other pack mates how to play nicely.

Mom will do whatever it takes to get the pups to be gentle. She will give a hard look, growl, or remove herself entirely until all the pups get the idea that they need to be gentle. This is their first lesson in bite inhibition. Puppies taken from their mothers before eight weeks of age often do not have an adequate bite inhibition with other dogs and are too rough with people as well. Bite inhibition is an important lesson in growing up.

The pups learn from each other as well. They learn not to play too rough, how to be ignored, and how to entice someone else to play. Those that do not learn these basic lessons may find it difficult to accept discipline from other dogs and people later in life and harder to have good canine relationships with other dogs.

Seven to Twelve Weeks

From seven to twelve weeks, it is important for the puppy to be socialized as much as possible. Get all the friends and family members that you can over to see the new puppy. While vets quail at the idea of the puppy being out socializing before it has all of its vaccinations, if you can find a training facility that requires canine students to be vaccinated, you may not run much of a risk.

Socialization is so important that it is worth a certain amount of risk. It is crucial that little boxers meets as many other dogs during this time as possible, especially if you intend to show them later in obedience or conformation. Your boxer really needs to have the experience of meeting other dogs at this critical time in his life. Spending his time with other dogs and people will build his confidence in thinking he is safe and can cope with the demands of meeting other dogs and people. This is invaluable in a show or competition dog and in a safe, well-adjusted pet.

Fear Periods

The time between eight to twelve weeks is sometimes called the fear imprint period. It is generally believed that any painful or particularly frightening experience leaves a lasting impression on a pup at this time, even more than if that same experience happened at some other time in life. This time coincides with the period in the wild during which the mother would be doing the final weaning of the pups, so it might be that this period occurs with an initial realization on the part of the canine puppy that he won't always be taken care of.

 Fact

Because of the fear period, some breeders and competition dog owners used to go to almost extreme measures to ensure that the pup not come into a new home later than day forty-nine. They believed that an older puppy would never bond right or be as readily trainable.

If a breeder has been responsibly socializing the puppies while still in the litter, this is unlikely to be a problem in your average well-bred boxer litter. In fact, most vets who do ear crops want to wait until the pup is about ten weeks old or at least ten pounds. That event falls within the fear period, and most puppies that are cropped are not emotionally traumatized by the experience.

The real message here is to make sure that the pup is not overwhelmed by anything. A cool, calm, matter-of-fact approach will go far to ensure that your pup will come out of this fear period with no emotional scars.

Beyond Twelve Weeks

In the time between about twelve weeks and eight months, your boxer puppy will go through many different phases emotionally and physically. It is possible that he will go through other fear periods to a lesser extent.

If your pup shows any fear reactions that do not seem normal, you can assume that they fall into one of the fear period categories. Do *not* attempt to make him get over it by dragging him to the object he fears. If you make a big deal of his fear, you reinforce to him that there is a good reason to be afraid of whatever triggered his reaction. The best course of action is none. Leave him alone, ignore his reaction, and the behavior will pass. Or let him investigate on his own with no encouragement from you. He will discover that in most cases, what he feared is perfectly safe and harmless to him.

There is some suggestion in research that those later fear periods are due to calcium deficiencies attributed to growth spurts. This is another reason why it is important to feed an optimum diet. During this time it is important to keep training and reinforcing the basic obedience commands (sit, down, stay, come, and leave it) with patient persistence. Changes, physically and mentally, are happening at a very fast rate in your boxer's life, so you want to give him every opportunity to learn how to be a good dog as much as he can at every stage of his life.

 **Essential**

> It is important to provide your pup with things to chew on, as around three to four months of age and beyond he will really need to chew to help him with teething. He can't help it, so make sure you hide your valuable items, especially shoes. Teething pups have the tendency to chew shoes beyond the point of recognition.

Finally, remember that somewhere between four to eight months, your boxer will move from puppyhood to adulthood. In other words, at some point in time during this age, other dogs will come to regard him as a young adult, capable of better behavior. They will not tolerate the same degree of pushiness or play from him as they would have in the past. You should expect better behavior of him, too.

The Eight- to Fourteen-Month Fear Period

Sometimes called the secondary fear period, this fear period also appears to have its roots in canine evolution. Many boxers show no signs of this secondary fear period, but some do. In the wild, young canines would be taken hunting with the pack for the first time during this period. They would know that any time they saw or smelled something unfamiliar, they should treat it like danger. For many canines, wild or domestic, danger means fear. It was nature's way of instilling watchfulness into wild canines.

Sexual awareness, or the kick-in of hormones, can make your boxer very aware that he might have some competitors in other males, and this can make him feel insecure. This is an important time to keep training and socializing him and to avoid letting him think that the world is big and dangerous.

Preventing Separation Anxiety

Separation anxiety is not an ordinary bid for attention. It is a full-blown canine melt-down that occurs when your boxer finds that he is alone or away from you. His bark might become high-pitched and he might pant, drool, or, at an extreme, even involuntarily uri-nate or defecate in his crate. He might frantically paw to get out of his crate or scratch at the door where he last saw his favorite person or persons leave. The negative consequences of all this are visited not just on your boxer but on the neighborhood, which might not be as sympathetic about nonstop, high-pitched barking.

 fact

Separation anxiety usually occurs when your boxer becomes overly bonded with a member of the family or the family in general. To avoid this, redirect your boxer's attention from just one person to toys, or to other people, such as a neighbor, a friend, or dog walker. It is also very important to keep the human departures and returns very unemotional and matter of fact.

Coming and Going

Usually, separation anxiety starts with something that the human family is doing to cue the dog to their imminent departure. It might be as simple as feeling bad that you need to leave the puppy for several hours. A good way to prevent separation anxiety from becoming an established behavior is to ignore your boxer for a half hour before the family leaves and for another half hour after returning. This is hard when the boxer is little and needs to potty more often and on a more immediate basis, so the solution is to take him out on a leash, very matter-of-factly, praise him very moderately when he potties, then whisk him back into his crate or confinement area at least a few minutes before you leave. This helps to ensure that he doesn't just associate going out to potty one last time with your leaving.

 Essential

If your boxer has an especially bad case of separation anxiety, try leaving on the television or radio. Lots of dogs respond well to classical music. There are other possible solutions. You can make a tape of your voice and put it on continuous play so he hears you all day. Or make sure he has so many toys and treats that he couldn't possibly miss you. Try buying interactive toys, hire a dog walker, or take your boxer to doggy day care where he can play all day with other dogs.

When you come back, you need to be equally calm. After you take him out to potty, on leash, you can put him back into his crate or confinement area for a few minutes to give you time to change clothes, pick up your mail, and rewind a little from your day. Then you can get him out to play. By changing your pattern of coming and going to a very calm, ho-hum version, you will go far to prevent separation anxiety from occurring.

Trips to the Vet and Groomer

Some dogs exhibit separation-anxiety–like symptoms when taken to see their vet or groomer. If you do not cue your boxer to be afraid of either his vet or groomer, chances are that he will be like most boxers and adore these outings, regardless of what they do to him. So, if you have been doing your training and socializing homework, these trips will just be one more happy experience that your boxer is more than delighted to share with you.

Play Dates

One of the benefits of taking your boxer to training and puppy socialization is that you will meet some new human friends while your boxer meets some new canine friends. And you and your new human friends may decide to get together to arrange some doggy play dates.

▲ Boxers love other dogs as much as they love humans! Be sure to socialize them at an early age to avoid aggression.

First of all, play dates are not essential if you are training and exercising your boxer as much as you should be. But if he has a particular friend, it might be fun for all. Second, you will need to watch things progress carefully, especially if your male boxer's friend is a male, too. They may get to a point where they feel that they need to compete with each other. So watch that the play doesn't get too rough and lead to something more than play. Bear in mind also that boxers tend to play rough and to use their paws like human boxers. That can totally flummox other breeds that are not used to this.

 **Alert!**

Your boxer should never ride in a car unrestrained. The crate is really the best way for your boxer to ride while traveling in a car with you. However, if you have a small car that doesn't accommodate a crate, then a seatbelt harness, which can be purchased at most pet stores, is a good option, as is a pet barrier that is placed at the back of SUVs and vans. Never let your boxer ride unrestrained in a car.

In general, many boxers get along very well with other breeds. Labs, goldens, and weimaraners, all much the same size dogs as boxers, often get along very well with boxers, though boxers also make good friends of dogs that are much larger and smaller, such as Irish wolfhounds and miniature poodles. Play dates with these much bigger or smaller dogs would require a great deal of supervision.

Territoriality

Your boxer will probably tend to be territorial on his property. This is not unusual in boxers, a guard dog breed. It is natural for dogs of most breeds to want to define and protect their territories against intruders. This is an instinctive response on the part of most dogs. If you live out in the country, where your boxer's barking will bother no one, territoriality may not be an issue. However, if you live in a residential neighborhood or apartment, where your boxer's barking will annoy the neighbors, barking is a problem.

If you have yet to curb bad barking habits, you need to go back to basic training and develop strong leadership skills with an excellent "Leave it" and or "No bark" command. This is one of the many places where good leadership skills can stop any unwanted actions. If you stop unwanted barking often enough, your boxer will look to you to see if it is okay to be territorial. Obviously, in most circumstances, it is not okay to bark, but there may come a time when you do want your boxer to sound the alarm.

CHAPTER  17

Behavioral Issues

Behavioral issues can really put a damper on dog owner-ship. Suppose, for example, that your boxer growled at someone, barked through the last three nights, ate the tires off your car, or ran away. You probably feel angry and betrayed by this dog you have worked so hard to care for and train. Perhaps you rescued your boxer and you are now faced with problems you hadn't anticipated. This chapter has advice on what to do in such scenarios.

Problem Prevention

If you got your boxer as a little pup, problem prevention is made up of consistent lessons over time and training your boxer to learn all the things that a good boxer needs to know. Your boxer has been around other dogs enough that he knows he needn't defend whatever territory he's on and how to get along well with people. He is socialized. This is the best problem-prevention tool you can give any dog.

Warning Signs

If you see your dog being a little too pushy or aggressive around other puppies or in some of his other training classes, this is the time to correct him by giving him his "No bad looks" education and dis-tracting him by getting him to focus on you. Remember that once you have broken the hard stare of a dog, you have defused about 75 percent of the problem of a challenge. However, if he is still not responding, then it is time to do a very alpha thing. Put your hand over his muzzle (like the letter U) and tell him to knock it off in a very strong voice, usually using the command "No" or "Leave it."

This maneuver is usually effective in asserting dominance, since you are doing it from a dominant position over and above his head, and you will get through to him. Hopefully, he will understand that hard stares are unacceptable to you as his pack leader, and he will knock it off. If he tries to get his muzzle out from under your hand, or snaps or even fake snaps at you, your boxer needs to go back to doggy boot camp and get on the NILIF ("nothing in life is free") training program.

 **Essential**

"Nothing in Life Is Free," or NILIF, means that your boxer must work for every bit of food, attention, love or affection that he gets. He must sit, down, or both at your command and do it quickly. He understands commands and control by now, and he will respect that you have taken control of the situation. Unlike humans, who would rather fight over issues of dominance, your strong leadership will probably be reassuring to him. It tells him that someone is in charge (not him) and that he doesn't have to run things. Dogs like to know who is in charge.

This is a serious wake-up call to you that your boxer is not respecting your authority as the pack leader. Whether this is due to lack of adequate training, lack of adequate socialization, or simply an end run on his part to see if he can move up the alpha dog ladder makes no difference. Any time you see even the beginning of any behavioral problem, you need to go back to training the basics and training extensively.

What's the Cause?

If bad behavior is an issue that you really have not seen coming, have your boxer checked out by your vet to make sure there are no underlying health problems that may be causing a defensive reaction in his behavior. On the other hand, if this is a problem in your home, say with the children teasing or trying to pull a hiding boxer out from under the bed when he no longer wanted to play, and he snapped or even bit, you need to get back to training your family on how to live with and respect a canine. Although boxers are very good with children, you can hardly expect any canine to put up with abuse and teasing.

Canine Good Citizen (CGC)

Started in 1989, the Canine Good Citizen (CGC) is a certification program designed to reward dogs that have good manners at home and in the community. The CGC is a two-part program that stresses responsible pet ownership for owners and basic good manners for dogs. All dogs that pass the ten-step CGC test receive a certificate from the AKC. Any good boxer can pass if he has had all the lessons and training in how to be a good dog. (See Chapter 18 for a full discussion of the CGC test.)

Many dog owners choose CGC training as the first step in training their dogs. The program lays the foundation for other AKC activities such as rally, obedience, agility, tracking, and other performance events. As you work with your boxer to teach him CGC skills, you'll discover the many benefits and joys of training.

Barking, Biting, Lunging, and Growling

Perhaps your boxer is so big now that you can no longer handle him, or you just haven't trained him, so you can't take him anywhere. Don't worry—there's still room for improvement. Since dogs can always learn new tricks, your relationship with your boxer and his with the outside world can still be fixed.

In order to be successful, you must make time to work at it with him. He can't learn those things that you won't teach him. In other words, he can only become as good a dog as you are willing to work and train him to be. And without adequate education and training from you, your boxer's behavior can worsen to the point that it's difficult to live with.

 **Alert!**

> Owners who are not prepared to train their boxers to cope with the increasingly complex real world around them are disrespectful to their dogs and probably should not have one. Not only does an untrained boxer pose a possible threat to people and other animals, but the owner who does not adequately train a boxer to live within the rules of society gives even responsible boxer owners a bad rap.

Humans can't function in society without knowing the rules. Canines can't either. It is imperative that you make certain that your boxer can function in society. If you evaluated your lifestyle and made owning a boxer a lifestyle choice, but you didn't put in your time training your boxer, you need to do so now.

Barking

If your boxer gets frenzied in public and barks too much, and you have not trained a "No bark" or "Leave it" command, revisit the section on barking in Chapter 15.

Start this exercise first in your home and your yard so that your boxer has some baseline understanding about your expectations before you take him back into public. An aggressively barking dog pulling at his leash is very frightening to others. In the short term, it might be best to take your boxer out of situations that over-stimulate him to bark or behave aggressively until you get it under control, as you don't want this behavior to become a self-reward-ing or self-perpetuating behavior.

 **Fact**

A self-rewarding or self-perpetuating behavior is one that is intrinsi-cally rewarding. This is how habits start in humans too. It's part of how we learn. In dogs, barking and being aggressive tends to develop an adrenaline rush that some become addicted to and which can be very hard to retrain. That's why it is very important to prevent these sort of self-rewarding behaviors from happening.

Biting

If your boxer has bitten a person or another dog, you are in a serious situation legally and with respect to your dog ownership—even if the victim was a family member. With some dogs, once the bite-inhibition gulf has been crossed, they have less respect for humans than before. It is worth it to train your boxer so he'll never even think of doing this in the first place.

Alert!

Although humane muzzles allow the dog to eat, drink, and pant, there is some risk that a boxer could still overheat with one on, so you must monitor him carefully. Never leaved a muzzled boxer unat-tended, and never use a basket-type muzzle or one that does not allow the boxer to pant or to drink water.

If your boxer has bitten someone, consider muzzling him with a neoprene-type humane muzzle (one that allows him to eat, drink water, and to pant, but not to extend his canines to bite and do much damage) when interacting with humans and other dogs.

This is a short-term solution until you can retrain him or get help with this issue.

Lunging

If your boxer is lunging at other dogs or people, you need to step back and get him under control. You may need to do some retraining, but in the short term you are best off taking him out of situations where it is likely to happen. If he is lunging, he is not thinking good thoughts for the most part, and you need to make sure he doesn't injure another person or dog with his lunging and the intent behind it.

This may be a good time to take your boxer back to an obedience class where he must both socialize and learn at the same time. This is not the time to cut him any slack on his behavior. You are right to expect quick responses and a precise performance. Remember, the more you expect of your boxer at this point in time, the more he will respect your leadership. This is also the time to be totally consistent and firm.

Growling

If your boxer is growling at other dogs, you need to be very careful that he doesn't provoke some other dog into a fight. If he is growling at people, you need to remove him from situations in which he can intimidate others until you have this behavior under control.

Proofing to make sure you've completely gotten rid of a bad behavior such as growling is also a good idea. Proofing is what trainers call the process of testing your dog's behavior. It usually occurs after the dog has learned what you want and can perform the exercises in a variety of different situations. It is a way for you to find out how much and how well he has learned what you have taught him. People who do competitive obedience always proof their dogs before they show in obedience rings, but the concept is valid for all other aspects of canine training as well.

Food Guarding

In an ideal world, we would all have separate places to eat—humans at the table, and dogs outside or in their own room. However, in the real world, chances are pretty good that if your boxer eats outside, it's on the patio at best. It is more likely, however, that he normally eats in the kitchen or the laundry room.

If you take no steps to prepare your boxer to accept at least some limitations on his instincts toward food guarding and simply taking food from those that are weaker and less likely to put up resistance, you risk a bite to a family member or guest around the issue of food. If you have failed to have your children prepare his food, and take it away at least once per meal now and then for a few seconds, and if you have failed to sometimes pet your boxer while he eats, he probably thinks he owns his food bowl and the territory where he eats. Should a child or guest make the mistake of trying to pet him while he is eating, it is not unlikely that he might growl, or worse, bite.

 **Essential**

Your boxer should be so accepting of your leadership that you should be able to take anything that you want out of his mouth. For safety's sake, in case he accidentally ingests something toxic or poisonous, you and family members should be able to pet him while he is eating, especially if he eats in the kitchen, and people are around while he is eating.

If you need to retrain this, you will again go back to the doggy boot camp concept. You boxer needs to learn that you control the food, and that he must earn it. If he bites or growls at anyone over his food, you need to make him work for every morsel. That means that he must sit, down, come, or whatever he is learning at the time, and get treated with his ordinary dinner if he responds correctly.

When you are satisfied that he is responding well to basic commands again, you can return his food to him, but you need to take it away for a few seconds. Again, this is not done to tease or harass him but simply to show your dominance. In a pack, the leader or any particular canine's superior does this with food at times. In domestic packs, it is not uncommon for an older or more dominant dog to control the toys or sometimes a bone. However, in canine terms, the superior always gives the food or toys back when he has made his point, so your boxer will understand that you are making your point.

If eating becomes a stressful issue, it is best to try to find a peaceful spot where your boxer will not be overstimulated by hectic surroundings to eat peacefully. While that is ideal, for safety's sake, it is still best that he is used to others controlling his food, so that he does not react in an unfortunate way if someone makes a mistake around him. Most well-bred boxers can easily be trained to accept their human's handling of their food with no problem.

Shyness

Shyness in a boxer is not acceptable in terms of what boxers were developed for and bred to do. The boxer should be a calm, confident, careful dog that is brave in defense of and loyal to his owner. Shyness does not fit into that description.

 Fact

Some shy dogs are also fear biters, or dogs that bite out of fear rather than aggression. The key with a fear biter is to work slowly and gently through all the training and socialization steps. Never corner any dog, as this is a virtual guarantee to make him bite. Shy dogs and potential fear biters are most comfortable when they know what is expected of them, so training and a predictable routine are critical with this type of dog.

Shyness is a big problem in a show dog, and if it is genuine shyness of the less dominant member of the pack, socialization is the only answer. If the shyness is the result of lack of calcium uptake due to a growth spurt or stress, the result might be as bad, but the cause is different. In both cases, dietary support should be optimum, and in both cases, it is important to keep socializing your boxer in a nonthreatening way. If he doesn't want to go near things, again, don't force it, but don't quit. The minute you quit socializing your boxer, you condemn him to a life of fear and anxiety in new situations. He doesn't have to participate fully, but he should be able to at least be in new situations meeting a few nice, low-key people without falling apart. This is one situation where the only way past it is to go through it, so you need to keep socializing your boxer. Shy dogs can only gain in confidence through learning that they can cope with new situations and people, and confident dogs flourish with the attention, so as before, train with patient persistence.

Aggression

There are many different potential causes of aggression. It may be hereditary, although it shouldn't be if you got your boxer from a reputable breeder. Genuine hereditary aggression is rare in domesticated dogs of most breeds. Aggression may also result from a health issue. However, the most common cause of aggression is the result of lack of adequate socialization and training, which includes some basic misunderstandings and poor timing or mismanagement of a situation.

Owners frequently reward undesirable behavior inadvertently. This might be as subtle as taking a secret little pride in your boxer's protective or macho side, or as obvious as not correcting him when he growls. This can have the unfortunate result of making it occur again and again. Aggression may also occur as a fundamental misunderstanding that socialization must continue to occur throughout your boxer's life, and it has not on the part of the humans involved.

 Essential

Aggression is a natural and, to some extent, a necessary phenomenon in domestic canines at times. After all, it is the only method that
really allows them to make a point after everything else has failed.
It does not necessarily mean the end of your relationship with your
boxer, but it does mean that you need to step back and re-evaluate
the situation.

If you have missed out on some of your boxer's early education, or missed some cues that all is not going well, and your boxer
has acted inappropriately, what's the solution? First, you can work
harder at exercising your boxer physically and mentally. This may
mean longer walks and longer training sessions and even more
playtime. Whatever makes your boxer tired and happy will help
to work off the inclination to be aggressive. This is an example of
expending the energy of aggression.

Alternatively, you can change channels on your boxer. Boxers,
which tend to be the drama kings and queens of the dog world,
are very susceptible and responsive to a change of attitude. So, if
your boxer is showing signs of dominance or aggression to other
dogs, for instance, you can say something like "Phooey" and show
disappointment, or shame or ridicule, "Oh no, you're being bad,"
or "You've got to be kidding." Your boxer will probably shift attitudes right along with you.

Of course, like any other type of training reinforcement, you
have to be vigilant about when this type of attitude occurs. Try
not to miss any opportunities over a period of about a month or
more, during which you should reinforce constantly to your boxer
that you don't approve of or agree with his negative assessment of
the situation. When you do this, you need to move out of the area
of the dog in question just in case your boxer *is* picking up something bad in the other dog's attitude. Usually, if you remove your
boxer from the situation, the other dog will give it up as well.

◀ If your boxer is aggressive with other dogs you must keep him away from others until he can behave.

Aggression and Drive Triggers

In any event, you need to carefully assess what triggers your boxer's aggression. For those dogs that have high prey drives (many dogs in agility and obedience), almost anything that moves can trigger this drive. That may be bikers, joggers, smaller dogs, cats, squirrels, cars, or even children.

The first solution is not to let your boxer off leash so that he can chase anything he wishes, and to work on your recall games to strengthen that part of the equation. Secondly, lots of exercise is a must, and a lot of retrieving will often help. The boxer often does well with scent training, as it makes him use his brain, and that is always challenging for a dog. You can do this by hiding his toys around the house and having him find them, or by teaching formal scent-retrieve exercises. He will need to be put on a sit/stay or someone should hold him back while you hide the toy. After a few rounds of this game, your boxer will be tired, as scenting wears most dogs out more than almost any other exercise.

Dominance Aggression

For a dog that is naturally dominant, you need to use a different tactic. The dominant pup is often one that gets things quickly and appears to be following all the rules. What he is really doing is figuring out how long it's going to take him to take over. Often, with a pup like this, the first thing that shows you a sign of him being dominant aggressive is that he growls at a lesser pack member or guest when told to get off the couch.

 Essential

> To curb aggression in a dominant dog, play tug of war with your boxer. If he's a pup, be careful not to let him tug to the point of dislocating his jaw or pulling his bite out of alignment. Always let your boxer win, but when the play session is done, be sure to take possession of all the tug toys and put them away. Another trick for a dominant dog is to practice lots of long downs. This reinforces to your boxer that you are the ultimate pack leader, and the exercise gives him time and a lowly position to consider it.

This is the pup that needs strong guidance and a strong pack leader, and he needs to have rules firmly enforced by other family members as well. If your boxer is a very dominant pup, when he grows up, he will be the one who puts his head across another dog's shoulders or neck. If the other dog agrees that your boxer is dominant, he will crouch down and accept your boxer's position. If not, a fight will ensue. Try to avoid this. Some boxers learn to love to fight, and they often win.

While games and more training should help ease aggression, sometimes these methods aren't enough. If you are afraid of your boxer but don't want to give up on him just yet, get a humane muzzle. This takes the decision-making ability away from him and reinforces your position as the dominant one. The muzzle is a not-so-subtle dominance inhibitor. Once the muzzle is on, you can go back and retrain, hopefully making up for those things that he missed in his early education.

Early Separation from the Litter

One type of aggression tends to occur in those pups that have been taken from their mother and pack before the age of seven weeks. If you got your boxer from a reputable breeder, this probably won't happen. However, if you got your boxer from somewhere else, your boxer could show signs of aggression to people with no warning. He could attack other dogs with no warning and might be inclined to not stop biting even after the other dog submits.

If your boxer left the pack before about seven weeks of age, he may have missed those lessons on bite inhibition. He can't interpret body language well and isn't entirely aware of the consequences of his actions. In these cases, if a fight ensues, it can be very hard to stop. In a multidog household, these sorts of attacks can arise if your boxer becomes jealous of another dog getting attention. It is sometimes also a problem with older dogs and rescues.

 **Alert!**

Aggression is a double-edged sword. On the one hand, it can have some very negative ramifications, but on the other, it can tell you a lot about your boxer that can help you to take a positive direction with him. Aggression does not have to be the end of your canine/human relationship.

The principle retraining of this dog is to reward him for being calm in an ever-diminishing territory. Put your boxer on a leash and have a person walk by, first at a distance and then closer. Give your boxer a treat every time he does *not* react in any way to the person's presence. In this way, you familiarize your boxer with nonthreatening strangers or other people. The best social solution for this dog is that you tell people to ignore your boxer when they come to the house, especially if he is not acting out in an aggressive way. Give your boxer the chance to accept them and to work up the courage to make friends, or at least keep his distance.

Fixing Problem Areas

If there are no underlying health issues that might be contributing to your boxer's bad behavior, then you have let training slide and/ or you have overlooked clues that your boxer has decided to work his way up the alpha dog ladder.

Once you know what has gone wrong, you are ready to begin retraining if that is what you want to do. Your entire family must be committed to training and changing their behaviors that have lead to the bad behavior on your boxer's part. If your entire family is not in agreement and committed to do the work that will result in a positive change in your boxer's behavior, it won't work. If training requires patient persistence to have a good boxer, retraining requires almost ten times the effort because you have to work to get rid of habits and self-rewarding behaviors that reinforce the bad behavior.

First, you must determine what you want to change. If it's barking, you know you need to work on training a "No bark" and "Leave it" command. If it's biting, you must carefully look at the circumstances around any biting that occurred and see what you missed and what you need to do differently. If you need help retraining your boxer, by all means hire an in-house trainer or a behaviorist. And you may need the humane muzzle. If your boxer has bitten another male in a fight, neutering him may be the best thing to do. Some dogs handle their hormones better than others. But don't neuter him thinking that that will solve all of his behavioral problems—it usually doesn't. However, in combination with dedicated retraining, it can have a good effect.

In the meantime, your boxer can learn to live with a muzzle on, which is in itself a dominance-reducing tool.

 **Question?**

Muzzles seem so cruel. Is it really okay to use them?
Leaving an untrained dog free to harm someone is much crueler than using a protective muzzle until training is reinforced. Just one inappropriate application of teeth can be catastrophic. If your dog bites your neighbor's child, for example, the neighbor might take legal action and insist that your dog be put to sleep. Don't risk it!

Once you have the situation under control, you need to find a way to teach your boxer acceptable behavior. Training any and all behaviors competes with aggressive behavior. The more positive behaviors you can put on command in places where your boxer might like to be aggressive, the more you reduce his tendency to be an aggressive dog.

The more you fade the rewards of negative self-rewarding or self-perpetuating behavior and replace them with good behaviors, the better off you and your boxer will be. Your boxer will now have a whole resume of good behaviors that will earn him praise. This goes a long way to eliminate the inclination to want to do the bad behaviors.

Help from a Behaviorist

Let's say that the problem you are having with your boxer is overwhelming to you, but the thought of giving him up is unacceptable. You've tried more training, more exercise, and rewarding good behaviors, but nothing works. What should you do?

First of all, you can contact your vet, your local obedience club, and local trainers for help. If they cannot help, they will probably refer you to a behaviorist. While anyone can call himself a behaviorist, when you check his credentials, you might want to ask about his background and some other basic questions, such as the following:

- What is your breed of preference?
- What is your experience in training dogs?
- What type of methods do you use in retraining problem dogs?
- Have you ever worked with boxers before?

The reason for asking these questions is that a lot of people with a behavioral background have little or no real dog-training experience, and they tend at times to overlook the practical value of training a dog. If the behaviorist you're interviewing has never worked with a boxer or other working breed, he is apt to overestimate the drives that an ordinary boxer might have and to underestimate the breed's intelligence.

These miscalculations lead some in behavioral circles to believe that boxers are superstitious because they frequently understand the cause/effect of a certain behavior almost too readily. However, there is nothing superstitious about this. Most boxers are simply smart enough to figure out how to step back in the course of events. Paradoxically, they are sometimes willing to be bad so that they can then be rewarded later for being good. Boxers are very smart, and they figure out causal events much more thoroughly than they get credit for. This is actually very good news when it comes to training.

If you are uncomfortable with what one behaviorist recommends for your boxer, keep searching until you find a professional whose methods don't make you uncomfortable. There are many good trainers and behaviorists out there who can help with a wide range of boxer behavioral problems.

Competitive Obedience

Even if your boxer does not shine quite like a 200 dog (a nickname derived from the highest score possible in obedience competition), you can still have the positive experience of training your boxer for AKC obedience titles as a continuation of what he has already learned about being a good dog. Really good competitive obedience teams make it look so easy with teamwork, precision, and positive attitude. However, many hours of long, hard work go into making a competitive obedience team shine.

About Obedience Titles

Nowhere will you find better dog trainers than those obedience trainers who are successful at the upper level titles. They train a complex set of skills that not only ask the dog to give a lot but also serve to demonstrate the dog's intelligence, biddability, and drives.

Originally printed in the obedience competitors' magazine, *Front and Finish*, Sandra Mowry's essay, entitled "What Is an Obedience Title, Really?," represents the spirit of dedication to obedience and training that is still alive and well in dog shows every weekend all across America.

"Not just a brag, not just a stepping stone to a higher title, not just an adjunct to competitive scores; a title is a tribute to the dog that bears it, a way to honor the dog, an ultimate memorial. It will remain in the record and in the memory, for about as long as anything in this world can remain.

And though the dog himself doesn't know or care that his achievements have been noted, a title says many things in the world of humans, where such things count.

A title says your dog was intelligent, adaptable, and good natured. It says that your dog loved you enough to do the things that please you, however crazy they may have sometimes seemed.

In addition, a title says that you love your dog. That you loved to spend time with him because he was a good dog and that you believed in him enough to give him yet another chance when he failed and in the end your faith was justified.

A title proves that your dog inspired you to that special relationship enjoyed by so few; that in a world of disposable creatures, this dog with a title was greatly loved, and loved greatly in return.

And when that dear short life is over, the title remains as a memorial of the finest kind, the best you can give to a deserving friend. Volumes of praise in one small set of initials after the name.

An obedience title is nothing less than love and respect, given and received and recorded permanently."

Getting an obedience title on a boxer puts that boxer among the most elite of the breed. It is truly an achievement to be proud of. Substitute the name of your boxer for "dog" in the essay, and see if you are not moved to want to demonstrate to the world your love for him and your pride in him.

Almost every weekend of the year, you can find trials occurring in all kinds of places in all fifty states. Many all-breed kennel clubs offer trials with their conformation point shows. There are also obedience-only clubs that offer trials only. Some boxer clubs offer trials with their annual or semiannual specialties, while other breed clubs may offer all-breed trials with their annual specialty and trial. That means trials can occur in many different venues, all of which can offer legs toward a title.

In addition to the AKC trials, the United Kennel Club offers shows and trials around the country, but their obedience exercises are slightly different. The Australian Shepherd Club of America also gives obedience trials and titles to other breeds than Australian shepherds. If you get bitten by the trialing bug, you have other options.

Novice

In order to be eligible to show in the novice class, your boxer must be registered with the AKC. Alternately, he must have an indefinite listing privilege (ILP) number from the AKC. See below for a detailed explanation of the ILP.

 **Essential**

The Indefinite Listing Privilege is a number that the AKC will grant to a dog that appears to be a purebred dog of a particular breed, but that, for whatever reason, has no AKC registration. The ILP allows the dog to participate in all events that boxers are eligible to compete in other than conformation. This includes rescue boxers.

Requirements for Novice Class

The Novice class is the first class in traditional obedience in which a dog can compete. The exercises that the dog must perform are the following:

- Heel on leash and figure eight
- Stand for examination
- Heel free
- Recall
- Long sit for one minute
- Long down for three minutes

Do any of these look familiar? They should because they are all either direct exercises or variations on those that you have learned in this book.

If your boxer can do more than half the point value for each of these exercises under three different licensed AKC judges at three different licensed AKC trials, the AKC will send you a certificate that states what title your boxer has achieved. The maximum score that your boxer could receive would be a 200, and the minimum that he could receive and still get a titling leg would be 170 minimum with no less than 50 percent of each exercise. The title that you would earn is called the Novice Companion Dog (abbreviated CD).

 **Fact**

The American Kennel Club Obedience Title Certificate has the official seal of the AKC on it and is signed by the president. Once you have one of these, you will probably want more, and you will never want any adult boxer you own ever to be without one. This title certificate proves that your boxer is a very elite and loved boxer indeed.

Novice A Versus Novice B

A slightly confusing fact, until you know more about how obedience trials are run, is that there is an A and a B class for Novice, Open, and Utility. Novice A is for those people who have never titled a dog before in AKC obedience. This means that you and your boxer get to compete against people who are about as inexperienced as yourselves for your first title. There is some comfort in that. You can all be inexperienced and nervous together.

Novice B is for everyone who has titled a dog before. You only get one Novice A dog, but you can have as many Novice B dogs as you can successfully train. And you can show indefinitely in

Novice B or until you earn a "High In Trial." "High in Trial" is an award for having the highest score among the regular classes at a trial—all novice, open, and utility classes.

Open or Companion Dog Excellent

The next titling class after Novice is Open. It is harder than Novice but builds on the skills that you have polished for Novice. To show in Open, you must have successfully earned a Novice title or the CD.

The exercises in Open A are the following:

- Heel free and figure eight
- Drop on recall
- Retrieve on the flat
- Retrieve over the high jump
- Broad jump
- Long sit for three minutes (owner out of sight)
- Long down for five minutes (owner out of sight)

There are six different variations of Open B. In this case, Open A is for the handler of any dog who has never put an Obedience Trial Championship (OTCH, the ultimate obedience title) on a dog. Open B is for those people who have put an OTCH on a dog and for those people who are showing for Utility Dog Excellent legs and OTCH points, or for those people who want to continue to show in Open, but are sixty days past earning their Open title in the A classes.

You will see that there is no on-leash work and that jumps and retrieving are part of the exercises. Your boxer must therefore be able to heel off leash and to take jumps correctly and safely. You may need obedience class instruction in order to teach him how to do these exercises, or maybe not, depending upon how determined you are.

In order to earn the open title or CDX (Companion Dog Excellent), you must qualify in each of the separate exercises, earning more than half the points available to each exercise three times under three different judges, again with a 200 point maximum and a 170 minimum with no less than 50 percent of the points in each exercises.

Utility and Utility Excellent

To earn the Utility Dog title, or UD, you must have your CDX. The exercises are as follows in Utility A:

- Signal exercise
- Scent discrimination article number 1
- Scent discrimination article number 2
- Directed retrieve
- Moving stand for examination
- Directed jumping

In order to earn the Utility Dog (UD) title, you must earn more than half of the points for each exercise and qualify under three different judges three times with a 200 point maximum, a 170 minimum and no less than 50 percent of the points in any exercise. You may show in Utility A if you have not previously earned an OTCH title, and for sixty days after you originally earn the third leg of your utility title.

The exercises that are included in the utility title are advanced far beyond what every boxer needs to know to be a good dog, but they are certainly not out of reach for any well-bred boxer. There are six different arrangements of these same exercises in Utility B.

The Utility Excellent title, or UDX, is the title after the Utility title. To earn a Utility Dog Excellent title, the dog must qualify in both open and utility B ten times at the same trial on the same day. Obviously, a dog of any breed that obtains this title is exceptional and has an owner who is very devoted to training the dog.

 **fact**

As of the writing of this book, 101 utility titles have been earned by boxers since the AKC established the title in the late 1940s. There have been fifteen Utility Dog Excellent titles earned by boxers since the title was established in the 1990s.

Obedience Trial Champions

The Obedience Trial Championship, or OTCH, as it is generally known, is the apex of virtually any dog's obedience career. The OTCH is the result of earning 100 points by defeating other dogs in the Open and Utility B classes. The number of points earned is dependent upon the number of dogs entered and on the placement that the dog earns to defeat other dogs. While OTCH points are awarded to dogs in the top four places, the truth is that in order for there to be points, especially in the Open B classes, a lot of dogs must be entered in that class. If you live in an area where there aren't a lot of obedience trials, it can take a while to earn this prestigious title.

In addition to the 100 points, the OTCH dog must also have a first place in Utility and Open B and one more first place in either class for a total of a minimum of three first places in Utility and Open B. This is a very competitive title, and only two boxers have earned the right to be called an Obedience Trial Champion since the AKC instituted the title in the mid-1990s.

Rally Obedience

In 2005, the AKC instituted a new titling event called rally obedience. Based upon the old obedience doodling exercises that were done to help polish exercises for regular obedience, rally obedience titles are meant to be the bridge between the Canine Good Citizen test and the Novice classes in obedience or agility. Rally is one of the most successful new titling events that the AKC has ever introduced.

Rally obedience (or Rally-O, as it's sometimes called) is an event in which the dog and handler perform a course that the judge prepares. Certain exercises are done at numbered stations. The judge tells the handler when to begin, and the dog and handler proceed through a course that has ten to twenty stations, depending upon the level of the class. The dog and handler proceed at a brisk pace and proceed through the numbered stations, doing whatever the sign says to do at that station.

While rally obedience is subject to the rules that govern regular obedience, the points that you lose for mistakes happen in specific increments, as follows:

One-point deductions for each of the following:

- Tight leash
- Dog interfering with the handler's forward movement
- Poor sits
- Slow, delayed, or resistant response
- Touching or tickling a post, pylon, or person
- Out of position

Three-point deductions occur for the following:

- Repeat of a station
- Pylon/post knocked over on figure eight, spiral, or serpentine
- Lack of control
- Loud command or intimidating signal
- Excessive barking
- Handler error

Ten-point deduction for each of the following:

- Incorrectly performed station

- Hitting the jump
- Handler error

One to ten-point deduction for the following:

- Lack of teamwork

Non-qualifying scores (NQ) shall be given for:

- Minimum requirements not met
- Dog unmanageable
- Station not attempted
- Consistently tight lead
- Substantially out of position/not completing the honor exercise
- Elimination in the ring during judging
- Bar knocked off the uprights/using jump as an aid to going over
- Handler error

While errors will take points off, any ties in placements are broken by time. Each rally run is timed. Timing begins when the judge says "Forward" and ends when the dog and handler team cross the finish line. In case of a tie, the dog and handler completing the course in the least amount of time will receive the higher placement and a plus (+) after the score.

 Essential

One basic, fundamental difference between what this book describes as "what all good boxers need to know" and competitive obedience is that your boxer will need to learn to work despite distractions. And your boxer will need to learn to work in a variety of situations. Until your boxer has generalized or learned the exercise and can perform it in a variety of circumstances, he doesn't really know it.

Again, in Rally-O there is a difference between the A and B classes. In this case, the Novice A class is for those handlers who have not put an obedience title on a dog.

Rally Novice (RN)

In the rally Novice class, all exercises are judged with the dog on leash. There are ten to fifteen stations. No more than five that are stationary stations, or the kind of exercises that require dog and handler to come to a complete halt, such as "Halt, down your dog," "Halt, one step, two steps, three steps back," or "Halt, walk around your dog." That means that the other exercises are moving exercises, such as "Spiral left, dog inside," slows, fasts, and so on.

Rally Advanced (RA)

The rally Advanced class must have between twelve and seventeen stations, with no more than seven stationary exercises per course. One jump must be used for this class. It may be any jump used as standard equipment in AKC obedience classes, such as a broad jump, high jump, or bar jump. Four-foot-wide jumps may be used in place of five-foot-wide jumps.

Rally Excellent (RE)

The rally Excellent class must have between fifteen and twenty stations with no more than seven stationary exercises per course. Two jumps must be used for this class. Again, these may be any jump used as standard equipment in AKC obedience classes, such as a broad jump, high jump, or bar jump.

One additional exercise that is part of rally Excellent is the honor exercise. Prior to the class, the judge will designate either the sit or the down for the honor exercise as well as the placement in the ring. The judge will also designate where the handler will stand in the ring during the exercise, whether next to the dog or in front, facing the dog. The essence of the honor exercise is for the dog to be able to work with a distraction in the ring.

Canine Good Citizen (CGC) Certification

The new Canine Good Citizenship (CGC) test, discussed briefly in Chapter 17, includes the Responsible Dog Owners Pledge, which all owners must sign. In signing, the owners agree to take care of their dog's health needs, safety, exercise, training, and quality of life. Owners also agree to show responsibility in their dog ownership by cleaning up after their dogs in public places and never letting their dogs infringe on the rights of others.

The CGC test for the dog includes the following:

- **Accepting a friendly stranger:** This part of the test demonstrates that the dog will allow a friendly stranger to approach him and speak to the owner or handler in a natural, ordinary fashion.
- **Sitting politely for petting:** This test demonstrates that the dog will allow a friendly stranger to touch him while he is out with his handler.
- **Appearance and grooming:** This is a practical test that demonstrates that the dog will welcome being groomed and examined and will permit someone, such as a vet, groomer, or friend of the owner, to do so. It also demonstrates the owner's care, concern, and sense of responsibility in grooming their dog. The dog must appear to be in healthy condition (at a good weight, clean, healthy, well-groomed, and alert).
- **Out for a walk (walking on a loose lead):** This test demonstrates that the handler is in control of the dog.
- **Walking through a crowd:** This test demonstrates that the dog can move politely in pedestrian traffic and is under control in public places. The dog and handler walk through a crowd of people, passing close to at least three. The dog may show some interest in the people, but should continue to walk with the handler, without evidence of overexuberance, shyness, or resentment.

- **Sit and down on command and staying in place:** This test demonstrates that the dog has training, and will respond to the handler's commands to sit and down in an area where the handler indicates, and that the dog will stay in the place where the handler has commanded.
- **Coming when called:** This test demonstrates that the dog will call when called by the handler. The handler walks ten feet from the dog, turns and faces the dog, and calls the dog. The handler may use encouragement to get the dog to come.
- **Reaction to another dog:** This test demonstrates that the dog can behave politely around other dogs.
- **Reaction to distraction:** This test demonstrates that the dog is confident at all times when faced with common distracting situations.
- **Supervised separation:** This test demonstrates that a dog can be left with a trusted person, if necessary, and will maintain training and good manners.

▲ Boxers are exceptional show and performance dogs that excel in all forms of competition.

Any dog that eliminates during the test must be marked as having failed. The only exception to this rule is the supervised separation test when held outdoors.

Furthermore, any dog that growls, snaps, bites, attacks, or attempts to attack a person or another dog is not a good citizen and must be dismissed from the test.

Many obedience clubs, training club, specialty clubs, and kennel clubs hold CGC testing and training. Many basic obedience classes start with training that will help any dog and handler team that practices the exercises faithfully to pass the test at the end of the training class. You can contact the AKC for more information on how to find a test in your area.

The CGC exam basically tests all the things that every good dog needs to know. If the dog can demonstrate that he does know all these things and passes the test, the AKC will provide a certificate that states the dog is a canine good citizen—a worthy endeavor for every boxer owner.

CHAPTER 19

Other Advanced Training

If you and your boxer have tackled competitive obedience and are looking for another challenge, perhaps it's time to pursue some more advanced training. Events such as conformation, agility, and tracking require intense education and training time for dog and handler and result in highly skilled and happy dogs. Therapy dogs and assistance dogs remind us that dogs of all breeds are companions to human beings, and sensitive and gracious ones at that. This chapter discusses all of these advanced training options.

Conformation

If you bought your boxer with the specific aim of competing in conformation, he should show outstanding promise of being a breed type or the promise of very closely approximating the boxer standard. Otherwise, it may not be possible to get his breed championship. However, even if your boxer is going to do conformation, he needs to know how to be a good dog, and more since he will routinely have an AKC judge and others go over his mouth and his private parts as part of the examination.

As the legendary boxer breeder Eleanor Linderholm-Wood of Merrilane Boxers said, "as few dogs are reincarnated Best in Show winners, obedience training will make show training easier."

Conformation Basics

If your boxer knows how to do good walkies (no pulling on the leash, no lagging, and no sniffing), and if he has been properly socialized and educated since puppyhood and is used to spending time in his crate or x-pen, conformation show training itself will not pose any difficulties.

Basically, what your boxer needs to do in the show ring is to stand a certain way (squarely over his paws), let the judge go over his mouth, body. and testicles, and hold that stand during the exam with no shyness, aggression, or even too much enthusiasm. Even if your boxer is friendly and well socialized, this will take more effort than just being friendly. To let a stranger touch his mouth and private parts takes training!

 Essential

It is best that you know the usual ring procedures before you go off to show your boxer at his first show. Nothing is more irritating to many judges than someone who does not know the rules of the sport. You may want to attend handling classes to learn how to set your boxer up, basic ring patterns, ring etiquette, and how to get your boxer to perform in front of a judge. All this will help your training to be more efficient once you get into the conformation ring.

In addition, your boxer has to be able to gait or trot nicely around the ring with you or a professional handler. He has to do this to show the judge his movement on the down-and-back exercise and while going around the ring, and he needs to be able to do a free stack. Boxers are one of the breeds that are hand-stacked and have to have a nice free stack as well.

Hand stacking a dog means that the handler bends down and places each of the dog's four paws so that the dog's weight is evenly distributed, and so that his front paws are squarely beneath his shoulders and his back paws and legs are comfortably placed behind him. His neck should be nicely arched, and he needs to be looking straight ahead. In boxers, this also means that his tail should be up.

Free stacking means that the dog has basically learned how to put himself together without the handler's help. This is usually done on the down-and-back, when the handler and your boxer return to stop in front of the judge. It makes a very nice impression if your boxer can put himself together and stack in front of the judge without help from the handler, with his feet squarely planted, neck arched, tail up, and his expression one of animated and happy containment.

Show Training

The best way to begin show training is simply to pick the puppy up when he is quite young, from in front of his chest and beneath his back end, and set him down squarely, which is roughly what a show stack is. He should land with his paws under his shoulders and his feet comfortably balancing him from behind. Hold the pup in this position for just a few moments, and then praise him or give him a treat.

Eventually, your boxer will need to learn to be hand stacked and to do a free stack on his own.

 **Alert!**

Conformation is the only sport where amateurs routinely compete against professionals. There are professional handlers in every breed in AKC shows. You can pay these handlers to present your dog to an AKC judge at an AKC show and sometimes train your dog to be shown. While this can be quite expensive, showing in the boxer ring is quite competitive, and your boxer will likely be more successful in winning with a professional handler. However, you should still learn how to train your boxer to do this yourself, as it can be a lot of fun and very gratifying to win!

Agility

Agility competition began in England and was brought to the United States by Bud Kramer in the 1980s. By 1998, agility had become an AKC titling event, and it is a popular one. In addition to AKC agility, there are a number of other registries that provide agility trials, including USDAA (United States Dog Agility Association) and UKC agility.

▲ **Due to their strength and obedience, boxers are very successful in competitions such as agility.**

The titles that can be earned are in three different categories: standard, jumpers, and preferred. In standard agility, dogs, under the direction of their handlers, negotiate a complex obstacle course that includes jumps, weaves, tunnels, a three- to four-foot-high dog walk, a teeter-totter, an A-frame, and a table in a sequence that is drawn out by the judge who judges the course. The standard class includes contact objects such as the dog-walk, the A-frame, table, jumps and seesaw. Each of the contact objects has a safety zone painted on the object, and the dog must place at least one paw in that area to successfully complete that obstacle.

Jumpers is a class that consists only of jumps with weaves, which has no contact objects in it, and preferred is a class which has contact objects but a lowered jump height. The preferred classes follow the same format as the standard class.

The standard agility titles are Novice Agility (NA), Open Agility (OA), Agility Excellent (AX), the Master Agility title in which the dog must have earned the AX title, then qualify ten more times. The Master Agility Championship (MACH) title requires the dog to achieve a minimum of 750 championship points and twenty double-qualifying scores. A championship point in agility is awarded for each full second a dog runs under course time. Dogs can only earn those points from the Excellent B standard agility class or the Excellent B jumpers with weaves class. Dogs placing first in their class double their championship points, and dogs placing second in their class receive one and a half times their standard championship points. At this point in time, three boxers have earned the MACH.

 **fact**

AKC agility is available to every AKC breed. The classes are divided by jump heights in order to make the competition equal between the different sizes of dogs. Most boxers jump heights of twenty or twenty-four inches in standard agility.

The jumpers with weaves titles are as follows: Novice Jumpers with Weaves (NAJ), Open Jumpers with Weaves (OAJ), Advanced Agility with Weaves (AXJ), and Master Agility with Weaves (MXJ). Since jumping is such an important component of agility, each dog participating must have a valid official jump height card that can be presented at check-in or be measured prior to competing.

Tracking

When it comes to the canine nose, nothing compares. Dog noses have as many as 20,000 more scent receptors than human noses. Dogs can track old scent over rough terrain, through water (don't believe those movie scenes where the bad guy jumps into a stream and gets away!), can tell the scent of a live person as opposed to a corpse (even under water), and can smell drugs, bombs, cancer, and almost anything we ask of them. Boxers have been success-ful cadaver dogs (specifically trained to search for dead bodies) in earthquakes, fires, and bombings, and a number of them have been on search-and-rescue teams throughout the United States and with federal marshals.

Canine Search-and-Rescue

There are many search-and-rescue groups throughout the United States that need volunteers to train their dogs to search for missing persons of all ages and in many different types of cir-cumstances. This is one wonderful way in which dog owners can give back to their communities. Practically every dog is capable of tracking and making a contribution if their owner is capable of the rigorous training that is required of a search-and-rescue dog-and-handler team.

 **Essential**

The volunteers in rescue groups who search for lost people must spend hundreds of hours training and conditioning not only their dogs but also themselves for challenging physical circumstances. They are on call twenty-four hours a day. They live with a beeper or pager at all times, and must be prepared to leave their jobs, taking vacation time if they must, and occasionally face real threats of dan-ger in order to participate in the searches.

Tracking As a Sport

As an AKC sport, the Tracking Dog (TD) and Tracking Dog Excellent titles (TDX) indicate the dog's ability to follow a track laid by a person under a variety of conditions on moderate terrain and to find an article dropped by that person at the end of the track. Before a team can compete for either of these titles, they must pass a preliminary certification test administered by an AKC judge. The AKC also awards a Versatile Tracker (VTD) and a Champion Tracker (CHT) title. To date, no boxer has won either of these titles.

Contrary to what many people think, boxers make excellent scenting dogs. They are often good air-scenters, able to pick a scent out of the air and follow it, as opposed to many dogs that tend to follow the scent on the ground. As a sport, tracking fanciers like to see dogs follow the scent on the ground in a step-by-step fashion, but for search-and-rescue purposes, it is good to have at least some dogs that can air scent well.

Therapy Dogs

Therapy dogs do a variety of community-service jobs. The term used to apply to dogs that visited nursing homes, but now the medical profession has found that therapy dogs are helpful in much broader applications.

 Fact

People who are disoriented, such as Alzheimer's patients, or those who have problems with focus, such as children with high-functioning autism or learning disabilities, can often benefit from interaction with therapy dogs. The pleasure of concentrating on a dog can require these patients to think again about what is going on right here and now.

The use of therapy dogs has grown a great deal in the last decade for a number of reasons. Therapy dogs boost morale. Keeping good morale in long-term care facilities can be difficult, but most people become dog lovers around a well-trained dog. Also, it has long been established that people who have pets live longer and have less stress in general, a boon for patients in long-term care facilities, or people who are recovering from illnesses that enforce inactivity, depression is very common. Dogs help to break up the boredom of the day, and they provide a bright spot to people who often have few other things to look forward to in their lives.

Dogs often help to facilitate greater cooperation within the staff, and people that they take care of. This is partly a function to increased morale, but a good, loving therapy dog manages to elicit cooperation from many.

 Essential

The training that a therapy dog undergoes is extensive in terms of developing the dog's people skills. After all, in a therapeutic situation, a dog may encounter people whose movement is impaired or erratic, who may lash out at the dog, and who may cry or carry on in ways that are alarming to the dog. Therapy Dogs International and Delta Pet Partners have extended training programs for their canine candidates, but many programs start with Canine Good Citizen certification as the basis.

Therapy dogs also help with social stimulation. One reason therapy dogs boost morale, help with depression, and improve relationships is that dogs invite conversation. People talk to dog owners, and they talk about dogs. Sometimes therapy dogs are the only visitors these long-term care patients have, and the dogs become the reason they get up and interact with others.

Another way that therapy dogs help is by providing an outlet for all people's need for touch. For those long-term patients who have few friends or relatives to visit, therapy dogs provide someone who not only will touch the patients, but who also will touch back if the patient desires. This is also critical for high-functioning autistic children. Therapy dogs are safe to touch and to communicate with.

Therapy dogs are a wonderful way to expose children to nice dogs in a setting where the dogs can help make a positive difference for other reasons. Pediatric oncology units now use therapy dogs at times to help children get through painful procedures. Therapy dogs provide a positive and sympathetic distraction. For children in the READ program (a volunteer program that helps children who are having difficulty learning to read or comprehending what they read), dogs provide a very safe listening audience, and therapists have found that children find it less threatening to explain to a dog what a certain passage means than when asked to explain material to an adult. A statement such as, "I don't think that my boxer understood that last part. Could you explain it to him?" is much less threatening to a child struggling with reading than a therapist or volunteer asking the child to explain the passage.

Assistance Dogs

The Americans with Disabilities Act (ADA) has done much to guarantee that people with disabilities are entitled unlimited use of their assistance dog within parameters in which regular dogs are not allowed. The most obvious use of an assistance dog is guide dogs for the blind. Boxers were one of the first dogs used as guide dogs for the blind, and they are still used today, though the more popular German shepherds, Labrador retrievers, and golden retrievers have become more common.

More assistance dogs are used by the deaf and hearing-impaired to alert the people to doorbells and knocks on the door and the telephone ringing. Dogs are also used by those who are wheelchair bound to help by picking up dropped objects, helping people in and out of the wheelchair, alerting at signs of a seizure, and a whole host of other issues. Dogs have finally come into their own as a true working companion in the field of assistance dogs.

Special Consideration for Canine Athletes

Boxers are considered among the most athletic of dogs, and for that reason, they are sometimes overworked at an early age, whether intentionally or by accident. This can lead to a whole host of bone overgrowth problems such as panosteitis and osteochrondroitis in some cases, or simple injuries to anterior cruciate ligaments, knees, groin muscles, and so on.

One caution to take with any puppy is to try to limit his rough play while he is growing up. There is no point in the pup injuring himself when he is young and creating a condition that is going to cause painful arthritis when he is an old dog.

 **Alert!**

Most vets and specialists who are knowledgeable about how dogs grow tend to recommend that the larger breed dogs (boxers are included in this group) not be jumped at their full height (usually the height at their withers) until their growth plates close. For most boxers, especially the males and the females at the taller shoulder heights, that doesn't occur until between eighteen months and two years of age. Until then, exercise that is repetitive in nature or that pounds the joints should be avoided.

There is a belief among a lot of boxer people that if their boxers don't get lots of physical exercise then the dogs will be deprived. Thus, many take their boxer puppies for long jogs before their bones, joints, and muscles are ready for repetitive exercise. Truthfully, the best exercise that a growing boxer puppy can get is the kind that he can self-regulate. Even better are lessons that fatigue the little boxer mind. That means no more than twenty minutes of continuous running or playing at any one time, and no jumping higher than elbow height.

Assessing the Canine Athlete

According to Chris Zink, D.V.M., one of the leading national canine sports vets, in a canine athlete, the angle formed by a line perpendicular to the ground and the articulation of the scapula should be about 30 degrees. A well-bred boxer should have about this degree of angulation. Obviously, a boxer should also have good hips, but if he has poor shoulders, he will have almost as much trouble jumping and landing as if he has bad hips. In agility competition, he will have more trouble on the sharply angled A-frames.

Zink also mentions a weight-to-height ratio that is ideal in the canine athlete, particularly those that compete in agility. Her recommendation is to divide the dog's weight by its height at the shoulders. If the ratio is under 2.0, then the dog is at little risk of injury from repeated jumping. This is roughly equivalent to the ectomorphic type of human being who is very thin. This ratio includes whippets, Border collies, and Shelties, the last two of which are very good agility dogs.

The risk of injury increases if the ratio of weight to height is between 2.0 and 3.5. Most boxers fall into this category, so they are at moderate risk of injury with repetitive impact to their joints simply because of the ratio of their weight to their height. Boxers are fairly heavy dogs for their size. This isn't because they are fat but because they are generally very muscled and have relatively good bone density.

Zink says that if the ratio of weight to height is over 3.5, people should be very careful about jumping their dogs for fear of injury. Only an overweight boxer would fall into that category, and Zink recommends that dogs be very thin for performance. No performance dog should carry any subcutaneous fat, and boxers should never be fat.

Boxers could probably be considered mesomorphic. They are not whippet thin, and not mastiff heavy, but somewhere in between. The ectomorph would always have the advantage when it comes to anything that involves jumping and landing. Mesomorphs like boxers would be midrange in the risk categories. All boxers at a good weight would be in the cautionary range, but not really close to the true danger zone. The lower the boxers' weight, the less risk of injury he will suffer from jumping.

Veterinary Chiropractic

Veterinary chiropractic, which excels in the treatment of bio-mechanical problems, is relatively new. It minimizes, if not elimi-nates, gaiting oddities due to spinal or other joint misalignments. Conformation dogs have been getting adjusted for years as they are largely judged on their gait. In more recent years, competition obedience and agility dog owners have seen the value of chiro-practic adjustments in extending the length of time the dog can comfortably compete.

 **Fact**

Chiropractic for humans or canines is a method of treatment based upon the theory that disease is caused by interference of the nerve function. By manipulating the spine and the joints of the body, normal nerve function can be re-established and the body is able to heal itself.

More importantly, veterinary chiropractic can enhance overall health for any boxer. Spinal misalignments can create disorders within the internal organs of the dog. Here is a partial list of prob-lem misalignments and their common effects, as developed by the American Veterinary Chiropractic Association:

- Cervical subluxations, especially of the atlas vertebra, the occiput, and axis (all in the upper neck region), can be related to behavioral abnormalities and problems, such as aggression, slow learning, hyperactivity, attention deficit, blurred vision, fear biting, recurrent ear infections, and some kinds of seizures.
- Mid- and lower-cervical subluxations can relate to motion sickness, some anxiety states, lick granulomas, and hypothyroidism.
- Subluxations of the thoracic area (between the shoulder blades) can relate to hypothyroidism, heart problems, especially mitral valve insufficiency in older dogs, and some liver disorders.
- Farther down the back, thoracolumbar junction subluxations are the most common in dogs, and can be related to cystitis and diarrhea. Caudal lumbar subluxations with sacral rotations are related to acute onset incontinence and constipation. Back pain from overdoing it can also cause incontinence.

Alert!

Personality changes can be signs of some part of the back being out of alignment. Some dogs bite or look like they've got a headache. Other signs include a tail that does not wag symmetrically or a stiff back. A boxer that previously rolled that no longer rolls or rolls only to a certain point, then stops may also have an alignment issue. Owners should also keep an eye out for a lumpy, bumpy spine, especially near the back of the rib cage; head tilt; scuffing foot; stilted rear gait, or a rear gait that is always wide; lack of symmetry to the limbs; tail clamped to the body; or a boxer that wiggles or shakes when a certain part of his body is touched.

An important fact to note here is that if you see any of the conditions above, you might wish to find a veterinary chiropractor, but you should definitely take your boxer to the vet if you suspect any injury.

Dogs that are regularly adjusted have longer show careers than those who do not receive chiropractic treatment as part of their regular veterinary care. Old obedience competition boxers who were adjusted regularly have been known to jump their full AKC obedience regulation heights days before dying at advanced ages. Chiropractic adjustments have positive benefits to a dog with spondylosis as the result of an action injury as well. If your boxer is active in performance competition, it is wise to find a veterinary chiropractor to help you and your boxer with maintaining health and fitness.

CHAPTER 20

Travel Considerations for Your Boxer

T raveling with your boxer can be one of your biggest adventures or one of your biggest headaches. The difference depends upon how much traveling your boxer has done as a pup and how much he has learned about traveling. Obviously, the earlier your boxer travels with you, the easier and more natural it will be to him. However, if you only take your boxer in the car to places he sees as unpleasant, such as to the veterinarian, it is unlikely that he will ever become a great traveler.

Car Travel

As part of training, you have crate trained your boxer. This is very important, as the safest place for your boxer to be in a car is in the crate. If the crate cannot fit in your car, your boxer should be otherwise restrained, whether by a harness or behind a secure barrier in the back. While restraining your boxer is a must, there are other precautions to take as well.

One important consideration is safeguarding your car. You probably want to be able to leave your valuables in it, and the most irreplaceable of your valuables is your boxer. Obviously, you can lock your car, but you need to provide adequate ventilation for your boxer if you are going to leave him in your car for any length of time.

Alert!

If you are crossing state lines for travel of any kind, it is best to have a health certificate for your boxer, especially if you are staying in hotels. Vaccination requirements vary by state, and a health certificate, which includes your vet's name, address, and phone number, will help prove to authorities that your boxer is unlikely to be a disease carrier. Without a health certificate, your boxer could be quarantined.

A second safeguard is to plan for ample medication to cover your trip, should your boxer need any, and what to do about fleas and any other unaccustomed pests. Even if you don't ordinarily use topical flea or tick products, it might be a good idea to do so before you leave home. The fleas and ticks in areas new to you may be even less friendly than the ones that inhabit grass and trees where you live.

You may even find these pests in hotels rooms, and the last thing that you want to do is to be in a position where family or friends that you might stay with suspect your boxer of bringing in a flea epidemic when you and he come to visit. This can easily be avoided through use of a topical flea product.

Essential

It is a good idea to take along a doggy first-aid kit that will include Kaopectate in case of diarrhea on the road, ipecac to induce vomiting in case your boxer ingests something that he really shouldn't, rescue remedy for emergencies or other startling experiences, Traumeel or arnica (an herbal remedy) in case of a muscle injury, a splint with vet wrap, tweezers, and first-aid scissors.

Your vehicle should also be well stocked with baggies or other plastic bags to pick up any waste that your boxer leaves. When you travel, this is of the utmost importance if you want to be invited back and to pave the way diplomatically for visits from other dogs and their owners. Every time a dog owner does not pick up after her dog, it is more difficult for other responsible dog owners to avoid a bad reputation. Every time you pick up after your boxer, you help all responsible dog owners everywhere.

Air Travel

If you are planning an airline trip with your boxer, you cannot do so without planning in advance. Not only are there certain times of the year when airlines will not fly dogs or pets as excess baggage (in extreme hot or cold temperatures), there are also times when you can't fly your boxer because another pet may be flying as excess baggage. Many airlines no longer fly dogs at all.

Planning for Your Flight

You will need to contact the airline you wish to use to check with them if they fly pets. If your boxer is flying as excess baggage (at an additional charge to you), he will need to fly in an airline approved crate or one that is made out of strong, impact-resistant plastic. Most pet stores carry airline crates.

If for some reason your boxer is not crate trained, now is the time to get him used to his crate. He will need to be in the crate in the hold while the plane is being loaded, or on the ground waiting to be loaded, and while being prepared for take-off, landing, and while in the air. It is often a considerable amount of time that your boxer needs to learn to tolerate.

You will need a health certificate that the airlines can examine in order for him to board. All health certificates are valid for a period of thirty days, but most people get them as close to the time that they leave as possible, which usually means a day or two before the trip.

 **Alert!**

It is a good idea to feed your boxer lightly as early as possible before you need to leave for the airport the day you fly. If your boxer's stomach is too empty for too long, it will typically only become more upset as time goes by than if he has a little something in his stomach to digest. Half of breakfast or dinner is good, or just a couple of treats. But don't let your boxer overeat before he gets on a plane!

Decorating the Airline Crate

When you buy your airline crate, it will have two or more stickers to put on the outside of the crate that read something on the order of, "Caution Live Animal." This is to alert airline staff of the fact that they are dealing with a live animal. However, in this busy, impersonal day and age, many who travel with their beloved boxers go much farther than that simple alert. They attach a picture of their boxer and personal note from the boxer that reads something like this: "Hi, I'm Bonzo, a well-trained boxer, and I'm happy to be flying with you to the American Boxer Club National Specialty in _____. I'm normally very friendly, but I'm away from my person, John Smith, and I may be worried." A personalized note like this can do much to remind airline workers that your boxer is a nice dog, and he will be treated accordingly.

Alert!

When you buy your airline crate for your boxer, buy it only as large as it needs to be so that your boxer can stand and turn around somewhat comfortably in it. If the crate is bigger than that, it defeats the purpose of helping contain your boxer in case you run into turbulence in the sky, and he gets bounced around. It the crate is too large, your boxer can also get stiff from having to brace himself.

Some airlines require you to attach a small amount of food to the crate for your dog, and most require that you have an available supply of water in the crate. What many experienced dog owners do when flying is to freeze water in the cup that comes with the airline crate. This helps to insure that your boxer's water won't spill in turbulence, and he is less likely to become dehydrated if the flight takes more time than expected.

Assistance Dogs

If you require an assistance dog to help you in life in general, the American Disabilities Act helps to ensure that you can fly with your boxer in the cabin of the plane, although he must be out of the way at all times. You will need to make arrangements for this with advanced planning if you want to take your boxer with you. He needs specific certification as an assistance dog that you will need to provide to the airline, plus all the other items any dog requires to travel.

VIP Dogs

Some domestic airlines have special programs that allow your boxer to fly in the cabin in a seat, strapped in as if he were wearing a seat belt. To fly inside the cabin, he must have proof that he is well trained as well as a health certificate. This service varies by airline, and is only provided by a few. If you would like to fly like this with your boxer, you will need to plan well in advance and do your research.

International Flights

If you are planning to travel by air with your boxer to a foreign country, you will need to contact the appropriate consulates or departments of agriculture of the country or countries you are planning to visit for information on their vaccination requirements. You may need to check on this frequently, as much as six months in advance as well as just days before you travel. These laws can change quickly and often, so the requirements for vaccinations can change with little or no notice.

Recreational Vehicle (RV) Travel

Recreational vehicles (RVs) are the dog-show transport choice of many, and recreational vehicles have become a popular way to travel and see the country. Since an RV functions as a home-away-from-home on wheels, it is only natural that you would want to take your boxer with you when you travel in your RV.

Types of RVs

Recreational vehicles come in two basic types: trailers types and self-contained, enclosed vehicles. Each has different implications for traveling with your boxer. The most basic type of trailer is the tow pop-up. These are the smallest and simplest of the trailers. They are almost like a pop-up tent on a trailer that can be towed by a car or truck. With this type of RV, it is essential that you have room for your boxer's crate in the towing vehicle so that he can ride safely as you travel. Otherwise, he needs his own doggy seat belt or a barrier restraint. The bottom line is that you need to make arrangements for safe travel in the tow vehicle for your boxer. You will want a place for your boxer to sleep at night while you are camping.

 **Fact**

The category of tow vehicles includes what are called fifth wheels. Fifth wheels are a specific type of trailer designed to hook onto the bed of a pick-up truck. These types of trailers can be quite large and elegant.

The second type of trailer is the more traditional, heavier trailer that can be anywhere from about eighteen to thirty-five feet long. These trailers require a vehicle with a larger engine to tow them. You will need a heavier vehicle the larger and longer your trailer is. Almost any vehicle can tow a trailer, but smaller cars and trucks without sufficient weight and braking ability cannot hold the weight of the trailer safely downhill.

In all trailers, regardless of size, you will need to have a crate in the towing vehicle and a bed for your boxer to sleep on in the trailer.

▲ If you bring your boxer on a trip, make sure to include some toys from home so he feels comfortable traveling.

Some of the smaller trailers that are sparsely furnished have room to leave a crate in the trailer, which might be easier for you to manage. Don't do this unless you can guarantee sufficient ventilation to the trailer, as this type usually has no heat or air conditioning while you drive. However, if the weather is nice, if you can check every hour or so, and if your boxer doesn't mind, this can be a fine way for him to travel. Otherwise, it might be safer and he might be happier to ride in the car or truck with you.

The second general type of recreational vehicle is the self-contained, enclosed type that looks like a private bus. Often, these are built on bus chassis. They usually include a kitchen, bedrooms, and bathroom.

Bigger RVs usually include the elements of a Class A RV on a van or truck body with a larger van or truck engine. The driver's and passenger's seats are much like they would be in a van or bus, whereas the driver's and passenger's seats in a Class A RV are more elegant. Class C RVs are generally not as big or expensive as Class A RVs. With both the Class A and Class C RVs, it is best for your boxer to travel crated. This way, he cannot accidentally interfere with the driver, and he is safer should an accident occur.

 Alert!

While there are many different RV parks across America, not all are created equal as far as dogs are concerned. Some have wonderful dog runs and walk-and-play areas where your boxer can stretch his legs and enjoy being a dog for a while. Others will not accept dogs over forty pounds, which eliminates most adult boxers. Check with each RV park as you travel.

Remember, just as your unrestrained dog can basically become a missile in a car accident, the same thing can happen if he's riding unrestricted in a RV. It is best to plan for your boxer's safety while traveling.

Staying in Hotels

Like every other aspect of traveling with your boxer, you will need to find which hotels take dogs in the areas you wish to visit. Hotels don't require health certificates, but they may require a pet deposit that you can get back upon checking out if nothing has been destroyed, or they may simply charge you more for the privilege of staying in a hotel with your dog.

The good-manners approach to traveling with your boxer is best. It requires that you take your crate into your room when your boxer is with you and that you never leave your boxer in a strange hotel room, loose and unattended. The risk of his chewing something or barking is too great. And every time a guest dog damages a hotel room, dog lovers everywhere lose a place where they can stay with their dogs. Remember, in a hotel room, you can order in, so there really is no need to leave your boxer alone in the room.

Room Location

It is a good idea to get a room on the ground floor of a hotel or motel you are staying in with your boxer. If you can, get a far corner of the building or complex. That way, if your boxer needs to go out at night to potty, you don't have far to go, and you will disturb fewer people––always a good thing as a dog owner.

If you must leave your boxer for any length of time, leave him in his crate with the television or a radio on (at modest decibels!) as a distraction for him. This is also a good time to provide him with his favorite type of chew toy to reduce his level of stress and boredom.

If you can't get a ground-floor room, and must take an elevator, try to take your boxer up on the elevator with just him and his family on his first elevator trip. That will make it seem less odd and scary to him. Put him in a sit/stay at your side in heel position. If you act as if you and he do this all the time, he'll likely be fine with the new experience.

Know Your Boxer

The biggest key to staying in a hotel room with your boxer is to know him and his stressors and to be a savvy and compassionate boxer owner. Make sure he has all his comforts of home with him in his crate, and don't expect him to be the perfectly calm dog the very first time in a hotel. Make sure he doesn't mess anything up—feeding him in his crate or outside in the car in his crate if he's a messy eater will help ensure that you get your pet deposit back if you've been sensible and not let him get nervous enough to chew anything else. If he has damaged anything, however, expect to lose your pet deposit and some other cash as well.

Boarding Kennels

As sad as it is, sometimes you just can't travel with your boxer. So what do you do when you will have to travel and your boxer simply can't come with you? One very common option is to board your boxer in a kennel. Some vets will board their patients, so this is a good place to start looking for a suitable kennel. Even if your vet doesn't have a boarding kennel attached to the veterinary hospital, she may be able to refer you to a good boarding kennel. Other good sources for finding a good boarding kennel are your obedience classes, other dog friends, and your breeder.

 **Fact**

If your breeder lives in the area, she will probably be more than willing to board your boxer for short periods of time now and then, and certainly in an emergency. Who would take better care of your boxer than his ethical, reputable breeder? Of course, your breeder likely won't be willing to do this for free, so be prepared to pay just as you would at a kennel.

No matter how you find the boarding kennel, you should visit the facility to see if you feel comfortable with it before you send your boxer there. Ask yourself the following questions:

- Is it this somewhere you would feel comfortable leaving your beloved boxer?
- Is the kennel bonded and insured? Are the kennel help experienced with a variety of breeds of dogs?
- Is it clean and well tended?

- Are the facilities adequate to the weather? Will your boxer be warm in winter and cool in summer?
- Does your boxer have protection from rain, snow, and excessive heat?
- What is the human-to-canine ratio?
- Is there a vet on call twenty-four hours a day? If not, what arrangements are in place for canine emergencies?
- If your boxer needs medication, will they give it to him? Special diets?
- Will they give him his own food?
- How about quality time and attention? What can you expect for your boxer if you kennel him there? What type of service contract does the kennel provide?

Only you can make the call on these questions, but your boxer needs adequate protection from the elements, access to veterinary care in case of an emergency (for him), medication, and fresh food and water at minimum. The rest of the considerations might be optional in case of an emergency situation that takes you out of town on a short notice for a brief amount of time.

Pet Sitters

An alternative to boarding your boxer in a kennel is to find a trustworthy pet sitter. You can find a good pet sitter from many of the same sources that you looked into to find a good kennel. Ask your vet, your obedience classmates, and your dog-lover friends. Or you can look pet sitters up on the Internet and find people who have affiliations with various different organizations who might live in your area. Pet Sitters International, online at *www.petsit.com*, can provide you with links to trustworthy local pet sitters.

Qualifications of Pet Sitters

Many of the qualifications of pet sitters are the same as those you would look for in a good kennel. For instance, ask yourself what your gut instinct tells you about this person. This is even tougher because you are not only leaving your boxer, but you are leaving your home open to a relative stranger. For those reasons, you will want to feel very secure about the person you hire as a pet sitter. Find out the following:

- Is she bonded and insured?
- Can she provide references (in case you need to interview a stranger, or someone who no one you know knows)?
- Does your boxer like her and vice versa?
- Does she provide a service contract?
- Is she interested, courteous, and informed?
- Is she someone you are comfortable having your home?
- Is she professional?
- Does she have regular office hours, and will she answer any questions promptly?
- Does she have access to twenty-four-hour veterinary service?

If you feel good about the person you are considering hiring as a pet sitter, and you find one that you like, you may be very happy with the outcome. Just do your homework so that you do not receive any unpleasant surprises.

Doggy Day Care

Doggy day care is a relatively recent phenomenon in America. The service provides a way to give your boxer some attention and stimulation during the day when you cannot be there with him. In most doggy day care facilities, there are other dogs that your boxer can play with. In this sense, it is much like day care for children.

All the same questions about insurance, experience, and access to veterinary care apply. But if you need to travel, doggy day care might provide a way to care for your boxer in your absence. Some kennel dogs for more than the day, but some do not. Most might be able to accommodate your boxer for a day or two now and then.

In Case of a Disaster

The Federal Emergency Management Agency, Department of Homeland Security, and the Humane Society all agree that in case of any emergency—earthquake, fire, terrorist attack, flood, mud slides, hurricane, or tornado—you need to include your boxer, and every family pet, in your disaster plans.

According to the U.S. Secretary of Homeland Security, the most important thing to do is to decide what to do in advance—will you stay in your home, or will you travel outside of the area? In each case, you need to devise a plan to deal with the situation should it arise.

For your boxer, you need to plan for the following:

- A safe place if you stay or if you go
- A seven-day supply of food and water
- Spare water and food dishes
- Pet carriers and leashes
- ID, vet records, and medications
- Blankets and toys
- Litter and waste containers

You also need to arrange for someone to care for your boxer should you be away at the time a disaster strikes. If you have found a kennel, a pet sitter, or a doggy day care center, they may provide the solution that you need. Or you might check with local animal shelters to see if they could care for your boxer. You need to do whatever it takes so that your boxer will not be left behind in the event of a large-scale disaster or emergency.

CHAPTER 21

The Senior Boxer

Just as it suddenly occurred to you that your boxer was no longer a puppy, you will realize one day that your boxer has become an older dog. Maybe he no longer plays as much as when he was young, he sleeps more, has become gray, or has a little limp. However you make this realization, you need to accept that your boxer has changed, as have his needs. Your boxer is now a senior.

What Is Old for a Boxer?

"Old" is a relative term. Obviously, if you have a boxer that is over ten, you will be the envy of many. Ten for a healthy boxer is about sixty-one in human terms, an age in human terms that covers a wide variety of conditions and situations. Some people run marathons at this age, and some are completely bedridden.

Even with the Hollywood attitude that fifty is the new thirty, sixty-one still encompasses a lot of variations. Some boxers go over their full AKC jump height at age twelve and older, while some cannot jump after the age of six. A lot of this has to do with the line that your boxer came from, and a lot has to do with the fitness level that you have helped him maintain throughout his life.

If he has had sensible, regular physical exercise, as well as regular mental stimulation through life-long training and high-quality food, the chances are that he will be doing very well. Many upper-level obedience dogs (dogs showing for their UDX and OTCH titles) are still in active competition from the ages of six to ten (which has often been called the "Golden Age of Obedience"). Some boxers have had honorable mention in *Front and Finish*, the obedience competition magazine, at advanced ages as old as eleven, and some boxers have finished their Novice A agility titles at eight. Aging often really depends upon the physical and mental stimulation your boxer gets, in combination with good genes and good food.

 **fact**

Holistic practices look at aging in dogs a little differently than the old "seven years to each human year" rule that used to be the standard in determining a dog's age in human years. Some holistic practitioners feel that the first year of a puppy's life is like fourteen human ones; the second year is like seven in human terms; and each year after that is about five years in human terms.

Senior Health Exams

When your boxer turns about seven, your vet will probably start doing more blood work and might recommend doing exams twice a year rather than annually. Health tests and screenings for the geriatric boxer may include a blood smear for a complete blood count, serum chemistry profile with electrolytes, urinalysis, blood pressure check, electrocardiogram, check of the eyes, thyroid panel, a joint-and-limb evaluation, and a dental exam.

This preventive program helps to ensure a longer, healthier life for the aging boxer. The most common problems of the aging boxer are loss of sight and hearing, arthritis, kidney and liver failure or disease, heart disease, and Cushing's syndrome (a disorder of the adrenal glands).

 fact

You may find that your older boxer does not wake up as quickly or readily as he once did. This could be because of loss of hearing, but it is common in older dogs. He may sleep more than he used to during the day, and it is possible that he will sleep less at night. He may start to snore if he has not snored before, and he may become very particular about where he wants to sleep.

Nutrition for the Senior Dog

There are a variety of nutritional needs that arise as any dog ages. Boxers are no different. For one thing, you want to keep control over your boxer's weight, which you should have been doing throughout his life. Also, nutritional supplements may be needed to protect against injuries and conditions such as arthritis.

Weight Control

If you are feeding an optimum kibble or raw-food diet, weight should not be an issue for your senior dog. However, if you have not, and your boxer is overweight, it is important to trim him down. Excess weight puts additional stress on the body's vital organs, to say nothing of joints, muscles, and ligaments. If it is hard to keep your senior boxer's weight down, you may want to supplement with more vegetables. Vegetables provide a lot of fiber with relatively few extra calories, and they may help to make your boxer feel like he's eating more while not packing on the pounds.

Supplements for Aging Boxers

Boxers that remain active throughout old age tend to suffer at least one injury along the way. This may crop up as a problem when they age, usually in the form of arthritis. Many older boxers are on glucosamine/chondroitin supplements for joint problems, or MSM for pain associated with soft tissue and ligament injuries or stress from arthritic joints.

Like many aging mammals, boxers may need extra digestive enzymes to fully utilize the nutrition in their food. There may also come a time when your boxer may need a vitamin or mineral supplement. Many boxers seem to need supplements such as the following:

- A kelp or seaweed formula
- Calcium
- Essential fatty acids in the form of fish oils, such as cod liver or salmon oil, flaxseed oil, or evening of primrose oil
- Extra vitamins C and E

The need for these things is best determined by your veterinary nutritionist, or holistic vet, although there are many pet supplements in pet stores and catalogs that address these issues in providing extra nutritional support.

Problems of Aging

While a few boxer lines go gray earlier, six years of age seems to be a common time for most lines of boxers to start to go grow gray hairs around the face and muzzle. At first, that is the primary area where they will turn gray, but eventually, gray hair will begin to appear throughout the entire body, and the fawn or brindle color that they used to be will simply start to fade. As early as age six, your boxer will also begin to lose muscle mass.

Hearing Loss

This may happen gradually, but many older boxers start to lose hearing around age ten or so. Brindles seem to lose their hearing more commonly than fawns. Once this starts to happen, it is essential to keep your boxer on-leash almost all the time. He will not be able to hear you when you call, and he could become endangered if he goes onto a street. If he doesn't hear you, he probably also won't hear a car approaching. Loss of hearing may account for not coming on recall when you call him as well.

 **Alert!**

Be aware that becoming hard of hearing might be very frightening or disorienting to your boxer. He may startle more and might be aggressive if awakened abruptly. He may respond aggressively if startled. If your boxer appears to be losing his hearing, make sure that your actions are calm and methodical to avoid startling or frightening him.

Hearing loss can be confusing. Sometimes, it is as if the hearing comes and goes a bit, and sometimes, the older, more opinionated boxer will exhibit a bit of selective hearing! It is important to watch this carefully. If you see a sign of hearing becoming a problem, make sure that your boxer is safely on-leash in situations that could be potentially dangerous to a hard-of-hearing dog. This might be a good time, if you have not taught your boxer signals before this, to teach him hand signals for a recall, down, and stay. Signals might be a lifesaver.

Confusion

There may be times when your boxer seems confused. Part of this might be a loss of cognitive function. However, it is just as likely that if your boxer's hearing is going, he is confused about that. Since he is a dog, he doesn't understand what is happening, and this may cause a less confident demeanor and hesitation in approaching you and other people, attitudes that were never an issue earlier in his life.

However, if your boxer is losing his cognitive faculties, you may find that he is going outside, and just standing there, unsure of what to do next. He may begin to hide. He may hear you calling him, but he may forget what that means and not come for that reason. He may walk around in patterns or without a real destination. He may forget where his food or water bowls are, or he may not recognize familiar people.

 Essential

> If your boxer is suffering from cognitive dysfunction of aging, he might become fearful of ordinary things in life that never bothered him before, such as furniture, heaters, thunder, passing traffic, other loud noises, and strangers. He could react aggressively if he becomes too fearful.

Potty Accidents

Possibly the most distressing problem of aging to both you and to your boxer are housetraining accidents that have not been issues since he was a little pup. As dogs age, like humans, the frequency of the need to urinate can increase greatly. Without greater access to outside areas where he can potty, your boxer may find it necessary to urinate in the house. This will distress him if he isn't suffering from cognitive dysfunctions that can be associated with aging. It is very important to make sure that your boxer can get outside or that his walks increase accordingly.

It is also possible that your boxer will have accidents and defecate in the house. While that may be the result of having to potty more frequently or problems with his sphincter muscles, defecating in the house tends to relate more to cognitive dysfunction.

At any rate, if you see potty accidents occurring in the house, you need to make sure that he has a chance to potty outside more frequently.

 Fact

Old-dog syndrome, also called cognitive dysfunction syndrome (CDS), is the gradual deterioration of a dog's cognitive abilities. Most of these are indicated by a change in the dog's behavior, most commonly routine responses, and responses in training. More than half of all dogs show some signs of CDS. In addition, most of the problems of aging have some relationship to old-dog syndrome although these problems can also occur without a full-blown diagnosis of CDS.

Failing to Respond to Social Stimuli

Whereas before your return home after work was the most exciting event in your boxer's day, now he might approach you slowly and almost fearfully, possibly cringing or cowering before it seems to dawn on him that his beloved person is home. Only then does his happiness reveal itself. This may go even further in that your boxer no longer tolerates being petted for periods of time or even much human contact at all. If your boxer is at this point, then you are truly dealing with a geriatric patient (regardless of chronological age), and you must decide what steps to take to safeguard him in this condition.

 Alert!

Old age problems that require immediate veterinary attention include your boxer whimpering when he moves, convulsions or seizures, drinking massive amounts of water (and urinating accordingly), more frequent vomiting, and refusal of food.

This is not a great time to make big changes in your or your boxer's life. Some boxers that change households after age seven or so seem to mourn lost yards or surroundings. They seem to take change in their routines and surroundings (territory) very seriously. If your boxer has begun to avoid social stimuli, you need to evaluate big changes carefully with his needs in mind. Since his days are probably numbered, you may want to put off big moves, house remodels, or changes in household members or routines.

If your boxer is at this stage, it is also unwise to consider bringing in a new pup. If your boxer is still alive when the pup becomes a juvenile, the pup's protective pack instincts could kick in and cause him or her to try to drive your boxer out of the pack, as canines in the wild would do. Driving the old and infirm and the weak out of the pack is a protective measure so that the pack will not be slowed down or made vulnerable because of the illness or infirmity of one of its members, making the entire group an easier target for predators or competitors for control of the territory.

Comfort Seeking

When your boxer starts to age, you will find that he becomes more and more of a comfort seeker. If you have been successful at keeping your boxer off the furniture and your bed up until now, unless he has a wonderful bed in a nice warm corner of the house which he totally loves, he might decide to opt for comfort over doing what he was once taught.

 **Fact**

Even if your boxer did not suffer from separation anxiety as a pup, and especially if he did, you may find this problem rearing its head in his old age. It might show up in the form of stressing by drooling (sometimes enough to cover an entire kitchen floor), nonstop pacing while you are gone, or it might take the form of nonstop, high-pitched barking until you return.

If comfort seeking becomes a problem, you might want to get him a large, very comfortable bed with a back support for him to lean up against or to put his head on. Boxers tend to like to do that, especially as they age. The old-fashioned wicker basket beds are very popular with a lot of boxers for that reason—they provide a firm backrest, although some of the new beds that have a backrest built in are very popular, too. Some companies make orthopedic beds for dogs. If your boxer has become arthritic, this might be the best option, or he might prefer a combination of the above.

◄ The older boxer is a quieter, more reserved companion, but he still needs as much love and attention as when he was a pup.

You might find, as well, that your boxer gets colder than he once did. Be sure to have his thyroid checked now, if you have not done this before, as low body temperature is one sign of thyroid disease. Even if he does not have thyroid disease, he may come to feel the cold more, so you might want to get him a coat. You can find these at pet stores and in pet catalogs and at some dog shows. Your boxer will probably thank you for this. Likewise, you might find that he finds heat more problematic and may need a wet coat (described on page 138) to help him to cool down.

As he approaches the end, you may also find that he becomes more and more picky about his food. This is the one time in his life where it is okay to get the really cheap canned dog food. It has a lot of chemical additives to enhance flavor, and it might appeal to your boxer's diminishing taste buds. Once he starts to refuse his normal food on a regular basis and is not sick, you are at the beginning of the end of your boxer's time.

When to Say Goodbye

It is hard to imagine, feeling the great joy you feel when your boxer is a puppy, that at some point in time you will be in the position of having to contemplate putting him to sleep. It is sobering to consider that how your boxer lives and how he dies is up to you. It is part of our great responsibility to canine (and other animal) companions. Your boxer had been loyal and true to you, so you owe him your best at this important point in his life, too.

This is not the time to be cowardly and hope that he simply fades away nicely. He deserves better than that from you. Most boxers die of cancer or some other canine illness. Those that actually live long enough to have old-dog syndrome are not that common, although some do. Letting your boxer die by inches of old age or infirmity is cruel and unnecessary in this day and age.

If your boxer is in any way suffering more than just a bit of discomfort, you owe it to him to do the right thing. Take him to your vet for a humane euthanasia, regardless of his age, but be particularly sure to do this if he is old and the prognosis for his recovery is poor. If he is suffering from old-dog syndrome and his cognitive functions are diminished, if not altogether gone, it is probably kinder to put him to sleep. Boxers are proud dogs, and most would not want to live like strangers, not recognizing beloved humans, family, and friends in the home and territory they loved and cherished guarding.

 **Essential**

Euthanasia comes from Greek roots that literally mean "good death." A good death is a painless one with dignity surrounded by the people who loved you and whom you loved. Euthanasia for dogs is usually an injection of an overdose of an anesthesia or barbiturate. The experience is painless, although some veterinarians administer a sedative before the anesthesia to ensure that the dog is totally relaxed and comfortable just in case the dog reacts to its human's anxious feelings about the experience.

But what if he is just losing his physical faculties and has retained his cognition? It might be that your boxer is chagrined about his behavior, to say nothing of confused about why it is happening. Some of what may masquerade as old-dog syndrome may in fact be your boxer being depressed about his physical state and not understanding it. After all, he cannot talk to you to tell you how he's feeling, so for all we know he may regret letting you down.

If you have any real doubts about your boxer's true quality of life, physically, mentally, or emotionally, it is probably time to do the kindest thing and to make an appointment with your vet for his last visit.

What to Do with Your Boxer's Remains

You have a number of options with what to do with your boxer's remains. You can bury him in the back yard, have him cremated, donate his body to a science research project, or simply let him go to the laboratory that picks up laboratory waste from your veterinarian.

If you have your boxer cremated, you will pay a fee, and get his ashes back from the cremation in a week or two. You can bury him in the back yard with a marker. If you choose to bury your boxer in the back yard, you should either use a canine casket or make sure that you bury him very deep so that the smell of his decomposing body does not attract wild animals or encourage other dogs to dig there. Your boxer deserves more respect than being dug up again. If you bury him deeply, you should not have this problem, and you can put a marker on the spot where he rests.

The final option is to simply let his body go by leaving it with the vet after he is put to sleep. The spirit and personality of the boxer that was your boxer is gone. You have him in memories, and, undoubtedly, countless photos. That may be enough.

After Your Boxer Is Gone

While you will always miss your boxer, it is likely that after a time of mourning your loss of him, you will be thinking of the early, exciting, and happy days when you were looking for a pup. You will remember the joy you felt when you found him, the pride you felt as he mastered his lessons that every good dog needs to know, and the contentment you felt with his companionship. When that happens, it is time to go in search of the perfect boxer puppy. You will never find another boxer just like the one you lost, but there is another pup out there that will be the new boxer companion of your dreams.

Bibliography

Books

The Allergy Solution for Dogs, Shawn Messonier, DVM. Prima Publishing, Roseville, CA. 2000.

Anti-Aging for Dogs, John M. Simon, DVM, with Steve Duno. St. Martin's Press, New York, NY. 1998.

Biting, Barking, Lunging, Growling, Cheryl Smith. Kemptville, Ontario, Canada. 1997.

Body Posture and Emotions: Shifting Shapes, Shifting Minds, Suzanne Clothier. Flying Dog Press, St. Johnsville, NY. 1996.

The Boxer, Dan M. Gordon, M.D. Judy Publishing Company, Chicago. 1953.

Boxer, William Scolnik. Kennel Club Books, Allenhurst, NJ. 1999.

The Boxer, Elizabeth Somerfield. ARCO Publishing Company, Inc. New York. 1970.

The Boxer, John P. Wagner. Orange Judd Publishing Company, Inc. New York. 1946.

The Boxer: An Owner's Guide to a Happy, Healthy Pet, Stephanie Abraham. Howell Book House, New York, NY. 1996.

Boxers, Herta E. Kraupa-Tuskany. Barron's Educational Series, Inc., Hauppage, NY. 1988.

Boxers, Beverly Pisano. T.F.H. Publications, Inc., Neptune City, NJ. 1977.

Clicker Training for Obedience, Morgan Spector. Sunshine Books, Waltham, MA. 1999.

The Complete Boxer, Milo G. Denlinger. Denlinger's Publishers. Silver Springs, MD. 1950.

Dog Logic: Companion Obedience, Joel M. McManis. Howell Book House, New York, NY. 1992.

Dogs, Diet And Disease, Caroline D. Levin, RN, Lantern Publications, Oregon City, OR. 2001.

Dog Training for Dummies, Jack Volhard and Wendy Volhard. Wiley Publishing, Inc., New York, NY. 2001.

Finding a Balance: Issues of Power in the Human/Dog Relationship, Suzanne Clothier. Flying Dog Press, St. Johnsville, NY. 1996.

Flower Essence Repertory, Patricia Kaminski and Richard Katz. The Flower Essence Society, Nevada City, CA. 1994.

Four Paws, Five Directions, Cheryl Schwartz, DVM. Celestial Arts, Berkeley, CA. 1996.

Genetics of the Dog, Malcolm B. Willis. Howell Book House, New York, NY. 1989.

The Holistic Guide for a Healthy Dog, Wendy Volhard & Kerry Brown, DVM. Howell Book House, New York, NY. 1995.

K9 Kitchen: Your Dogs' Diet: The Truth Behind the Hype, Monica Segal. Doggie Diner, Inc., Toronto, Canada. 2002.

My Life with Boxers, Friederun Stockmann. Coward-McCann, Inc. New York. 1968.

My Life with Boxers, A New Translation, Friederun Stockmann, translation by Calvin D. Gruver. Classic Pet Books, Sauk Rapids, MN. 1998

Mystical Dogs, Jean Houston. Inner Ocean Publishing, Makowao, HI. 2002.

Natural Health Bible for Dogs and Cats, Shawn Messonier, DVM. Three Rivers Press, Prima Publishing, New York, NY. 2001.

The New Boxer, Billie McFadden. Howell Book House, New York, NY. 1989.

The New Owner's Guide to the Boxer, Richard Tomita. TFH Publications, Inc. Neptune City, NJ. 1996.

On Talking Terms with Dogs: Calming Signals, Turid Rugas. Legacy by Mail, Inc., Carlsborg, WA. 1997.

Open and Utility Training, The Motivational Method, Jack and Wendy Volhard. Howell Book House, New York, NY. 1992.

Physical Therapy for the Canine Athlete, Suzanne Clothier & Sue Ann Lesser, DVM. Flying Dog Press, St. Johnsville, NY. 1996.

Reigning Cats and Dogs, Pat McKay, Oscar Publications, South Pasadena, CA. 1992.

Second Hand Dog: How to Turn Yours into a First-Rate Pet, Carol Lea Benjamin. Macmillan Publishing, New York, NY. 1988.

Therapy Dogs: Training Your Dog to Reach Others, Kathy Diamond Davis. Howell Book House, New York, NY. 1992

Think Dog: An Owner's Guide to Canine Psychology, John Fisher. Trafalgar Square Publishing, North Pomfret, VT. 1991.

Understanding and Teaching Self Control, Suzanne Clothier. Flying Dog Press, St. Johnsville, NY. 1996.

Understanding Puppy Testing, Suzanne Clothier. Flying Dog Press, St. Johnsville, NY. 1996.

Understanding Your Dog, Dr. Michael W. Fox. Coward, McCann & Geoghegan, Inc., New York, NY. 1972.

When Good Dogs Do Bad Things, Mordecai Siegal and Matthew Margolis. Little, Brown and Company. New York, NY. 1986.

The World of the Boxer, Richard Tomita. TFH Publications, Inc., Neptune City, NJ. 1998.

Articles

"Aortic Ejection Velocity in Healthy Boxers with Soft Cardiac Murmurs and Boxers Without Cardiac Murmurs: 201 Cases (1997–2001), Koplitz, Meurs, Spier, Bonagura, Fuentes, and Wright. Dept. of Veterinary Clinical Sciences, College of Veterinary Medicine. The Ohio State University, Columbus, OH.

"Canine Dilated Cardiomyopathy-Recognition & Clinical Management," Kathryn Meurs, DVM, Ph.D., Diplomate ACVIM (Cardiology), The Ohio State University. Walthum/OSU Symposium. Small Animal Cardiology, 2002.

"Canine Hypothyroidism: Prevalence of Positive TGAA in 871 Laboratory Samples from Boxers." Ray Nachreiner, DVM, Ph.D., College of Veterinary Medicine, Michigan State University, East Lansing, MI. Presented to the American Boxer Club, 2002.

"Degenerative Myelopathy and Excitotoxins," Shawn Messonier, DVM. *Boxer Review*, March 2005. Northridge, CA.

"Dilated Cardiomyopathy in the Boxer Dog," Kathryn M. Meurs, DVM, Ph.D., Diplomate ACVIM (Cardiology). Ohio State University–College of Veterinary Medicine. 1997.

"Familial Ventricular Arrhythmia in Boxers," Meurs, Spier, Miller, Lekmkuhl, and Towbin. Ohio State University–College of Veterinary Medicine. 2002.

"Progress Report to the ABC: ABCF Foundation Boards," by Kathryn M. Meurs, DVM, Ph.D. Diplomate ACVIM (Cardiology) May 7, 2002.

Boxer Resources

Clubs

The American Boxer Club
Corresponding Secretary
6310 Edward Drive
Clinton, MD 20735-4135
www.americanboxerclub.org

The American Kennel Club
5580 Centerview Drive
Raleigh, NC 27606
(919) 816-3627
www.akc.org

The publication offices of the AKC (the *AKC Gazette,* the *AKC Events Calendar,* and the *AKC Records*) may be reached at the following address:
The American Kennel Club
260 Madison Avenue
New York, NY 10016
(919) 233-9767

Publications and Internet Resources

Boxer Review
This is the longest running and oldest Boxer publication.

8840 White Oak Avenue
Northridge, CA 91325
(818) 885-7220
www.boxerreview.com

The Boxer Mail List (BML)
This is your best online bet for general information on boxers. It is very helpful to puppy owners and first-time boxer owners. The BML is the oldest boxer mail list on the Internet, dating back to 1995. The official way to join the BML is to e-mail the following address: *listserv@listserv.ipui.edu.* Leave the subject line empty. The message should say, "Subscribe boxer." Doing that will generate a request for confirmation. Reply to that with the message, "OK."

That will automatically forward copies of the subscription request to list owners, Maryann Watkins and Dale Ulmer, so they can take the appropriate action. One of them will then send a copy of the BML rules to the applicant. When that person tells the list owner that the rules are acceptable, the list owner will enter the subscription.

The ShowBoxer-L
This is the best mail list on the Internet for information on showing in conformation, health issues, and general discussions on showing. The ShowBoxer-L is the oldest of the show lists for boxers.

www.showboxer-l.com

The ObedcompBoxer List

The longest-running and best list on the Internet for boxers in competitive AKC (and similar venues) obedience titles, including rally obedience, and tracking. Going to the Web site will give you an opportunity to generate a request to the list owner, which will be confirmed by the list owner.

http://groups.yahoo.com/group/ObedcompBoxer

The Boxer Underground: The Alternative Boxer News Magazine

An online magazine created to answer the desire of many boxer breeders and exhibitors.

www.boxerunderground.com

Index

A

Adoption fees, 32
Adult boxers, 34–35, 41–43, 71–75, 84–86
Aggression, 148, 156, 219–20, 227–32
Agility competition, 252–53
Aging, 31, 277–78
Air travel, 60–61, 265–68
AKC Gazette: The Official Journal for the Sport of Purebred Dogs, 49
Allergies, 120–21
Alpha leader, 194–96
Alpha rolling, 172–73
American Boxer Club, 9, 22, 26, 45, 51, 52
American Boxer Rescue Association (ABRA), 41
American Kennel Club (AKC), xiii, 1, 4–5, 9, 13–14, 48–52, 237–38, 252
Appearance, 14–15
Assistance dogs, 257–58, 267
Athletic considerations, 258–62

B

Backyard breeders, 24
Bacterial infections, 93, 94
Balance, 39–40
BARF diet, 91–92. *See also* Raw diets

Bark collars, 203–4
Barking, 193–94, 201–4, 222–23
Bathing, 161–63
Bedding, 63, 70
Begler, Frank, 8
Behavioral issues, 180–83, 196, 219–34
Behaviorists, 233–34
Bell ringing, 80–81
Bennett, Chauncey Z., 52
Billinghurst, Ian, 91
Bioavailability, 90
Bitches, 21, 35–36. *See also* Female boxers
Biting, 8, 223–24
Bleeding, 130, 134, 142
Bloat, 96, 153–55
Boarding kennels, 272–73
Body, v, 14–15, 18–19
Bones, broken, 130
Bones, chewing, 99, 141
Bordatella (kennel cough), 104
Bowel disease, 126, 152
Boxer cardiomyopathy (BCM), 143–46
Boxer colitis, 151–53
Boxer Rescue Foundation (BRF), 41
Boxer Rescue of Los Angeles, Inc., 41
Boxer rescue organizations, 14, 32, 34, 41, 43, 72
Bracycephalic breeds, 12, 109, 137, 156

The Everything® Breed-Specific Series

Trade Paperback, $12.95
ISBN: 1-59337-316-3

Trade Paperback, $12.95
ISBN: 1-59337-048-2

Trade Paperback, $12.95
ISBN: 1-59337-424-0

Trade Paperback, $12.95
ISBN: 1-59337-121-7

Available wherever books are sold!

The definitive, must-have guides for the most popular breeds!

Trade Paperback, $12.95
ISBN: 1-59337-314-7

Trade Paperback, $12.95
ISBN: 1-59337-047-4

Trade Paperback, $12.95
ISBN: 1-59337-423-2

Trade Paperback, $12.95
ISBN: 1-59337-122-5

To order, call 800-289-0963, or visit us at *www.everything.com*

The definitive, must-have guides for the most popular breeds!

THE
EVERYTHING
CHIHUAHUA
B O O K

A complete guide to raising, training, and caring for your chihuahua

Joan Hustace Walker

Trade Paperback, $12.95
ISBN: 1-59337-527-1

THE
EVERYTHING
BOXER
B O O K

A complete guide to raising, training, and caring for your boxer

Karla Spitzer

Trade Paperback, $12.95
ISBN: 1-59337-526-3

To order, call 800-289-0963, or visit us at www.everything.com

Everything® and everything.com® are registered trademarks of F+W Publications, Inc.